THE AUTOBIOGRAPHY OF
BENJAMIN FRANKLIN

THE AUTOBIOGRAPHY OF BENJAMIN FRANKLIN

Benjamin Franklin

WORDSWORTH AMERICAN LIBRARY

This edition published 1996 by
Wordsworth Editions Limited
Cumberland House, Crib Street
Ware, Hertfordshire SG12 9ET

ISBN 1 85326 564 0

Typeset by Antony Gray
Printed and bound in Great Britain by
Mackays of Chatham plc, Chatham, Kent

INTRODUCTION

Benjamin Franklin spent the last twenty years of his life trying to complete his autobiography, one of the earliest and most famous to be written by an American. On at least three occasions he quit working on the manuscript altogether, once for thirteen years. Even when he had revised its four parts for publication, the story ended in 1758, with thirty years of life and his greatest diplomatic triumphs left to tell. Part One, written in 1771, takes the form of a letter to his son, William, and chronicles the adventures of young Franklin in Philadelphia. Part Two, begun in 1784 while Franklin was in France, replaces the pretence of the letter with a simple inscription, 'Continuation of the Account of my Life'. Parts Three and Four chronicle, in sometimes plodding detail, his work on civic projects in Philadelphia, in science, and in Pennsylvanian and colonial politics.

If the act of composing the *Autobiography* was somewhat curious, so has been its life in print. Part One first appeared in a 1791 French translation, an incomplete version that circulated in Europe and America. In 1818, Franklin's grandson, William, published what was thought to be a complete version but was missing the final part. Only in 1868 was a version published containing all four parts.

Franklin had begun writing this project at the urging of friends who convinced him that it was his duty to write the story of such a distinguished and illustrative life. And what a remarkable life it was. His natural intelligence and skills made him a successful printer, but his real vocation was what the critic Vernon L. Parrington has called 'the field of civic betterment'. In this field Franklin filled every role: political figure (he helped to write both the Declaration of Independence and the Constitution); scientist (his experiments with electricity were known worldwide); inventor (of the Franklin stove and the bifocals); prolific author; philosopher (founder of the American Philosophical Society); diplomat; and public benefactor (he founded Philadelphia's lending library, police department and fire brigade).

Given this list of accomplishments, it hardly seems surprising that Franklin took so long to complete the *Autobiography*. Here was a life too full and demanding to allow itself to be set on paper. As much as to his hectic schedule, though, Franklin's ambivalence can be attributed to his temperament. Benjamin Franklin was by most accounts (including his own) a genuinely humble, unassuming person, and he may well have feared what many autobiographers fear: that his telling of his own life might be taken as just the kind of self-serving public posturing that he so despised, and had so often made the target of his own quick wit. One sees his caution throughout the book, but especially in Part One, as when Franklin tells his readers, 'I mention this industry the more particularly and the more freely, tho' it seems to be talking in my own praise, that those in my posterity, who shall read it, may know the use of that virtue . . . '

The difficulty, of course, was that Franklin's very project obligated him to promote his life and himself, if not as examples of perfection then as ideals worthy of study and imitation. This is why Franklin begins with such a dramatic account of his early years of struggle and triumph in Philadelphia. As must all writers of autobiography, Franklin creates himself as a character in a drama: young Ben Franklin, clever but broke, arriving in the big city to seek his fortune. With nothing but his own industry, frugality and virtue, he succeeds in life and in business, despite dishonest businessmen and idle companions. Along the way, he learns simple but hard-earned lessons. 'I grew convinced,' Franklin tells his reader, 'that truth, sincerity and integrity in dealings between man and man were of the utmost importance to the felicity of life.'

How much of Franklin's success story is based on fact is difficult to say, though some of it is almost certainly what the critic J. A. Lemay has called 'artful fiction'. But documenting the brute facts and figures of his life was never Franklin's aim. Neither was confessing his every weakness or failure, though he does offer a sprinkling of what he calls *errata*, minor errors of judgement or failures to keep his own resolutions. Rather, Franklin's purposes were two: to create a believable model of a life that would inspire and teach through its example, and to 'fix the idea of the American Dream in the reader's mind', as Lemay puts it. In this, Franklin's *Autobiography* participates in an important eighteenth-century genre, the 'promotional tract', writing that celebrates the great promise of a young nation. (For other examples, see Jefferson's *Notes on the State of Virginia* and Crevecoeur's *Letters from an American Farmer*, both published in 1782.)

The triumph of young Ben Franklin is the ideal American story, a rise 'from the poverty and obscurity in which I was born and bred, to a state of affluence and some degree of reputation in the world'. The key to prosperity in America, Franklin amply illustrates, was not inheritance and class privilege, but merit and sweat. This is why we are shown young Ben working late to finish a printing job, and why Franklin tells us, 'this industry, visible to our neighbours, began to give us character and credit'. He tells his rags-to-riches story, Franklin reminds his reader, not out of vanity but so that 'you may in your mind compare such unlikely beginnings with the figure I have since made there'.

Franklin tells his life story extremely well, but his real skill as a writer came in distilling his anecdotes into the diamond-hard resolutions and maxims for living, now so much a part of our language that we often forget their author. Like the puritan 'conduct book' on which it is partly modelled (Franklin acknowledged Cotton Mather's *Essays to do Good*), the *Autobiography* uses anecdotes not to move readers closer to God but to show how common-sense living can lead to a good and successful life on earth. Its simple and elegant truths, written in Franklin's direct and accessible style, continue to bring generations of readers to study this text, not as a historical curiosity but as a practical guide to living. In the words of the critic Howard Mumford Jones, Franklin's *Autobiography* has become our 'secular Bible'.

RICHARD JENSETH
St Lawrence University

FURTHER READING

Catherine Drinker Bowen, *The Most Dangerous Man in America: Scenes from the Life of Benjamin Franklin*, 1974

D. H. Lawrence, *Studies in Classic American Literature*, 1923

J. A. Lemay, 'Benjamin Franklin', 1972

Vernon Parrington, *The Colonial Mind*, 1927

Edmund Wright, *Franklin of Philadelphia*, 1986

CONTENTS

THE AUTOBIOGRAPHY OF
BENJAMIN FRANKLIN

Franklin's Draft Scheme of the Autobiography

Copie d'un Projêt tres Curieux de Benjamin Franklin –
1ere Esquisse de ses Mémoires. Les additions à l'encre-
*rouge sont de la main de Franklin.**

My writing. Mrs Dogood's letters. Differences arise between my Brother and me (his temper and mine); their cause in general. His Newspaper. The Prosecution he suffered. My Examination. Vote of Assembly. His manner of evading it. Whereby I became free. My attempt to get employ with other Printers. He prevents me. Our frequent pleadings before our Father. The final Breach. My Inducements to quit Boston. Manner of coming to a Resolution. My leaving him and going to New York (return to eating flesh); thence to Pennsylvania. The journey, and its events on the Bay, at Amboy. The road. Meet with Dr Brown. His character. His great work. At Burlington. The Good Woman. On the River. My Arrival at Philadelphia. First Meal and first Sleep. Money left. Employment. Lodging. First acquaintance with my afterward Wife. With J. Ralph. With Keimer. Their characters. Osborne. Watson. The Governor takes notice of me. The Occasion and Manner. His character. Offers to set me up. My return to Boston. Voyage and accidents. Reception. My Father dislikes the proposal. I return to New York and Philadelphia. Governor Burnet. J. Collins. The Money for Vernon. The Governor's Deceit. Collins not finding employment goes to Barbados much in my Debt. Ralph and I go to England. Disappointment of Governor's Letters. Colonel French his Friend. Cornwallis's Letters. Cabbin. Denham. Hamilton. Arrival in England. Get employment. Ralph not. He is an expense to me. Adventures in England. Write a Pamphlet and print 100. Schemes. Lyons. Dr Pemberton. My diligence, and yet poor through Ralph. My Landlady. Her character. Wygate. Wilkes. Cibber.

* This memorandum, probably in the handwriting of M. le Veillard, immediately precedes the Outline in the MS – B.

Plays. Books I borrowed. Preachers I heard. Redmayne. At Watts's. Temperance. Ghost. Conduct and Influence among the Men. Persuaded by Mr Denham to return with him to Philadelphia and be his clerk. Our voyage and arrival. My resolutions in Writing. My Sickness. His Death. Found D. R. married. Go to work again with Keimer. Terms. His ill-usage of me. My Resentment. Saying of Decow. My Friends at Burlington. Agreement with H. Meredith to set up in Partnership. Do so. Success with the Assembly. Hamilton's Friendship. Sewell's History. Gazette. Paper money. Webb. Writing Busy Body. Breintnal. Godfrey. His character. Suit against us. Offer of my Friends, Coleman and Grace. Continue the Business, and M. goes to Carolina. Pamphlet on Paper Money. Gazette from Keimer. Junto credit; its plan. Marry. Library erected. Manner of conducting the project. Its plan and utility. Children. Almanac. The use I made of it. Great industry. Constant study. Father's Remark and Advice upon Diligence. Carolina Partnership. Learn French and German. Journey to Boston after ten years. Affection of my Brother. His Death, and leaving me his Son. Art of Virtue. Occasion. City Watch amended. Post-office. Spotswood. Bradford's Behaviour. Clerk of Assembly. Lose one of my Sons. Project of subordinate Juntos. Write occasionally in the papers. Success in Business. Fire companies. Engines. Go again to Boston in 1743. See Dr Spence. Whitefield. My connection with him. His generosity to me. My returns. Church Differences. My part in them. Propose a College. Not then prosecuted. Propose and establish a Philosophical Society. War. Electricity. My first knowledge of it. Partnership with D. Hall, etc. Dispute in Assembly upon Defence. Project for it. Plain Truth. Its success. Ten thousand Men raised and disciplined. Lotteries. Battery built. New Castle. My influence in the Council. Colours, Devices, and Mottoes. Ladies' Military Watch. Quakers chosen of the Common Council. Put in the commission of the peace. Logan fond of me. His Library. Appointed Postmaster-General. Chosen Assemblyman. Commissioner to treat with Indians at Carlisle and at Easton. Project and establish Academy. Pamphlet on it. Journey to Boston. At Albany. Plan of union of the colonies. Copy of it. Remarks upon it. It fails, and how. Journey to Boston in 1754. Disputes about it in our Assembly. My part in them. New Governor. Disputes with him. His character and sayings to me. Chosen Alderman. Project of Hospital. My share in it. Its success. Boxes. Made a Commissioner of the Treasury. My commission to defend the frontier counties. Raise Men and build Forts. Militia Law of my drawing. Made Colonel. Parade of my Officers. Offence to Proprietor. Assistance to Boston

Ambassadors. Journey with Shirley, etc. Meet with Braddock. Assistance to him. To the Officers of his Army. Furnish him with Forage. His concessions to me and character of me. Success of my Electrical Experiments. Medal sent me. Present Royal Society, and Speech of President. Denny's Arrival and Courtship to me. His character. My service to the Army in the affair of Quarters. Disputes about the Proprietor's Taxes continued. Project for paving the City. I am sent to England. Negotiation there. *Canada delenda est.* My Pamphlet. Its reception and effect. Projects drawn from me concerning the Conquest. Acquaintance made and their services to me – Mrs S. M. Small, Sir John P., Mr Wood, Sergeant Strahan, and others. Their characters. Doctorate from Edinburgh, St Andrew's. Doctorate from Oxford. Journey to Scotland. Lord Leicester. Mr Prat. De Grey. Jackson. State of Affairs in England. Delays. Eventful Journey into Holland and Flanders. Agency from Maryland. Son's appointment. My Return. Allowance and thanks. Journey to Boston. John Penn, Governor. My conduct toward him. The Paxton Murders. My Pamphlet. Rioters march to Philadelphia. Governor retires to my House. My conduct. Sent out to the Insurgents. Turn them back. Little thanks. Disputes revived. Resolutions against continuing under Proprietary Government. Another Pamphlet. Cool thoughts. Sent again to England with Petition. Negotiation there. Lord H. His character. Agencies from New Jersey, Georgia, Massachusetts. Journey into Germany, 1766. Civilities received there. Göttingen Observations. Ditto into France in 1767. Ditto in 1769. Entertainment there at the Academy. Introduced to the King and the Mesdames, Mad. Victoria and Mrs Lamagnon. Duc de Chaulnes, M. Beaumont, Le Roy, D'Alibard, Nollet. See Journals. Holland. Reprint my papers and add many. Books presented to me from many authors. My Book translated into French. Lightning Kite. Various Discoveries. My manner of prosecuting that Study. King of Denmark invites me to dinner. Recollect my Father's Proverb. Stamp Act. My opposition to it. Recommendation of J. Hughes. Amendment of it. Examination in Parliament. Reputation it gave me. Caressed by Ministry. Charles Townsend's Act. Opposition to it. Stoves and chimney-plates. Armonica. Acquaintance with Ambassadors. Russian Intimation. Writing in newspapers. Glasses from Germany. Grant of Land in Nova Scotia. Sicknesses. Letters to America returned hither. The consequences. Insurance Office. My character. Costs me nothing to be civil to inferiors; a good deal to be submissive to superiors, etc., etc. Farce of Perpetual Motion. Writing for Jersey Assembly. Hutchinson's Letters. Temple. Suit in Chancery.

Abuse before the Privy Council. Lord Hillsborough's character and conduct. Lord Dartmouth. Negotiation to prevent the War. Return to America. Bishop of St Asaph. Congress. Assembly. Committee of Safety. Chevaux-de-frise. Sent to Boston, to the Camp. To Canada, to Lord Howe. To France. Treaty, etc.

The Autobiography

DEAR SON – I have ever had pleasure in obtaining any little anecdotes of my ancestors. You may remember the inquiries I made among the remains of my relations when you were with me in England, and the journey I undertook for that purpose. Imagining it may be equally agreeable to you to know the circumstances of my life, many of which you are yet unacquainted with, and expecting the enjoyment of a week's uninterrupted leisure in my present country retirement, I sit down to write them for you. To which I have besides some other inducements. Having emerged from the poverty and obscurity in which I was born and bred, to a state of affluence and some degree of reputation in the world, and having gone so far through life with a considerable share of felicity, the conducing means I made use of, which with the blessing of God so well succeeded, my posterity may like to know, as they may find some of them suitable to their own situations, and therefore fit to be imitated.

That felicity, when I reflected on it, has induced me sometimes to say, that were it offered to my choice, I should have no objection to a repetition of the same life from its beginning, only asking the advantages authors have in a second edition to correct some faults of the first. So I might, besides correcting the faults, change some sinister accidents and events of it for others more favourable. But though this were denied, I should still accept the offer. Since such a repetition is not to be expected, the next thing most like living one's life over again seems to be a recollection of that life, and to make that recollection as durable as possible by putting it down in writing.

Hereby, too, I shall indulge the inclination so natural in old men, to be talking of themselves and their own past actions; and I shall indulge it without being tiresome to others, who, through respect to age, might conceive themselves obliged to give me a hearing, since this may be read or not as anyone pleases. And, lastly (I may as well confess it, since my denial of it will be believed by nobody), perhaps I shall a good deal gratify my own *vanity*. Indeed, I scarce ever heard or saw the introductory words, '*Without vanity I may say*,' etc., but some vain thing immediately followed. Most people dislike vanity in others, whatever share they have of it themselves; but I give it fair quarter wherever I meet with it, being persuaded that it is often productive of good to the possessor, and to others that are within his sphere of action; and therefore, in many cases, it would not be altogether absurd if a man were to thank God for his vanity among the other comforts of life.

And now I speak of thanking God, I desire with all humility to acknowledge that I owe the mentioned happiness of my past life to His kind providence, which led me to the means I used and gave them success. My belief of this induces me to *hope*, though I must not *presume*, that the same goodness will still be exercised toward me, in continuing that happiness, or enabling me to bear a fatal reverse, which I may experience as others have done; the complexion of my future fortune being known to Him only in whose power it is to bless to us even our afflictions.

The notes one of my uncles (who had the same kind of curiosity in collecting family anecdotes) once put into my hands, furnished me with several particulars relating to our ancestors. From these notes I learned that the family had lived in the same village, Ecton, in Northampton-shire, for three hundred years, and how much longer he knew not (perhaps from the time when the name of Franklin, that before was the name of an order of people, was assumed by them as a surname when others took surnames all over the kingdom), on a freehold of about thirty acres, aided by the smith's business, which had continued in the family till his time, the eldest son being always bred to that business; a custom which he and my father followed as to their eldest sons. When I searched the registers at Ecton, I found an account of their births, marriages and burials from the year 1555 only, there being no registers kept in that parish at any time preceding. By that register I perceived that I was the youngest son of the youngest son for five generations back. My grandfather Thomas, who was born in 1598, lived at Ecton till he grew too old to follow business longer, when he went to live with his son John, a dyer at Banbury, in Oxfordshire, with whom my father served an apprenticeship. There my grandfather died and lies buried. We saw his gravestone in 1758. His eldest son Thomas lived in the house at Ecton, and left it with the land to his only child, a daughter, who, with her husband, one Fisher, of Wellingborough, sold it to Mr Isted, now lord of the manor there. My grandfather had four sons that grew up, viz.: Thomas, John, Benjamin and Josiah. I will give you what account I can of them, at this distance from my papers, and if these are not lost in my absence, you will among them find many more particulars.

Thomas was bred a smith under his father; but, being ingenious, and encouraged in learning (as all my brothers were) by an Esquire Palmer, then the principal gentleman in that parish, he qualified himself for the business of scrivener; became a considerable man in the county; was a chief mover of all public-spirited undertakings for the county or town of Northampton, and his own village, of which many instances were related of him; and much taken notice of and patronised by the then Lord Halifax. He died in 1702, January 6th, old style, just four years to a day before I was born. The account we received of his life and character from some old people at Ecton, I remember, struck you as something extraordinary, from its similarity to what you knew of mine. 'Had he died on the same day,' you said, 'one might have supposed a transmigration.'

John was bred a dyer, I believe of woolens. Benjamin was bred a silk dyer, serving an apprenticeship at London. He was an ingenious man. I remember him well, for when I was a boy he came over to my father in Boston, and lived in the house with us some years. He lived to a great age. His grandson, Samuel Franklin, now lives in Boston. He left behind him two quarto volumes, MS, of his own poetry, consisting of little occasional pieces addressed to his friends and relations, of which the following, sent to me, is a specimen. He had formed a short-hand of his own, which he taught me, but, never practising it, I have now forgot it. I was named after this uncle, there being a particular affection between him and my father. He was very pious, a great attender of sermons of the best preachers, which he took down in his short-hand, and had with him many volumes of them. He was also much of a politician; too much, perhaps, for his station. There fell lately into my hands, in London, a collection he had made of all the principal pamphlets relating to public affairs, from 1641 to 1711; many of the volumes are wanting as appears by the numbering, but there still remain eight volumes in folio, and twenty-four in quarto and in octavo. A dealer in old books met with them, and knowing me by my sometimes buying of him, he brought them to me. It seems my uncle must have left them here when he went to America, which was above fifty years since. There are many of his notes in the margins.

This obscure family of ours was early in the Reformation, and continued Protestants through the reign of Queen Mary, when they were sometimes in danger of trouble on account of their zeal against popery. They had got an English Bible, and to conceal and secure it, it was fastened open with tapes under and within the cover of a joint-stool. When my great-great-grandfather read it to his family, he turned up the joint-stool upon his knees, turning over the leaves then under the tapes. One of the children stood at the door to give notice if he saw the apparitor coming, who was an officer of the spiritual court. In that case the stool was turned down again upon its feet, when the Bible remained concealed under it as before. This anecdote I had from my uncle Benjamin. The family continued all of the Church of England till about the end of Charles the Second's reign, when some of the ministers that had been outed for non-conformity holding conventicles in Northamptonshire, Benjamin and Josiah adhered to them, and so continued all their lives: the rest of the family remained with the Episcopal Church.

Josiah, my father, married young, and carried his wife with three children into New England, about 1682. The conventicles having been forbidden by law, and frequently disturbed, induced some considerable men of his acquaintance to remove to that country, and he was prevailed with to accompany them thither, where they expected to enjoy their mode of religion with freedom. By the same wife he had four children more born there, and by a second wife ten more, in all seventeen; of which I remember thirteen sitting at one time at his table, who all grew up to be men and women, and married; I was the youngest son, and the youngest child but two, and was born in Boston, New England. My mother, the second wife, was Abiah Folger, daughter of Peter Folger, one of the first settlers of New England, of whom honourable mention is made by Cotton Mather, in his church history of that country, entitled Magnalia Christi Americana, as 'a godly, learned Englishman', if I remember the words rightly. I have heard that he wrote sundry small occasional pieces, but only one of them was printed, which I saw now many years since. It was written in 1675, in the home-spun verse of that time and people, and addressed to those then concerned in the government there. It was in favour of liberty of conscience, and in behalf of the Baptists, Quakers, and other sectaries that had been under persecution, ascribing the Indian wars, and other distresses that had befallen the country, to that persecution, as so many judgements of God to punish so heinous an offence, and exhorting a repeal of those uncharitable laws. The whole appeared to me as written with a good deal of decent plainness and manly freedom. The six concluding lines I remember, though I have forgotten the two first of the stanza; but the purport of them was, that his censures proceeded from good-will, and, therefore, he would be known to be the author.

> Because to be a libeller (says he)
>   I hate it with my heart;
> From Sherburne town, where now I dwell
>   My name I do put here;
> Without offence your real friend,
>   It is Peter Folgier.

My elder brothers were all put apprentices to different trades. I was put to the grammar school at eight years of age, my father intending to devote me, as the tithe of his sons, to the service of the Church. My early readiness in learning to read (which must have been very early, as I do not remember when I could not read), and the opinion of all his friends, that I should certainly make a good scholar, encouraged him in this purpose of his. My uncle Benjamin, too, approved of it, and proposed to give me all his shorthand volumes of sermons, I suppose as a stock to set up with, if I would learn his character. I continued, however, at the grammar school not quite one year, though in that time I had risen gradually from the middle of the class of that year to be the head of it, and farther was removed into the next class above it, in order to go with that into the third at the end of the year. But my father, in the meantime, from a view of the expense of a college education, which having so large a family he could not well afford, and the mean living many so educated were afterwards able to obtain – reasons that he gave to his friends in my hearing – altered his first intention, took me from the grammar school, and sent me to a school for writing and arithmetic, kept by a then famous man, Mr George Brownell, very successful in his profession generally, and that by mild, encouraging methods. Under him I acquired fair writing pretty soon, but I failed in the arithmetic, and made no progress in it. At ten years old I was taken home to assist my father in his business, which was that of a tallow-chandler and soap-boiler; a business he was not bred to, but had assumed on his arrival in New England, and on finding his dyeing trade would not maintain his family, being in little request. Accordingly, I was employed in cutting wick for the candles, filling the dipping mold and the molds for cast candles, attending the shop, going of errands, etc.

I disliked the trade, and had a strong inclination for the sea, but my father declared against it; however, living near the water, I was much in and about it, learnt early to swim well, and to manage boats; and when in a boat or canoe with other boys, I was commonly allowed to govern, especially in any case of difficulty; and upon other occasions I was generally a leader among the boys, and sometimes led them into scrapes, of which I will mention one instance, as it shows an early projecting public spirit, tho' not then justly conducted.

There was a salt-marsh that bounded part of the mill-pond, on the edge of which, at high water, we used to stand to fish for minnows. By much tramping, we had made it a mere quagmire. My proposal was to build a wharf there fit for us to stand upon, and I showed my comrades a large heap of stones, which were intended for a new house near the marsh, and which would very well suit our purpose. Accordingly, in the evening, when the workmen were gone, I assembled a number of my play-fellows, and working with them diligently like so many emmets, sometimes two or three to a stone, we brought them all away and built our little wharf. The next morning the workmen were surprised at missing the stones, which were found in our wharf. Inquiry was made after the removers; we were discovered and complained of; several of us were corrected by our fathers; and, though I pleaded the usefulness of the work, mine convinced me that nothing was useful which was not honest.

I think you may like to know something of his person and character. He had an excellent constitution of body, was of middle stature, but well set, and very strong; he was ingenious, could draw prettily, was skilled a little in music, and had a clear pleasing voice, so that when he played psalm tunes on his violin and sung withal, as he sometimes did in an evening after the business of the day was over, it was extremely agreeable to hear. He had a mechanical genius too, and, on occasion, was very handy in the use of other tradesmen's tools; but his great excellence lay in a sound understanding and solid judgement in prudential matters, both in private and public affairs. In the latter, indeed, he was never employed, the numerous family he had to educate and the straightness of his circumstances keeping him close to his trade; but I remember well his being frequently visited by leading people, who consulted him for his opinion in affairs of the town or of the church he belonged to, and showed a good deal of respect for his judgement and advice: he was also much consulted by private persons about their affairs when any difficulty occurred, and frequently chosen an arbitrator between contending parties. At his table he liked to have, as often as he could, some sensible friend or neighbour to converse with, and always took care to start some ingenious or useful topic for discourse, which might tend to improve the minds of his children. By this means he turned our attention to what was good, just, and prudent in the conduct of life; and little or no notice was ever taken of what related to the victuals on the table, whether it was well or ill dressed, in or out of season, of good or bad flavour, preferable or inferior to this or that other thing of the kind, so that I was bro't up in such a perfect inattention to those matters as to be quite indifferent what kind of food was set before me, and so unobservant of it, that to this day if I am asked I can scarce tell a few hours after dinner what I dined upon. This has been a convenience to me in travelling, where my companions have been sometimes very unhappy for want of a suitable gratification of their more delicate, because better instructed, tastes and appetites.

My mother had likewise an excellent constitution: she suckled all her ten children. I never knew either my father or mother to have any sickness but that of which they dy'd, he at 89, and she at 85 years of age. They lie buried together at Boston, where I some years since placed a marble over their grave, with this inscription:

JOSIAH FRANKLIN
and
ABIAH his wife
lie here interred.
They lived lovingly together in wedlock
fifty-five years.
Without an estate, or any gainful employment,
By constant labor and industry,
with God's blessing,
They maintained a large family
comfortably,
and brought up thirteen children
and seven grandchildren
reputably.
From this instance, reader,
Be encouraged to diligence in thy calling,
And distrust not Providence.
He was a pious and prudent man;
She, a discreet and virtuous woman.
Their youngest son,
In filial regard to their memory,
Places this stone.
J. F. born 1655, died 1744, ætat 89
A. F. born 1667, died 1752, — 85

By my rambling digressions I perceive myself to be grown old. I us'd to write more methodically. But one does not dress for private company as for a public ball. 'Tis perhaps only negligence.

To return: I continued thus employed in my father's business for two years, that is, till I was twelve years old; and my brother John, who was bred to that business, having left my father, married, and set up for himself at Rhode Island, there was all appearance that I was destined to supply his place, and become a tallow-chandler. But my dislike to the trade continuing, my father was under apprehensions that if he did not find one for me more agreeable, I should break away and get to sea, as his son Josiah had done, to his great vexation. He therefore sometimes took me to walk with him, and see joiners, bricklayers, turners, braziers, etc., at their work, that he might observe my inclination, and endeavour to fix it on some trade or other on land. It has ever since been a pleasure to me to see good workmen handle their tools; and it has been useful to me, having learnt so much by it as to be able to do little jobs myself in my house when a workman could not readily be got, and to construct little machines for my experiments, while the intention of making the experiment was fresh and warm in my mind. My father at last fixed upon the cutler's trade, and my uncle Benjamin's son Samuel, who was bred to that business in London, being about that time established in Boston, I was sent to be with him some time on liking. But his expectations of a fee with me displeasing my father, I was taken home again.

From a child I was fond of reading, and all the little money that came into my hands was ever laid out in books. Pleased with the Pilgrim's Progress, my first collection was of John Bunyan's works in separate little volumes. I afterward sold them to enable me to buy R. Burton's Historical Collections; they were small chapmen's books, and cheap, 40 or 50 in all. My father's little library consisted chiefly of books in polemic divinity, most of which I read, and have since often regretted that, at a time when I had such a thirst for knowledge, more proper books had not fallen in my way, since it was now resolved I should not be a clergyman. Plutarch's Lives there was in which I read abundantly, and I still think that time spent to great advantage. There was also a book of Defoe's, called *An Essay on Projects*, and another of Dr Mather's, called *Essays to do Good*, which perhaps gave me a turn of thinking that had an influence on some of the principal future events of my life.

This bookish inclination at length determined my father to make me a printer, though he had already one son (James) of that profession. In

1717 my brother James returned from England with a press and letters to set up his business in Boston. I liked it much better than that of my father, but still had a hankering for the sea. To prevent the apprehended effect of such an inclination, my father was impatient to have me bound to my brother. I stood out some time, but at last was persuaded, and signed the indentures when I was yet but twelve years, old. I was to serve as an apprentice till I was twenty-one years of age, only I was to be allowed journeyman's wages during the last year. In a little time I made great proficiency in the business, and became a useful hand to my brother. I now had access to better books. An acquaintance with the apprentices of booksellers enabled me sometimes to borrow a small one, which I was careful to return soon and clean. Often I sat up in my room reading the greatest part of the night, when the book was borrowed in the evening and to be returned early in the morning, lest it should be missed or wanted.

And after some time an ingenious tradesman, Mr Matthew Adams, who had a pretty collection of books, and who frequented our printing-house, took notice of me, invited me to his library, and very kindly lent me such books as I chose to read. I now took a fancy to poetry, and made some little pieces; my brother, thinking it might turn to account, encouraged me, and put me on composing occasional ballads. One was called *The Lighthouse Tragedy*, and contained an account of the drowning of Captain Worthilake, with his two daughters: the other was a sailor's song, on the taking of *Teach* (or Blackbeard) the pirate. They were wretched stuff, in the Grub-Street-ballad style; and when they were printed he sent me about the town to sell them. The first sold wonderfully, the event being recent, having made a great noise. This flattered my vanity; but my father discouraged me by ridiculing my performances, and telling me verse-makers were generally beggars. So I escaped being a poet, most probably a very bad one; but as prose writing has been of great use to me in the course of my life, and was a principal means of my advancement, I shall tell you how, in such a situation, I acquired what little ability I have in that way.

There was another bookish lad in the town, John Collins by name, with whom I was intimately acquainted. We sometimes disputed, and very fond we were of argument, and very desirous of confuting one another, which disputatious turn, by the way, is apt to become a very bad habit, making people often extremely disagreeable in company by the contradiction that is necessary to bring it into practice; and thence, besides souring and spoiling the conversation, is productive of disgusts and, perhaps enmities where you may have occasion for friendship. I had caught it by reading my father's books of dispute about religion. Persons of good sense, I have since observed, seldom fall into it, except lawyers, university men, and men of all sorts that have been bred at Edinburgh.

A question was once, somehow or other, started between Collins and me, of the propriety of educating the female sex in learning, and their abilities for study. He was of opinion that it was improper, and that they were naturally unequal to it. I took the contrary side, perhaps a little for dispute's sake. He was naturally more eloquent, had a ready plenty of words; and sometimes, as I thought, bore me down more by his fluency than by the strength of his reasons. As we parted without settling the point, and were not to see one another again for some time, I sat down to put my arguments in writing, which I copied fair and sent to him. He answered, and I replied. Three or four letters of a side had passed, when my father happened to find my papers and read them. Without entering into the discussion, he took occasion to talk to me about the manner of my writing; observed that, though I had the advantage of my antagonist in correct spelling and pointing (which I ow'd to the printing-house), I fell far short in elegance of expression, in method and in perspicuity, of which he convinced me by several instances. I saw the justice of his remarks, and thence grew more attentive to the manner in writing, and determined to endeavour at improvement.

About this time I met with an odd volume of the *Spectator*. It was the third. I had never before seen any of them. I bought it, read it over and over, and was much delighted with it. I thought the writing excellent, and wished, if possible, to imitate it. With this view I took some of the papers, and, making short hints of the sentiment in each sentence, laid them by a few days, and then, without looking at the book, try'd to complete the papers again, by expressing each hinted sentiment at length, and as fully as it had been expressed before, in any suitable words that should come to hand. Then I compared my *Spectator* with the original, discovered some of my faults, and corrected them. But I found I wanted a stock of words, or a readiness in recollecting and using them, which I thought I should have acquired before that time if I had gone on making verses; since the continual occasion for words of the same import, but of different length, to suit the measure, or of different sound for the rhyme, would have laid me under a constant necessity of searching for variety, and also have tended to fix that variety in my mind, and make me master of it. Therefore I took some of the tales and turned them into verse; and, after a time, when I had pretty well forgotten the prose, turned them back again. I also sometimes jumbled my collections of hints into confusion, and after some weeks endeavoured to reduce them into the best order, before I began to form the full sentences and complete the paper. This was to teach me method in the arrangement of thoughts. By comparing my work afterwards with the original, I discovered many faults and amended them; but I sometimes had the pleasure of fancying that, in certain particulars of small import, I had been lucky enough to improve the method or the language, and this encouraged me to think I might possibly in time come to be a tolerable English writer, of which I was extremely ambitious. My time for these exercises and for reading was at night, after work or before it began in the morning, or on Sundays, when I contrived to be in the printing-house alone, evading as much as I could the common attendance on public worship which my father used to exact on me when I was under his care, and which indeed I still thought a duty, though I could not, as it seemed to me, afford time to practise it.

When about 16 years of age I happened to meet with a book, written by one Tryon, recommending a vegetable diet. I determined to go into it. My brother, being yet unmarried, did not keep house, but boarded himself and his apprentices in another family. My refusing to eat flesh occasioned an inconveniency, and I was frequently chid for my singularity. I made myself acquainted with Tryon's manner of preparing some of his dishes, such as boiling potatoes or rice, making hasty pudding, and a few others, and then proposed to my brother, that if he would give me, weekly, half the money he paid for my board, I would board myself. He instantly agreed to it, and I presently found that I could save half what he paid me. This was an additional fund for buying books. But I had another advantage in it. My brother and the rest going from the printing-house to their meals, I remained there alone, and, dispatching presently my light repast, which often was no more than a biscuit or a slice of bread, a handful of raisins or a tart from the pastry-cook's, and a glass of water, had the rest of the time till their return for study, in which I made the greater progress, from that greater clearness of head and quicker apprehension which usually attend temperance in eating and drinking.

And now it was that, being on some occasion made asham'd of my ignorance in figures, which I had twice failed in learning when at school, I took Cocker's book of Arithmetic, and went through the whole by myself with great ease. I also read Seller's and Shermy's books of Navigation, and became acquainted with the little geometry they contain; but never proceeded far in that science. And I read about this time Locke *on Human Understanding*, and the *Art of Thinking*, by Messrs du Port Royal.

While I was intent on improving my language, I met with an English grammar (I think it was Greenwood's), at the end of which there were two little sketches of the arts of rhetoric and logic, the latter finishing with a specimen of a dispute in the Socratic method; and soon after I procur'd Xenophon's Memorable Things of Socrates, wherein there are many instances of the same method. I was charm'd with it, adopted it, dropped my abrupt contradiction and positive argumentation, and put on the humble inquirer and doubter. And being then, from reading Shaftesbury and Collins, become a real doubter in many points of our religious doctrine, I found this method safest for myself and very embarrassing to those against whom I used it; therefore I took a delight in it, practis'd it continually, and grew very artful and expert in drawing people, even of superior knowledge, into concessions, the consequences of which they did not foresee, entangling them in difficulties out of which they could not extricate themselves, and so obtaining victories that neither myself nor my cause always deserved. I continu'd this method some few years, but gradually left it, retaining only the habit of expressing myself in terms of modest diffidence; never using, when I advanced anything that may possibly be disputed, the words *certainly*, *undoubtedly*, or any others that give the air of positiveness to an opinion; but rather say, I conceive or apprehend a thing to be so and so; it appears to me, or *I should think it so or so*, for such and such reasons; or *I imagine it to be so; or it is so, if I am not mistaken*. This habit, I believe, has been of great advantage to me when I have had occasion to inculcate my opinions, and persuade men into measures that I have been from time to time engag'd in promoting; and, as the chief ends of conversation are to *inform* or to be *informed*, to *please* or to *persuade*, I wish well-meaning, sensible men would not lessen their power of doing good by a positive, assuming manner, that seldom fails to disgust, tends to create opposition, and to defeat everyone of those purposes for which speech was given to us, to wit, giving or receiving information or pleasure. For, if you would inform, a positive and dogmatical manner in advancing your sentiments may provoke contradiction and prevent a candid attention. If you wish information and improvement from the knowledge of others, and yet at the same time express yourself as firmly fix'd in your present opinions, modest, sensible men, who do not love disputation, will probably leave you undisturbed in the possession of your error. And by such a manner, you can seldom hope to recommend yourself in *pleasing* your hearers, or to persuade those whose concurrence you desire. Pope says, judiciously:

> *Men should be taught as if you taught them not*
> *And things unknown propos'd as things forgot;*

farther recommending to us

> To speak, tho' sure, with seeming diffidence.

And he might have coupled with this line that which he has coupled with another, I think, less properly,

> For want of modesty is want of sense.

If you ask, Why less properly? I must repeat the lines,

> Immodest words admit of no defence
> For want of modesty is want of sense.

Now, is not *want of sense* (where a man is so unfortunate as to want it) some apology for his *want of modesty?* and would not the lines stand more justly thus?

> Immodest words admit *but* this defence,
> That want of modesty is want of sense.

This, however, I should submit to better judgements.

My brother had, in 1720 or 1721, begun to print a newspaper. It was the second that appeared in America, and was called the *New England Courant*. The only one before it was the *Boston News-Letter*. I remember his being dissuaded by some of his friends from the undertaking, as not likely to succeed, one newspaper being, in their judgement, enough for America. At this time (1771) there are not less than five-and-twenty. He went on, however, with the undertaking, and after having worked in composing the types and printing off the sheets, I was employed to carry the papers thro' the streets to the customers.

He had some ingenious men among his friends, who amus'd themselves by writing little pieces for this paper, which gain'd it credit and made it more in demand, and these gentlemen often visited us. Hearing their conversations, and their accounts of the approbation their papers were received with, I was excited to try my hand among them; but, being still a boy, and suspecting that my brother would object to printing anything of mine in his paper if he knew it to be mine, I contrived to disguise my hand, and, writing an anonymous paper, I put it in at night under the door of the printing-house. It was found in the morning, and communicated to his writing friends when they call'd in as usual. They read it, commented on it in my hearing, and I had the exquisite pleasure of finding it met with their approbation, and that, in their different guesses at the author, none were named but men of some character among us for learning and ingenuity. I suppose now that I was rather lucky in my judges, and that perhaps they were not really so very good ones as I then esteem'd them.

Encourag'd, however, by this, I wrote and convey'd in the same way to the press several more papers which were equally approv'd; and I kept my secret till my small fund of sense for such performances was pretty well exhausted, and then I discovered it, when I began to be considered a little more by my brother's acquaintance, and in a manner that did not quite please him, as he thought, probably with reason, that it tended to make me too vain. And, perhaps, this might be one occasion of the differences that we began to have about this time. Though a brother, he considered himself as my master, and me as his apprentice, and, accordingly, expected the same services from me as he would from another, while I thought he demean'd me too much in some he requir'd of me, who from a brother expected more indulgence. Our disputes were often brought before our father, and I fancy I was either generally in the right, or else a better pleader, because the judgement was generally in my favour. But my brother was passionate, and had often beaten me, which I took extremely amiss; and, thinking my apprentice-ship very tedious, I was continually wishing for some opportunity of shortening it, which at length offered in a manner unexpected.*

One of the pieces in our newspaper on some political point, which I have now forgotten, gave offence to the Assembly. He was taken up, censur'd, and imprison'd for a month, by the speaker's warrant, I suppose, because he would not discover his author. I too was taken up and examin'd before the council; but, tho' I did not give them any satisfaction, they content'd themselves with admonishing me, and dismissed me, considering me, perhaps, as an apprentice, who was bound to keep his master's secrets.

* I fancy his harsh and tyrannical treatment of me might be a means of impressing me with that aversion to arbitrary power that has stuck to me through my whole life.

During my brother's confinement, which I resented a good deal, notwithstanding our private differences, I had the management of the paper; and I made bold to give our rulers some rubs in it, which my brother took very kindly, while others began to consider me in an unfavourable light, as a young genius that had a turn for libelling and satire. My brother's discharge was accompany'd with an order of the House (a very odd one), that *'James Franklin should no longer print the paper called the New England Courant.'*

There was a consultation held in our printing-house among his friends, what he should do in this case. Some proposed to evade the order by changing the name of the paper; but my brother, seeing inconveniences in that, it was finally concluded on as a better way, to let it be printed for the future under the name of BENJAMIN FRANKLIN; and to avoid the censure of the Assembly, that might fall on him as still printing it by his apprentice, the contrivance was that my old indenture should be return'd to me, with a full discharge on the back of it, to be shown on occasion, but to secure to him the benefit of my service, I was to sign new indentures for the remainder of the term, which were to be kept private. A very flimsy scheme it was; however, it was immediately executed, and the paper went on accordingly, under my name for several months.

At length, a fresh difference arising between my brother and me, I took upon me to assert my freedom, presuming that he would not venture to produce the new indentures. It was not fair in me to take this advantage, and this I therefore reckon one of the first errata of my life; but the unfairness of it weighed little with me, when under the impressions of resentment for the blows his passion too often urged him to bestow upon me, though he was otherwise not an ill-natur'd man: perhaps I was too saucy and provoking.

When he found I would leave him, he took care to prevent my getting employment in any other printing-house of the town, by going round and speaking to every master, who accordingly refus'd to give me work. I then thought of going to New York, as the nearest place where there was a printer; and I was rather inclin'd to leave Boston when I reflected that I had already made myself a little obnoxious to the governing party, and, from the arbitrary proceedings of the Assembly in my brother's case, it was likely I might, if I stay'd, soon bring myself into scrapes; and farther, that my indiscreet disputations about religion began to make me pointed at with horror by good people as an infidel or atheist. I determin'd on the point, but my father now siding with my brother, I was sensible that, if I attempted to go openly, means would be used to prevent me. My friend Collins, therefore, undertook to manage a little for me. He agreed with the captain of a New York sloop for my passage, under the notion of my being a young acquaintance of his, that had got a naughty girl with child, whose friends would compel me to marry her, and therefore I could not appear or come away publicly. So I sold some of my books to raise a little money, was taken on board privately, and as we had a fair wind, in three days I found myself in New York, near 300 miles from home, a boy of but 17, without the least recommendation to, or knowledge of any person in the place, and with very little money in my pocket.

My inclinations for the sea were by this time worn out, or I might now have gratify'd them. But, having a trade, and supposing myself a pretty good workman, I offer'd my service to the printer in the place, old Mr William Bradford, who had been the first printer in Pennsylvania, but removed from thence upon the quarrel of George Keith. He could give me no employment, having little to do, and help enough already; but says he, 'My son at Philadelphia has lately lost his principal hand, Aquila Rose, by death; if you go thither, I believe he may employ you.' Philadelphia was a hundred miles further; I set out, however, in a boat for Amboy, leaving my chest and things to follow me round by sea.

In crossing the bay, we met with a squall that tore our rotten sails to pieces, prevented our getting into the Kill, and drove us upon Long Island. In our way, a drunken Dutchman, who was a passenger too, fell overboard; when he was sinking, I reached through the water to his shock pate, and drew him up, so that we got him in again. His ducking sobered him a little, and he went to sleep, taking first out of his pocket a book, which he desir'd I would dry for him. It proved to be my old favourite author, Bunyan's *Pilgrim's Progress*, in Dutch, finely printed on good paper, with copper cuts, a dress better than I had ever seen it wear in its own language. I have since found that it has been translated into most of the languages of Europe, and suppose it has been more generally read than any other book, except perhaps the Bible. Honest John was the first that I know of who mix'd narration and dialogue; a method of writing very engaging to the reader, who in the most interesting parts finds himself, as it were, brought into the company and present at the discourse. Defoe in his *Crusoe*, his *Moll Flanders*, *Religious Courtship*, *Family Instructor*, and other pieces, has imitated it with success; and Richardson has done the same in his *Pamela*, etc.

When we drew near the island, we found it was at a place where there could be no landing, there being a great surf on the stony beach.

So we dropped anchor, and swung round towards the shore. Some people came down to the water edge and hallow'd to us, as we did to them; but the wind was so high, and the surf so loud, that we could not hear so as to understand each other. There were canoes on the shore, and we made signs, and hallow'd that they should fetch us; but they either did not understand us, or thought it impracticable, so they went away, and night coming on, we had no remedy but to wait till the wind should abate; and, in the meantime, the boatman and I concluded to sleep, if we could; and so crowded into the scuttle, with the Dutchman, who was still wet, and the spray beating over the head of our boat, leak'd thro' to us, so that we were soon almost as wet as he. In this manner we lay all night, with very little rest; but, the wind abating the next day, we made a shift to reach Amboy before night, having been thirty hours on the water, without victuals, or any drink but a bottle of filthy rum, and the water we sail'd on being salt.

In the evening I found myself very feverish, and went into bed; but, having read somewhere that cold water drank plentifully was good for a fever, I follow'd the prescription, sweat plentiful most of the night, my fever left me, and in the morning, crossing the ferry, I proceeded on my journey on foot, having fifty miles to Burlington, where I was told I should find boats that would carry me the rest of the way to Philadelphia.

It rained very hard all the day; I was thoroughly soak'd, and by noon a good deal tired; so I stopped at a poor inn, where I stayed all night, beginning now to wish that I had never left home. I cut so miserable a figure, too, that I found, by the questions ask'd me, I was suspected to be some runaway servant, and in danger of being taken up on that suspicion. However, I proceeded the next day, and got in the evening to an inn, within eight or ten miles of Burlington, kept by one Dr Brown. He entered into conversation with me while I took some refreshment, and, finding I had read a little, became very sociable and friendly. Our acquaintance continu'd as long as he liv'd. He had been, I imagine, an itinerant doctor, for there was no town in England, or country in Europe, of which he could not give a very particular account. He had some letters, and was ingenious, but much of an unbeliever, and wickedly undertook, some years after, to travesty the Bible in doggerel verse, as Cotton had done Virgil. By this means he set many of the facts in a very ridiculous light, and might have hurt weak minds if his work had been published; but it never was.

At his house I lay that night, and the next morning reach'd Burlington, but had the mortification to find that the regular boats were gone a little before my coming, and no other expected to go before Tuesday, this being Saturday; wherefore I returned to an old woman in the town, of whom I had bought gingerbread to eat on the water, and ask'd her advice. She invited me to lodge at her house till a passage by water should offer; and being tired with my foot travelling, I accepted the invitation. She understanding I was a printer, would have had me stay at that town and follow my business, being ignorant of the stock necessary to begin with. She was very hospitable, gave me a dinner of ox-cheek with great good will, accepting only of a pot of ale in return; and I thought myself fixed till Tuesday should come. However, walking in the evening by the side of the river, a boat came by, which I found was going towards Philadelphia, with several people in her. They took me in, and, as there was no wind, we row'd all the way; and about midnight, not having yet seen the city, some of the company were confident we must have passed it, and would row no farther; the others knew not where we were; so we put toward the shore, got into a creek, landed near an old fence, with the rails of which we made a fire, the night being cold, in October, and there we remained till daylight. Then one of the company knew the place to be Cooper's Creek, a little above Philadelphia, which we saw as soon as we got out of the creek, and arriv'd there about eight or nine o'clock on the Sunday morning, and landed at the Market Street wharf.

I have been the more particular in this description of my journey, and shall be so of my first entry into that city, that you may in your mind compare such unlikely beginnings with the figure I have since made there. I was in my working dress, my best clothes being to come round by sea. I was dirty from my journey; my pockets were stuff'd out with shirts and stockings, and I knew no soul nor where to look for lodging. I was fatigued with travelling, rowing, and want of rest, I was very hungry; and my whole stock of cash consisted of a Dutch dollar, and about a shilling in copper. The latter I gave the people of the boat for my passage, who at first refus'd it, on account of my rowing; but I insisted on their taking it. A man being sometimes more generous when he has but a little money than when he has plenty, perhaps thro' fear of being thought to have but little.

Then I walked up the street, gazing about till near the market-house I met a boy with bread. I had made many a meal on bread, and, inquiring where he got it, I went immediately to the baker's he directed me to, in Second Street, and ask'd for biscuit, intending such as we had in Boston; but they, it seems, were not made in Philadelphia. Then I asked for a three-penny loaf, and was told they had none such. So not considering or knowing the difference of money, and the greater cheapness nor the names of his bread, I bad him give me three-penny worth of any sort. He gave me, accordingly, three great puffy rolls. I was surpris'd at the quantity, but took it, and, having no room in my pockets, walk'd off with a roll under each arm, and eating the other. Thus I went up Market Street as far as Fourth Street, passing by the door of Mr Read, my future wife's father; when she, standing at the door, saw me, and thought I made, as I certainly did, a most awkward, ridiculous appearance. Then I turned and went down Chestnut Street and part of Walnut Street, eating my roll all the way, and, coming round, found myself again at Market Street wharf, near the boat I came in, to which I went for a draught of the river water; and, being filled with one of my rolls, gave the other two to a woman and her child that came down the river in the boat with us, and were waiting to go farther.

Thus refreshed, I walked again up the street, which by this time had many clean-dressed people in it, who were all walking the same way. I joined them, and thereby was led into the great meeting-house of the Quakers near the market. I sat down among them, and, after looking round awhile and hearing nothing said, being very drowsy thro' labour and want of rest the preceding night, I fell fast asleep, and continued so till the meeting broke up, when one was kind enough to rouse me. This was, therefore, the first house I was in or slept in, in Philadelphia.

Walking down again toward the river, and, looking in the faces of people, I met a young Quaker man, whose countenance I lik'd, and, accosting him, requested he would tell me where a stranger could get lodging. We were then near the sign of the Three Mariners. 'Here,' says he, 'is one place that entertains strangers, but it is not a reputable house; if thee wilt walk with me, I'll show thee a better.' He brought me to the Crooked Billet in Water Street. Here I got a dinner; and, while I was eating it, several sly questions were asked me, as it seemed to be suspected from my youth and appearance, that I might be some runaway.

After dinner, my sleepiness return'd, and being shown to a bed, I lay down without undressing, and slept till six in the evening, was call'd to supper, went to bed again very early, and slept soundly till next morning. Then I made myself as tidy as I could, and went to Andrew Bradford the printer's. I found in the shop the old man his father, whom I had seen at New York, and who, travelling on horseback, had got to Philadelphia before me. He introduc'd me to his son, who receiv'd me civilly, gave me a breakfast, but told me he did not at present want a hand, being lately suppli'd with one; but there was another printer in town, lately set up, one Keimer, who, perhaps, might employ me; if not, I should be welcome to lodge at his house, and he would give me a little work to do now and then till fuller business should offer.

The old gentleman said he would go with me to the new printer; and when we found him, 'Neighbour,' says Bradford, 'I have brought to see you a young man of your business; perhaps you may want such a one.' He ask'd me a few questions, put a composing stick in my hand to see how I work'd, and then said he would employ me soon, though he had just then nothing for me to do; and, taking old Bradford, whom he had never seen before, to be one of the town's people that had a good will for him, enter'd into a conversation on his present undertaking and prospects; while Bradford, not discovering that he was the other printer's father, on Keimer's saying he expected soon to get the greatest part of the business into his own hands, drew him on by artful questions, and starting little doubts, to explain all his views, what interest he reli'd on, and in what manner he intended to proceed. I, who stood by and heard all, saw immediately that one of them was a crafty old sophister, and the other a mere novice. Bradford left me with Keimer, who was greatly surprised when I told him who the old man was.

Keimer's printing-house, I found, consisted of an old shatter'd press, and one small, worn-out font of English, which he was then using himself, composing an Elegy on Aquila Rose, before mentioned, an ingenious young man, of excellent character, much respected in the town, clerk of the Assembly, and a pretty poet. Keimer made verses too, but very indifferently. He could not be said to write them, for his manner was to compose them in the types directly out of his head. So there being no copy, but one pair of cases, and the Elegy likely to require all the letter, no one could help him. I endeavour'd to put his press (which he had not yet us'd, and of which he understood nothing) into order fit to be work'd with; and, promising to come and print off his Elegy as soon as he should have got it ready, I return'd to Bradford's, who gave me a little job to do for the present, and there I lodged and dieted. A few days after, Keimer sent for me to print off the Elegy. And now he had got another pair of cases, and a pamphlet to reprint, on which he set me to work.

These two printers I found poorly qualified for their business. Bradford had not been bred to it, and was very illiterate; and Keimer, tho' something of a scholar, was a mere compositor, knowing nothing of presswork. He had been one of the French prophets, and could act their enthusiastic agitations. At this time he did not profess any particular religion, but something of all on occasion; was very ignorant of the world, and had, as I afterward found, a good deal of the knave in his composition. He did not like my lodging at Bradford's while I work'd with him. He had a house, indeed, but without furniture, so he could not lodge me; but he got me a lodging at Mr Read's, before mentioned, who was the owner of his house; and, my chest and clothes being come by this time, I made rather a more respectable appearance in the eyes of Miss Read than I had done when she first happen'd to see me eating my roll in the street.

I began now to have some acquaintance among the young people of the town, that were lovers of reading, with whom I spent my evenings very pleasantly; and gaining money by my industry and frugality, I lived very agreeably, forgetting Boston as much as I could, and not desiring that any there should know where I resided, except my friend Collins, who was in my secret, and kept it when I wrote to him. At length, an incident happened that sent me back again much sooner than I had intended. I had a brother-in-law, Robert Holmes, master of a sloop that traded between Boston and Delaware. He being at Newcastle, forty miles below Philadelphia, heard there of me, and wrote me a letter mentioning the concern of my friends in Boston at my abrupt departure, assuring me of their good will to me, and that everything would be accommodated to my mind if I would return, to which he exhorted me very earnestly. I wrote an answer to his letter, thank'd him for his advice, but stated my reasons for quitting Boston fully and in such a light as to convince him I was not so wrong as he had apprehended.

Sir William Keith, governor of the province, was then at Newcastle, and Captain Holmes, happening to be in company with him when my letter came to hand, spoke to him of me, and show'd him the letter. The governor read it, and seem'd supris'd when he was told of my age. He said I appear'd a young man of promising parts, and therefore should be encouraged; the printers at Philadelphia were wretched ones; and, if I would set up there, he made no doubt I should succeed; for his part, he would procure me the public business, and do me every other service in his power. This my brother-in-law afterwards told me in Boston, but I knew as yet nothing of it; when, one day, Keimer and I being at work together near the window, we saw the governor and another gentleman (which proved to be Colonel French of Newcastle), finely dress'd, come directly across the street to our house, and heard them at the door.

Keimer ran down immediately, thinking it a visit to him; but the governor inquir'd for me, came up, and with a condescension and politeness I had been quite unus'd to, made me many compliments, desired to be acquainted with me, blam'd me kindly for not having made myself known to him when I first came to the place, and would have me away with him to the tavern, where he was going with Colonel French to taste, as he said, some excellent Madeira. I was not a little surprised, and Keimer star'd like a pig poison'd. I went, however, with the governor and Colonel French to a tavern, at the corner of Third Street, and over the Madeira he propos'd my setting up my business, laid before me the probabilities of success, and both he and Colonel French assur'd me I should have their interest and influence in procuring the public business of both governments. On my doubting whether my father would assist me in it, Sir William said he would give me a letter to him, in which he would state the advantages, and he did not doubt of prevailing with him. So it was concluded I should return to Boston in the first vessel, with the governor's letter recommending me to my father. In the meantime the intention was to be kept a secret, and I went on working with Keimer as usual, the governor sending for me now and then to dine with him, a very great honour I thought it, and conversing with me in the most affable, familiar, and friendly manner imaginable.

About the end of April, 1724, a little vessel offer'd for Boston. I took leave of Keimer as going to see my friends. The governor gave me an ample letter, saying many flattering things of me to my father, and strongly recommending the project of my setting up at Philadelphia as a thing that must make my fortune. We struck on a shoal in going down the bay, and sprung a leak; we had a blustering time at sea, and were oblig'd to pump almost continually, at which I took my turn. We arriv'd safe, however, at Boston in about a fortnight. I had been absent seven months, and my friends had heard nothing of me; for my br. Holmes was not yet return'd, and had not written about me. My unexpected appearance surpris'd the family; all were, however, very glad to see me, and made me welcome, except my brother. I went to see him at his printing-house. I was better dress'd than ever while in his service, having a genteel new suit from head to foot, a watch, and my pockets lin'd with near five pounds sterling in silver. He receiv'd me not very frankly, look'd me all over, and turn'd to his work again.

The journeymen were inquisitive where I had been, what sort of a country it was, and how I lik'd it. I prais'd it much, and the happy life I led in it, expressing strongly my intention of returning to it; and, one of them asking what kind of money we had there, I produc'd a handful of silver, and spread it before them, which was a kind of raree-show they had not been us'd to, paper being the money of Boston. Then I took an opportunity of letting them see my watch; and, lastly (my brother still grum and sullen), I gave them a piece of eight to drink, and took my leave. This visit of mine offended him extremely; for, when my mother some time after spoke to him of a reconciliation, and of her wishes to see us on good terms together, and that we might live for the future as brothers, he said I had insulted him in such a manner before his people that he could never forget or forgive it. In this, however, he was mistaken.

My father received the governor's letter with some apparent surprise, but said little of it to me for some days, when Capt. Holmes returning he showed it to him, ask'd him if he knew Keith, and what kind of man he was; adding his opinion that he must be of small discretion to think of setting a boy up in business who wanted yet three years of being at man's estate. Holmes said what he could in favour of the project, but my father was clear in the impropriety of it, and at last gave a flat denial to it. Then he wrote a civil letter to Sir William, thanking him for the patronage he had so kindly offered me, but declining to assist me as yet in setting up, I being, in his opinion, too young to be trusted with the management of a business so important, and for which the preparation must be so expensive.

My friend and companion Collins, who was a clerk in the post-office, pleas'd with the account I gave him of my new country, determined to go thither also; and, while I waited for my father's determination, he set out before me by land to Rhode Island, leaving his books, which were a pretty collection of mathematics and natural philosophy, to come with mine and me to New York, where he propos'd to wait for me.

My father, tho' he did not approve Sir William's proposition, was yet pleas'd that I had been able to obtain so advantageous a character from a person of such note where I had resided, and that I had been so industrious and careful as to equip myself so handsomely in so short a time; therefore, seeing no prospect of an accommodation between my brother and me, he gave his consent to my returning again to Philadelphia, advis'd me to behave respectfully to the people there, endeavour to obtain the general esteem, and avoid lampooning and libelling, to which he thought I had too much inclination; telling me, that by steady industry and a prudent parsimony I might save enough by the time I was one-and-twenty to set me up; and that, if I came near the matter, he would help me out with the rest. This was all I could obtain, except some small gifts as tokens of his and my mother's love, when I embark'd again for New York, now with their approbation and their blessing.

The sloop putting in at Newport, Rhode Island, I visited my brother John, who had been married and settled there some years. He received me very affectionately, for he always lov'd me. A friend of his, one Vernon, having some money due to him in Pennsylvania, about thirty-five pounds currency, desired I would receive it for him, and keep it till I had his directions what to remit it in. Accordingly, he gave me an order. This afterwards occasion'd me a good deal of uneasiness.

At Newport we took in a number of passengers for New York, among which were two young women, companions, and a grave, sensible, matron-like Quaker woman, with her attendants. I had shown an obliging readiness to do her some little services, which impress'd her I suppose with a degree of good will toward me; therefore, when she saw a daily growing familiarity between me and the two young women, which they appear'd to encourage, she took me aside, and said, 'Young man, I am concern'd for thee, as thou has no friend with thee, and seems not to know much of the world, or of the snares youth is expos'd to; depend upon it, those are very bad women; I can see it in all their actions; and if thee art not upon thy guard, they will draw thee into some danger; they are strangers to thee, and I advise thee, in a friendly concern for thy welfare, to have no acquaintance with them.' As I seem'd at first not to think so ill of them as she did, she mentioned some things she had observ'd and heard that had escap'd my notice, but now convinc'd me she was right. I thank'd her for her kind advice, and promis'd to follow it. When we arriv'd at New York, they told me where they liv'd, and invited me to come and see them; but I avoided it, and it was well I did; for the next day the captain miss'd a silver spoon and some other things, that had been taken out of his cabin, and, knowing that these were a couple of strumpets, he got a warrant to search their lodgings, found the stolen goods, and had the thieves punish'd. So, tho' we had escap'd a sunken rock, which we scrap'd upon in the passage, I thought this escape of rather more importance to me.

At New York I found my friend Collins, who had arriv'd there some time before me. We had been intimate from children, and had read the same books together; but he had the advantage of more time for reading and studying, and a wonderful genius for mathematical learning, in which he far outstripped me. While I liv'd in Boston, most of my hours of leisure for conversation were spent with him, and he continu'd a sober as well as an industrious lad; was much respected for his learning by several of the clergy and other gentlemen, and seemed to promise making a good figure in life. But, during my absence, he had acquir'd a habit of sotting with brandy; and I found by his own account, and what I heard from others, that he had been drunk every day since his arrival at New York, and behav'd very oddly. He had gam'd, too, and lost his money, so that I was oblig'd to discharge his lodgings, and defray his expenses to and at Philadelphia, which prov'd extremely inconvenient to me.

The then governor of New York, Burnet (son of Bishop Burnet), hearing from the captain that a young man, one of his passengers, had a great many books, desir'd he would bring me to see him. I waited upon him accordingly, and should have taken Collins with me but that he was not sober. The gov'r treated me with great civility, show'd me his library, which was a very large one, and we had a good deal of conversation about books and authors. This was the second governor who had done me the honour to take notice of me; which, to a poor boy like me, was very pleasing.

We proceeded to Philadelphia. I received on the way Vernon's money, without which we could hardly have finish'd our journey. Collins wished to be employ'd in some counting-house; but, whether they discover'd his dramming by his breath, or by his behaviour, tho' he had some recommendations, he met with no success in any application, and continu'd lodging and boarding at the same house with me, and at my expense. Knowing I had that money of Vernon's, he was continually borrowing of me, still promising repayment as soon as he should be in business. At length he had got so much of it that I was distress'd to think what I should do in case of being call'd on to remit it.

His drinking continu'd, about which we sometimes quarrell'd; for, when a little intoxicated, he was very fractious. Once, in a boat on the Delaware with some other young men, he refused to row in his turn. 'I will be row'd home,' says he. 'We will not row you,' says I. 'You must, or stay all night on the water,' says he, 'just as you please.' The others said, 'Let us row; what signifies it?' But, my mind being soured with his other conduct, I continu'd to refuse. So he swore he would make me row, or throw me overboard; and coming along, stepping on the thwarts, toward me, when he came up and struck at me, I clapped my hand under his crotch, and, rising, pitched him head-foremost into the river. I knew he was a good swimmer, and so was under little concern about him; but before he could get round to lay hold of the boat, we had with a few strokes pull'd her out of his reach; and ever when he drew near the boat, we ask'd if he would row, striking a few strokes to slide her away from him. He was ready to die with vexation, and obstinately would not promise to row. However, seeing him at last beginning to tire, we lifted him in and brought him home dripping wet in the evening. We hardly exchang'd a civil word afterwards, and a West India captain, who had a commission to procure a tutor for the sons of a gentleman at Barbados, happening to meet with him, agreed to carry him thither. He left me then, promising to remit me the first money he should receive in order to discharge the debt; but I never heard of him after.

The breaking into this money of Vernon's was one of the first great errata of my life; and this affair show'd that my father was not much out in his judgement when he suppos'd me too young to manage business of importance. But Sir William, on reading his letter, said he was too prudent. There was great difference in persons; and discretion did not always accompany years, nor was youth always without it. 'And since he will not set you up,' says he, 'I will do it myself. Give me an inventory of the things necessary to be had from England, and I will send for them. You shall repay me when you are able; I am resolv'd to have a good printer here, and I am sure you must succeed.' This was spoken with such an appearance of cordiality, that I had not the least doubt of his meaning what he said. I had hitherto kept the proposition of my setting up, a secret in Philadelphia, and I still kept it. Had it been known that I depended on the governor, probably some friend, that knew him better, would have advis'd me not to rely on him, as I afterwards heard it as his known character to be liberal of promises which he never meant to keep. Yet, unsolicited as he was by me, how could I think his generous offers insincere? I believ'd him one of the best men in the world.

I presented him an inventory of a little print'g-house, amounting by my computation to about one hundred pounds sterling. He lik'd it, but ask'd me if my being on the spot in England to choose the types, and see that everything was good of the kind, might not be of some advantage. 'Then,' says he, 'when there, you may make acquaintances, and establish correspondences in the bookselling and stationery way.' I agreed that this might be advantageous. 'Then,' says he, 'get yourself ready to go with Annis'; which was the annual ship, and the only one at that time usually passing between London and Philadelphia. But it would be some months before Annis sail'd, so I continu'd working with Keimer, fretting about the money Collins had got from me, and in daily apprehensions of being call'd upon by Vernon, which, however, did not happen for some years after.

I believe I have omitted mentioning that, in my first voyage from Boston, being becalm'd off Block Island, our people set about catching cod, and hauled up a great many. Hitherto I had stuck to my resolution of not eating animal food, and on this occasion I consider'd, with my master Tryon, the taking every fish as a kind of unprovoked murder, since none of them had, or ever could do us any injury that might justify the slaughter. All this seemed very reasonable. But I had formerly been a great lover of fish, and, when this came hot out of the frying-pan, it smelt admirably well. I balanc'd some time between principle and inclination, till I recollected that, when the fish were opened, I saw smaller fish taken out of their stomachs; then thought I, 'If you eat one another, I don't see why we mayn't eat you.' So I din'd upon cod very heartily, and continued to eat with other people, returning only now and then occasionally to a vegetable diet. So convenient a thing is it to be a *reasonable creature*, since it enables one to find or make a reason for everything one has a mind to do.

Keimer and I liv'd on a pretty good familiar footing, and agreed tolerably well, for he suspected nothing of my setting up. He retained a great deal of his old enthusiasms and lov'd argumentation. We therefore had many disputations. I used to work him so with my Socratic method, and had trepann'd him so often by questions apparently so distant from any point we had in hand, and yet by degrees led to the point, and brought him into difficulties and contradictions, that at last he grew ridiculously cautious, and would hardly answer me the most common question, without asking first, '*What do you intend to infer from that?*' However, it gave him so high an opinion of my abilities in the confuting way, that he seriously proposed my being his colleague in a project he had of setting up a new sect. He was to preach the doctrines, and I was to confound all opponents. When he came to explain with me upon the doctrines, I found several conundrums which I objected to, unless I might have my way a little to, and introduce some of mine.

Keimer wore his beard at full length, because somewhere in the Mosaic law it is said, '*Thou shalt not mar the corners of thy beard.*' He likewise kept the Seventh day, Sabbath; and these two points were essentials with him. I dislik'd both; but agreed to admit them upon condition of his adopting the doctrine of using no animal food. 'I doubt,' said he, 'my constitution will not bear that.' I assur'd him it would, and that he would be the better for it. He was usually a great glutton, and I promised myself some diversion in half starving him. He agreed to try the practice, if I would keep him company. I did so, and we held it for three months. We had our victuals dress'd, and brought to us regularly by a woman in the neighbourhood, who had from me a list of forty dishes, to be prepar'd for us at different times, in all which there was neither fish, flesh, nor fowl, and the whim suited me the better at this time from the cheapness of it, not costing us above eighteenpence sterling each per week. I have since kept several Lents most strictly, leaving the common diet for that, and that for the common, abruptly, without the least inconvenience, so that I think there is little in the advice of making those changes by easy gradations. I went on pleasantly, but poor Keimer suffered grievously, tired of the project, long'd for the fleshpots of Egypt, and order'd a roast pig. He invited me and two women friends to dine with him; but, it being brought too soon upon table, he could not resist the temptation, and ate the whole before we came.

I had made some courtship during this time to Miss Read. I had a great respect and affection for her, and had some reason to believe she had the same for me; but, as I was about to take a long voyage, and we were both very young, only a little above eighteen, it was thought most prudent by her mother to prevent our going too far at present, as a marriage, if it was to take place, would be more convenient after my return, when I should be, as I expected, set up in my business. Perhaps, too, she thought my expectations not so well founded as I imagined them to be.

My chief acquaintances at this time were Charles Osborne, Joseph Watson, and James Ralph, all lovers of reading. The two first were clerks to an eminent scrivener or conveyancer in the town, Charles Brogden; the other was clerk to a merchant. Watson was a pious, sensible young man, of great integrity; the others rather more lax in their principles of religion, particularly Ralph, who, as well as Collins, had been unsettled by me, for which they both made me suffer. Osborne was sensible, candid, frank; sincere and affectionate to his friends; but, in literary matters, too fond of criticising. Ralph was ingenious, genteel in his manners, and extremely eloquent; I think I never knew a prettier talker. Both of them great admirers of poetry, and began to try their hands in little pieces. Many pleasant walks we four had together on Sundays into the woods, near Schuylkill, where we read to one another, and conferr'd on what we read.

Ralph was inclin'd to pursue the study of poetry, not doubting but he might become eminent in it, and make his fortune by it, alleging that the best poets must, when they first began to write, make as many faults as he did. Osborne dissuaded him, assur'd him he had no genius for poetry, and advis'd him to think of nothing beyond the business he was bred to; that, in the mercantile way, tho' he had no stock, he might, by his diligence and punctuality, recommend himself to employment as a factor, and in time acquire wherewith to trade on his own account. I approv'd the amusing one's self with poetry now and then, so far as to improve one's language, but no farther.

On this it was propos'd that we should each of us, at our next meeting, produce a piece of our own composing, in order to improve by our mutual observations, criticisms, and corrections. As language and expression were what we had in view, we excluded all considerations of invention by agreeing that the task should be a version of the eighteenth Psalm, which describes the descent of a Deity. When the time of our meeting drew nigh, Ralph called on me first, and let me know his piece was ready. I told him I had been busy, and, having little inclination, had done nothing. He then show'd me his piece for my opinion, and I much approv'd it, as it appear'd to me to have great merit. 'Now,' says he, 'Osborne never will allow the least merit in anything of mine, but makes 1000 criticisms out of mere envy. He is not so jealous of you; I wish, therefore, you would take this piece, and produce it as yours; I will pretend not to have had time, and so produce nothing. We shall then see what he will say to it.' It was agreed, and I immediately transcrib'd it, that it might appear in my own hand.

We met; Watson's performance was read; there were some beauties in it, but many defects. Osborne's was read; it was much better; Ralph did it justice; remarked some faults, but applauded the beauties. He himself had nothing to produce. I was backward; seemed desirous of being excused; had not had sufficient time to correct, etc.; but no excuse could be admitted; produce I must. It was read and repeated; Watson and Osborne gave up the contest, and join'd in applauding it. Ralph only made some criticisms, and propos'd some amendments; but I defended my text. Osborne was against Ralph, and told him he was no better a critic than poet, so he dropped the argument. As they two went home together, Osborne expressed himself still more strongly in favour of what he thought my production; having restrain'd himself before, as he said, lest I should think it flattery. 'But who would have imagin'd,' said he, 'that Franklin had been capable of such a performance; such painting, such force, such fire! He has even improv'd the original. In his common conversation he seems to have no choice of words; he hesitates and blunders; and yet, good God! how he writes!' When we next met, Ralph discovered the trick we had played him, and Osborne was a little laughed at.

This transaction fixed Ralph in his resolution of becoming a poet. I did all I could to dissuade him from it, but he continued scribbling verses till *Pope* cured him. He became, however, a pretty good prose writer. More of him hereafter. But, as I may not have occasion again to mention the other two, I shall just remark here, that Watson died in my arms a few years after, much lamented, being the best of our set. Osborne went to the West Indies, where he became an eminent lawyer and made money, but died young. He and I had made a serious agreement, that the one who happen'd first to die should, if possible, make a friendly visit to the other, and acquaint him how he found things in that separate state. But he never fulfill'd his promise.

The governor, seeming to like my company, had me frequently to his house, and his setting me up was always mention'd as a fixed thing. I was to take with me letters recommendatory to a number of his friends, besides the letter of credit to furnish me with the necessary money for purchasing the press and types, paper, etc. For these letters I was appointed to call at different times, when they were to be ready; but a future time was still named. Thus he went on till the ship, whose departure too had been several times postponed, was on the point of sailing. Then, when I call'd to take my leave and receive the letters, his secretary, Dr Bard, came out to me and said the governor was extremely busy in writing, but would be down at Newcastle before the ship, and there the letters would be delivered to me.

Ralph, though married, and having one child, had determined to accompany me in this voyage. It was thought he intended to establish a correspondence, and obtain goods to sell on commission; but I found afterwards, that, thro' some discontent with his wife's relations, he purposed to leave her on their hands, and never return again. Having taken leave of my friends, and interchang'd some promises with Miss Read, I left Philadelphia in the ship, which anchor'd at Newcastle. The governor was there; but when I went to his lodging, the secretary came to me from him with the civillest message in the world, that he could not then see me, being engaged in business of the utmost importance, but should send the letters to me on board, wished me heartily a good voyage and a speedy return, etc. I returned on board a little puzzled, but still not doubting.

Mr Andrew Hamilton, a famous lawyer of Philadelphia, had taken passage in the same ship for himself and son, and with Mr Denham, a Quaker merchant, and Messrs Onion and Russel, masters of an iron work in Maryland; had engag'd the great cabin; so that Ralph and I were forced to take up with a berth in the steerage, and none on board knowing us, were considered as ordinary persons. But Mr Hamilton and his son (it was James, since Governor) return'd from Newcastle to Philadelphia, the father being recall'd by a great fee to plead for a seized ship; and, just before we sail'd, Colonel French coming on board, and showing me great respect, I was more taken notice of, and, with my friend Ralph, invited by the other gentlemen to come into the cabin, there being now room. Accordingly, we remov'd thither.

Understanding that Colonel French had brought on board the governor's dispatches, I ask'd the captain for those letters that were to be under my care. He said all were put into the bag together and he could not then come at them; but, before we landed in England, I should have an opportunity of picking them out; so I was satisfied for the present, and we proceeded on our voyage. We had a sociable company in the cabin, and lived uncommonly well, having the addition of all Mr Hamilton's stores, who had laid in plentifully. In this passage Mr Denham contracted a friendship for me that continued during his life. The voyage was otherwise not a pleasant one, as we had a great deal of bad weather.

When we came into the Channel, the captain kept his word with me, and gave me an opportunity of examining the bag for the governor's letters. I found none upon which my name was put as under my care. I picked out six or seven, that, by the handwriting, I thought might be the promised letters, especially as one of them was directed to Basket, the king's printer, and another to some stationer. We arriv'd in London the 24th of December, 1724. I waited upon the stationer, who came first in my way, delivering the letter as from Governor Keith. 'I don't know such a person,' says he; but, opening the letter, 'O! this is from Riddlesden. I have lately found him to be a complete rascal, and I will have nothing to do with him, nor receive any letters from him.' So, putting the letter into my hand, he turn'd on his heel and left me to serve some customer. I was surprised to find these were not the governor's letters; and, after recollecting and comparing circumstances, I began to doubt his sincerity. I found my friend Denham, and opened the whole affair to him. He let me into Keith's character; told me there was not the least probability that he had written any letters for me; that no one, who knew him, had the smallest dependence on him; and he laughed at the notion of the governor's giving me a letter of credit, having, as he said, no credit to give. On my expressing some concern about what I should do, he advised me to endeavour getting some employment in the way of my business. 'Among the printers here,' said he, 'you will improve yourself, and when you return to America, you will set up to greater advantage.'

We both of us happen'd to know, as well as the stationer, that Riddlesden, the attorney, was a very knave. He had half ruin'd Miss

Read's father by persuading him to be bound for him. By this letter it appear'd there was a secret scheme on foot to the prejudice of Hamilton (suppos'd to be then coming over with us); and that Keith was concerned in it with Riddlesden. Denham, who was a friend of Hamilton's, thought he ought to be acquainted with it; so, when he arriv'd in England, which was soon after, partly from resentment and ill-will to Keith and Riddlesden, and partly from good-will to him, I waited on him, and gave him the letter. He thank'd me cordially, the information being of importance to him; and from that time he became my friend, greatly to my advantage afterwards on many occasions.

But what shall we think of a governor's playing such pitiful tricks, and imposing so grossly on a poor ignorant boy! It was a habit he had acquired. He wish'd to please everybody; and, having little to give, he gave expectations. He was otherwise an ingenious, sensible man, a pretty good writer, and a good governor for the people, tho' not for his constituents, the proprietaries, whose instructions he sometimes disregarded. Several of our best laws were of his planning and passed during his administration.

Ralph and I were inseparable companions. We took lodgings together in Little Britain at three shillings and sixpence a week – as much as we could then afford. He found some relations, but they were poor, and unable to assist him. He now let me know his intentions of remaining in London, and that he never meant to return to Philadelphia. He had brought no money with him, the whole he could muster having been expended in paying his passage. I had fifteen pistoles; so he borrowed occasionally of me to subsist, while he was looking out for business. He first endeavoured to get into the playhouse, believing himself qualify'd for an actor; but Wilkes, to whom he apply'd, advis'd him candidly not to think of that employment, as it was impossible he should succeed in it. Then he propos'd to Roberts, a publisher in Paternoster Row, to write for him a weekly paper like the *Spectator*, on certain conditions, which Roberts did not approve. Then he endeavoured to get employment as a hackney writer, to copy for the stationers and lawyers about the Temple, but could find no vacancy.

I immediately got into work at Palmer's, then a famous printing-house in Bartholomew Close, and here I continu'd near a year. I was pretty diligent, but spent with Ralph a good deal of my earnings in going to plays and other places of amusement. We had together consumed all my pistoles, and now just rubbed on from hand to mouth. He seem'd quite to forget his wife and child, and I, by degrees, my engagements with Miss Read, to whom I never wrote more than one letter, and that was to let her know I was not likely soon to return. This was another of the great errata of my life, which I should wish to correct if I were to live it over again. In fact, by our expenses, I was constantly kept unable to pay my passage.

At Palmer's I was employed in composing for the second edition of Wollaston's *Religion of Nature*. Some of his reasonings not appearing to me well founded, I wrote a little metaphysical piece in which I made remarks on them. It was entitled 'A Dissertation on Liberty and Necessity, Pleasure and Pain'. I inscribed it to my friend Ralph; I printed a small number. It occasion'd my being more consider'd by Mr Palmer as a young man of some ingenuity, tho' he seriously expostulated with me upon the principles of my pamphlet, which to him appear'd abominable. My printing this pamphlet was another erratum. While I lodg'd in Little Britain, I made an acquaintance with one Wilcox, a bookseller, whose shop was at the next door. He had an immense collection of second-hand books. Circulating libraries were not then in use; but we agreed that, on certain reasonable terms, which I have now forgotten, I might take, read, and return any of his books. This I esteem'd a great advantage, and I made as much use of it as I could.

My pamphlet by some means falling into the hands of one Lyons, a surgeon, author of a book entitled *The Infallibility of Human Judgement*, it occasioned an acquaintance between us. He took great notice of me, called on me often to converse on those subjects, carried me to the Horns, a pale alehouse in — Lane, Cheapside, and introduced me to Dr Mandeville, author of *The Fable of the Bees*, who had a club there, of which he was the soul, being a most facetious, entertaining companion. Lyons, too, introduced me to Dr Pemberton, at Batson's Coffee-house, who promis'd to give me an opportunity, sometime or other, of seeing Sir Isaac Newton, of which I was extremely desirous; but this never happened.

I had brought over a few curiosities, among which the principal was a purse made of the asbestos, which purifies by fire. Sir Hans Sloane heard of it, came to see me, and invited me to his house in Bloomsbury Square, where he show'd me all his curiosities, and persuaded me to let him add that to the number, for which he paid me handsomely.

In our house there lodg'd a young woman, a milliner, who, I think, had a shop in the Cloisters. She had been genteelly bred, was sensible and lively, and of most pleasing conversation. Ralph read plays to her in the evenings, they grew intimate, she took another lodging, and he followed her. They liv'd together some time; but, he being still out of business, and her income not sufficient to maintain them with her child, he took a resolution of going from London, to try for a country school, which he thought himself well qualified to undertake, as he wrote an excellent hand, and was a master of arithmetic and accounts. This, however, he deemed a business below him, and confident of future better fortune, when he should be unwilling to have it known that he once was so meanly employed, he changed his name, and did me the honour to assume mine; for I soon after had a letter from him, acquainting me that he was settled in a small village (in Berkshire, I think it was, where he taught reading and writing to ten or a dozen boys, at sixpence each per week), recommending Mrs T— to my care, and desiring me to write to him, directing for Mr Franklin, schoolmaster, at such a place.

He continued to write frequently, sending me large specimens of an epic poem which he was then composing, and desiring my remarks and corrections. These I gave him from time to time, but endeavour'd rather to discourage his proceeding. One of Young's Satires was then just published. I copy'd and sent him a great part of it, which set in a strong light the folly of pursuing the Muses with any hope of advancement by them. All was in vain; sheets of the poem continued to come by every post. In the meantime, Mrs T—, having on his account lost her friends and business, was often in distresses, and us'd to send for me, and borrow what I could spare to help her out of them. I grew fond of her company, and, being at that time under no religious restraint, and presuming upon my importance to her, I attempted familiarities (another erratum) which she repuls'd with a proper resentment, and acquainted him with my behaviour. This made a breach between us; and, when he returned again to London, he let me know he thought I had cancell'd all the obligations he had been under to me. So I found I was never to expect his repaying me what I lent to him, or advanc'd for him. This, however, was not then of much consequence, as he was totally unable; and in the loss of his friendship I found myself relieved from a burthen. I now began to think of getting a little money beforehand, and, expecting better work, I left Palmer's to work at Watts's, near Lincoln's Inn Fields, a still greater printing-house. Here I continued all the rest of my stay in London.

At my first admission into this printing-house I took to working at press, imagining I felt a want of the bodily exercise I had been us'd to in America, where presswork is mix'd with composing. I drank only water; the other workmen, near fifty in number, were great guzzlers of beer. On occasion, I carried up and downstairs a large form of types in each hand, when others carried but one in both hands. They wondered to see, from this and several instances, that the *Water-American*, as they called me, was *stronger* than themselves, who drank *strong* beer! We had an alehouse boy who attended always in the house to supply the workmen. My companion at the press drank every day a pint before breakfast, a pint at breakfast with his bread and cheese, a pint between breakfast and dinner, a pint at dinner, a pint in the afternoon about six o'clock, and another when he had done his day's work. I thought it a detestable custom; but it was necessary, he suppos'd, to drink *strong* beer, that he might be *strong* to labour. I endeavoured to convince him that the bodily strength afforded by beer could only be in proportion to the grain or flour of the barley dissolved in the water of which it was made; that there was more flour in a pennyworth of bread; and therefore, if he would eat that with a pint of water, it would give him more strength than a quart of beer. He drank on, however, and had four or five shillings to pay out of his wages every Saturday night for that muddling liquor; an expense I was free from. And thus these poor devils keep themselves always under.

Watts, after some weeks, desiring to have me in the composing-room, I left the pressmen; a new bien venu or sum for drink, being five shillings, was demanded of me by the compositors. I thought it an imposition, as I had paid below; the master thought so too, and forbad my paying it. I stood out two or three weeks, was accordingly considered as an excommunicate, and had so many little pieces of private mischief done me, by mixing my sorts, transposing my pages, breaking my matter, etc., etc., if I were ever so little out of the room, and all ascribed to the chapel ghost, which they said ever haunted those not regularly admitted, that, notwithstanding the master's protection, I found myself oblig'd to comply and pay the money, convinc'd of the folly of being on ill terms with those one is to live with continually.

I was now on a fair footing with them, and soon acquir'd considerable influence. I propos'd some reasonable alterations in their chapel* laws, and carried them against all opposition. From my example, a great part of them left their muddling breakfast of beer, and bread, and cheese, finding they could with me be suppl'd from a neighbouring

---

* 'A printing-house is always called a chapel by the workmen, the origin of which appears to have been, that printing was first carried on in England in an ancient chapel converted into a printing-house, and the title has been preserved by tradition. The bien venu among the printers answers to the terms entrance and footing among mechanics; thus a journeyman, on entering a printing-house, was accustomed to pay one or more gallons of beer for the good of the chapel: this custom was falling into disuse thirty years ago; it is very properly rejected entirely in the United States.' – W. T. F.

house with a large porringer of hot water-gruel, sprinkled with pepper, crumb'd with bread, and a bit of butter in it, for the price of a pint of beer, viz., three half-pence. This was a more comfortable as well as cheaper breakfast, and kept their heads clearer. Those who continued sotting with beer all day, were often, by not paying, out of credit at the alehouse, and us'd to make interest with me to get beer; their *light*, as they phrased it, *being out*. I watch'd the pay-table on Saturday night, and collected what I stood engag'd for them, having to pay sometimes near thirty shillings a week on their accounts. This, and my being esteem'd a pretty good *riggite*, that is, a jocular verbal satirist, supported my consequence in the society. My constant attendance (I never making a St Monday) recommended me to the master; and my uncommon quickness at composing occasioned my being put upon all work of dispatch, which was generally better paid. So I went on now very agreeably.

My lodging in Little Britain being too remote, I found another in Duke Street, opposite to the Romish Chapel. It was two pair of stairs backwards, at an Italian warehouse. A widow lady kept the house; she had a daughter, and a maid servant, and a journeyman who attended the warehouse, but lodg'd abroad. After sending to inquire my character at the house where I last lodg'd she agreed to take me in at the same rate, 3s. 6d. per week; cheaper, as she said, from the protection she expected in having a man lodge in the house. She was a widow, an elderly woman; had been bred a Protestant, being a clergyman's daughter, but was converted to the Catholic religion by her husband, whose memory she much revered; had lived much among people of distinction, and knew a thousand anecdotes of them as far back as the times of Charles the Second. She was lame in her knees with the gout, and, therefore, seldom stirred out of her room, so sometimes wanted company; and hers was so highly amusing to me, that I was sure to spend an evening with her whenever she desired it. Our supper was only half an anchovy each, on a very little strip of bread and butter, and half a pint of ale between us; but the entertainment was in her conversation. My always keeping good hours, and giving little trouble in the family, made her unwilling to part with me; so that, when I talk'd of a lodging I had heard of, nearer my business, for two shillings a week, which, intent as I now was on saving money, made some difference, she bid me not think of it, for she would abate me two shillings a week for the future; so I remained with her at one shilling and sixpence as long as I stayed in London.

In a garret of her house there lived a maiden lady of seventy, in the most retired manner, of whom my landlady gave me this account: that she was a Roman Catholic, had been sent abroad when young, and lodg'd in a nunnery with an intent of becoming a nun; but, the country not agreeing with her, she returned to England, where, there being no nunnery, she had vow'd to lead the life of a nun, as near as might be done in those circumstances. Accordingly, she had given all her estate to charitable uses, reserving only twelve pounds a year to live on, and out of this sum she still gave a great deal in charity, living herself on water-gruel only, and using no fire but to boil it. She had lived many years in that garret, being permitted to remain there gratis by successive Catholic tenants of the house below, as they deemed it a blessing to have her there. A priest visited her to confess her every day. 'I have ask'd her,' says my landlady, 'how she, as she liv'd, could possibly find so much employment for a confessor?' 'Oh,' said she, 'it is impossible to avoid *vain thoughts*.' I was permitted once to visit her. She was cheerful and polite, and convers'd pleasantly. The room was clean, but had no other furniture than a mattress, a table with a crucifix and book, a stool which she gave me to sit on, and a picture over the chimney of Saint Veronica displaying her handkerchief, with the miraculous figure of Christ's bleeding face on it, which she explained to me with great seriousness. She look'd pale, but was never sick; and I give it as another instance on how small an income, life and health may be supported.

At Watts's printing-house I contracted an acquaintance with an ingenious young man, one Wygate, who, having wealthy relations, had been better educated than most printers; was a tolerable Latinist, spoke French, and lov'd reading. I taught him and a friend of his to swim at twice going into the river, and they soon became good swimmers. They introduc'd me to some gentlemen from the country, who went to Chelsea by water to see the College and Don Saltero's curiosities. In our return, at the request of the company, whose curiosity Wygate had excited, I stripped and leaped into the river, and swam from near Chelsea to Blackfriars, performing on the way many feats of activity, both upon and under water, that surpris'd and pleas'd those to whom they were novelties.

I had from a child been ever delighted with this exercise, had studied and practis'd all Thevenot's motions and positions, added some of my own, aiming at the graceful and easy as well as the useful. All these I took this occasion of exhibiting to the company, and was much flatter'd by their admiration; and Wygate, who was desirous of becoming a master, grew more and more attach'd to me on that account, as well as from the similarity of our studies. He at length proposed to me travelling all over Europe together, supporting ourselves everywhere by working at our business. I was once inclined to it; but, mentioning it to my good friend Mr Denham, with whom I often spent an hour when I had leisure, he dissuaded me from it, advising me to think only of returning to Pennsylvania, which he was now about to do.

I must record one trait of this good man's character. He had formerly been in business at Bristol, but failed in debt to a number of people, compounded and went to America. There, by a close application to business as a merchant, he acquir'd a plentiful fortune in a few years. Returning to England in the ship with me, he invited his old creditors to an entertainment, at which he thank'd them for the easy composition they had favoured him with, and, when they expected nothing but the treat, every man at the first remove found under his plate an order on a banker for the full amount of the unpaid remainder with interest.

He now told me he was about to return to Philadelphia, and should carry over a great quantity of goods in order to open a store there. He propos'd to take me over as his clerk, to keep his books, in which he would instruct me, copy his letters, and attend the store. He added, that, as soon as I should be acquainted with mercantile business, he would promote me by sending me with a cargo of flour and bread, etc., to the West Indies, and procure me commissions from others which would be profitable; and, if I manag'd well, would establish me handsomely. The thing pleas'd me; for I was grown tired of London, remembered with pleasure the happy months I had spent in Pennsylvania, and wish'd again to see it; therefore I immediately agreed on the terms of fifty pounds a year, Pennsylvania money; less, indeed, than my present gettings as a compositor, but affording a better prospect.

I now took leave of printing, as I thought, for ever, and was daily employed in my new business, going about with Mr Denham among the tradesmen to purchase various articles, and seeing them pack'd up, doing errands, calling upon workmen to dispatch, etc.; and, when all was on board, I had a few days' leisure. On one of these days, I was, to my surprise, sent for by a great man I knew only by name, a Sir William Wyndham, and I waited upon him. He had heard by some means or other of my swimming from Chelsea to Blackfriars, and of my teaching Wygate and another young man to swim in a few hours. He had two sons, about to set out on their travels; he wished to have them first taught swimming, and proposed to gratify me handsomely if I would teach them. They were not yet come to town, and my stay was uncertain, so I could not undertake it; but, from this incident, I thought it likely that, if I were to remain in England and open a swimming school, I might get a good deal of money; and it struck me so strongly, that, had the overture been sooner made me, probably I should not so soon have returned to America. After many years, you and I had something of more importance to do with one of these sons of Sir William Wyndham, become Earl of Egremont, which I shall mention in its place.

Thus I spent about eighteen months in London; most part of the time I work'd hard at my business, and spent but little upon myself except in seeing plays and in books. My friend Ralph had kept me poor; he owed me about twenty-seven pounds, which I was now never likely to receive; a great sum out of my small earnings! I lov'd him, notwithstanding, for he had many amiable qualities. I had by no means improv'd my fortune; but I had picked up some very ingenious acquaintance, whose conversation was of great advantage to me; and I had read considerably.

We sail'd from Gravesend on the 23rd of July, 1726. For the incidents of the voyage, I refer you to my Journal, where you will find them all minutely related. Perhaps the most important part of that journal is the *plan* to be found in it, which I formed at sea, for regulating my future conduct in life. It is the more remarkable, as being formed when I was so young, and yet being pretty faithfully adhered to quite thro' to old age.

We landed in Philadelphia on the 11th of October, where I found sundry alterations. Keith was no longer governor, being superseded by Major Gordon. I met him walking the streets as a common citizen. He seem'd a little asham'd at seeing me, but pass'd without saying anything. I should have been as much asham'd at seeing Miss Read, had not her friends, despairing with reason of my return after the receipt of my letter, persuaded her to marry another, one Rogers, a potter, which was done in my absence. With him, however, she was never happy, and soon parted from him, refusing to cohabit with him or bear his name, it being now said that he had another wife. He was a worthless fellow, tho' an excellent workman, which was the temptation to her friends. He got into debt, ran away in 1727 or 1728, went to the West Indies, and died there. Keimer had got a better house, a shop well supply'd with stationery, plenty of new types, a number of hands, tho' none good, and seem'd to have a great deal of business.

Mr Denham took a store in Water Street, where we open'd our goods; I attended the business diligently, studied accounts, and grew, in a little time, expert at selling. We lodg'd and boarded together; he counsell'd me as a father, having a sincere regard for me. I respected and loved him, and we might have gone on together very happy; but, in the beginning of February, 172⁶/₇, when I had just pass'd my twenty-first year, we both were taken ill. My distemper was a pleurisy, which very nearly carried me off. I suffered a good deal, gave up the point in my mind, and was rather disappointed when I found myself recovering, regretting, in some degree, that I must now, sometime or other, have all that disagreeable work to do over again. I forget what his distemper was; it held him a long time, and at length carried him off. He left me a small legacy in a nuncupative will, as a token of his kindness for me, and he left me once more to the wide world; for the store was taken into the care of his executors, and my employment under him ended.

My brother-in-law, Holmes, being now at Philadelphia, advised my return to my business; and Keimer tempted me, with an offer of large wages by the year, to come and take the management of his printing-house, that he might better attend his stationer's shop. I had heard a bad character of him in London from his wife and her friends, and was not fond of having any more to do with him. I tri'd for farther employment as a merchant's clerk; but, not readily meeting with any, I clos'd again with Keimer. I found in his house these hands: Hugh Meredith, a Welsh Pennsylvanian, thirty years of age, bred to country work; honest, sensible, had a great deal of solid observation, was something of a reader, but given to drink. Stephen Potts, a young countryman of full age, bred to the same, of uncommon natural parts, and great wit and humour, but a little idle. These he had agreed with at extreme low wages per week, to be rais'd a shilling every three months, as they would deserve by improving in their business; and the expectation of these high wages, to come on hereafter, was what he had drawn them in with. Meredith was to work at press, Potts at book-binding, which he, by agreement, was to teach them, though he knew neither one nor t'other. John —, a wild Irishman, brought up to no business, whose service, for four years, Keimer had purchased from the captain of a ship; he, too, was to be made a pressman. George Webb, an Oxford scholar, whose time for four years he had likewise bought, intending him for a compositor, of whom more presently; and David Harry, a country boy, whom he had taken apprentice.

I soon perceiv'd that the intention of engaging me at wages so much higher than he had been us'd to give, was, to have these raw, cheap hands form'd thro' me; and, as soon as I had instructed them, then they being all articled to him, he should be able to do without me. I went on, however, very cheerfully, put his printing-house in order, which had been in great confusion, and brought his hands by degrees to mind their business and to do it better.

It was an odd thing to find an Oxford scholar in the situation of a bought servant. He was not more than eighteen years of age, and gave me this account of himself; that he was born in Gloucester, educated at a grammar school there, had been distinguish'd among the scholars for some apparent superiority in performing his part, when they exhibited plays; belong'd to the Witty Club there, and had written some pieces in prose and verse, which were printed in the Gloucester newspapers; thence he was sent to Oxford; where he continued about a year, but not well satisfi'd, wishing of all things to see London, and become a player. At length, receiving his quarterly allowance of fifteen guineas, instead of discharging his debts he walk'd out of town, hid his gown in a furze bush, and footed it to London, where, having no friends to advise him, he fell into bad company, soon spent his guineas, found no means of being introduc'd among the players, grew necessitous, pawn'd his clothes, and wanted bread. Walking the street very hungry, and not knowing what to do with himself, a crimp's bill was put into his hand, offering immediate entertainment and encouragement to such as would bind themselves to serve in America. He went directly, sign'd the indentures, was put into the ship, and came over, never writing a line to acquaint his friends what was become of him. He was lively, witty, good-natur'd, and a pleasant companion, but idle, thoughtless, and imprudent to the last degree.

John, the Irishman, soon ran away; with the rest I began to live very agreeably, for they all respected me the more, as they found Keimer incapable of instructing them, and that from me they learned something daily. We never worked on Saturday, that being Keimer's Sabbath, so I had two days for reading. My acquaintance with ingenious people in the town increased. Keimer himself treated me with great civility and apparent regard, and nothing now made me uneasy but my debt to Vernon, which I was yet unable to pay, being hitherto but a poor economist. He, however, kindly made no demand of it.

Our printing-house often wanted sorts, and there was no letter-founder in America; I had seen types cast at James's in London, but without much attention to the manner; however, I now contrived a mould, made use of the letters we had as puncheons, struck the matrices in lead, and thus supply'd in a pretty tolerable way all deficiencies. I also engrav'd several things on occasion; I made the ink;

I was warehouseman, and everything, and, in short, quite a factotum.

But, however serviceable I might be, I found that my services became every day of less importance, as the other hands improv'd in the business; and, when Keimer paid my second quarter's wages, he let me know that he felt them too heavy, and thought I should make an abatement. He grew by degrees less civil, put on more of the master, frequently found fault, was captious, and seem'd ready for an outbreaking. I went on, nevertheless, with a good deal of patience, thinking that his encumber'd circumstances were partly the cause. At length a trifle snapped our connections; for, a great noise happening near the court-house, I put my head out of the window to see what was the matter. Keimer, being in the street, look'd up and saw me, call'd out to me in a loud voice and angry tone to mind my business, adding some reproachful words, that nettled me the more for their publicity, all the neighbours who were looking out on the same occasion being witnesses how I was treated. He came up immediately into the printing-house, continu'd the quarrel, high words pass'd on both sides, he gave me the quarter's warning we had stipulated, expressing a wish that he had not been oblig'd to so long a warning. I told him his wish was unnecessary, for I would leave him that instant; and so, taking my hat, walk'd out of doors, desiring Meredith, whom I saw below, to take care of some things I left, and bring them to my lodgings.

Meredith came accordingly in the evening, when we talked my affair over. He had conceiv'd a great regard for me, and was very unwilling that I should leave the house while he remain'd in it. He dissuaded me from returning to my native country, which I began to think of; he reminded me that Keimer was in debt for all he possess'd; that his creditors began to be uneasy; that he kept his shop miserably, sold often without profit for ready money, and often trusted without keeping accounts; that he must therefore fail, which would make a vacancy I might profit of. I objected my want of money. He then let me know that his father had a high opinion of me, and, from some discourse that had pass'd between them, he was sure would advance money to set us up, if I would enter into partnership with him. 'My time,' says he, 'will be out with Keimer in the spring; by that time we may have our press and types in from London. I am sensible I am no workman; if you like it, your skill in the business shall be set against the stock I furnish, and we will share the profits equally.'

The proposal was agreeable, and I consented; his father was in town and approv'd of it; the more as he saw I had great influence with his son, had prevail'd on him to abstain long from dram-drinking, and he hop'd might break him off that wretched habit entirely, when we came to be so closely connected. I gave an inventory to the father, who carry'd it to a merchant; the things were sent for, the secret was to be kept till they should arrive, and in the meantime I was to get work, if I could, at the other printing-house. But I found no vacancy there, and so remain'd idle a few days, when Keimer, on a prospect of being employ'd to print some paper money in New Jersey, which would require cuts and various types that I only could supply, and apprehending Bradford might engage me and get the job from him, sent me a very civil message, that old friends should not part for a few words, the effect of sudden passion, and wishing me to return. Meredith persuaded me to comply, as it would give more opportunity for his improvement under my daily instructions; so I return'd, and we went on more smoothly than for some time before. The New Jersey job was obtain'd, I contriv'd a copperplate press for it, the first that had been seen in the country; I cut several ornaments and checks for the bills. We went together to Burlington, where I executed the whole to satisfaction; and he received so large a sum for the work as to be enabled thereby to keep his head much longer above water.

At Burlington I made an acquaintance with many principal people of the province. Several of them had been appointed by the Assembly a committee to attend the press, and take care that no more bills were printed than the law directed. They were therefore, by turns, constantly with us, and generally he who attended, brought with him a friend or two for company. My mind having been much more improv'd by reading than Keimer's, I suppose it was for that reason my conversation seem'd to be more valu'd. They had me to their houses, introduced me to their friends, and show'd me much civility; while he, tho' the master, was a little neglected. In truth, he was an odd fish; ignorant of common life, fond of rudely opposing receiv'd opinions, slovenly to extreme dirtiness, enthusiastic in some points of religion, and a little knavish withal.

We continu'd there near three months; and by that time I could reckon among my acquired friends, Judge Allen, Samuel Bustill, the secretary of the Province, Isaac Pearson, Joseph Cooper, and several of the Smiths, members of Assembly, and Isaac Decow, the surveyor-general. The latter was a shrewd, sagacious old man, who told me that he began for himself, when young, by wheeling clay for the brick-makers, learned to write after he was of age, carri'd the chain for surveyors, who taught him surveying, and he had now by his industry, acquir'd a good estate; and says he, 'I foresee that you will soon work this man out of his business, and make a fortune in it at Philadelphia.' He had not then the least intimation of my intention to set up there or anywhere. These friends were afterwards of great use to me, as I occasionally was to some of them. They all continued their regard for me as long as they lived.

Before I enter upon my public appearance in business, it may be well to let you know the then state of my mind with regard to my principles and morals, that you may see how far those influenc'd the future events of my life. My parents had early given me religious impressions, and brought me through my childhood piously in the Dissenting way. But I was scarce fifteen, when, after doubting by turns of several points, as I found them disputed in the different books I read, I began to doubt of Revelation itself. Some books against Deism fell into my hands; they were said to be the substance of sermons preached at Boyle's Lectures. It happened that they wrought an effect on me quite contrary to what was intended by them; for the arguments of the Deists, which were quoted to be refuted, appeared to me much stronger than the refutations; in short, I soon became a thorough Deist. My arguments perverted some others, particularly Collins and Ralph; but, each of them having afterwards wrong'd me greatly without the least compunction, and recollecting Keith's conduct towards me (who was another freethinker), and my own towards Vernon and Miss Read, which at times gave me great trouble, I began to suspect that this doctrine, tho' it might be true, was not very useful. My London pamphlet, which had for its motto these lines of Dryden:

> Whatever is is right. Though purblind man
> Sees but a part o' the chain, the nearest link:
> His eyes not carrying to the equal beam,
> That poises all above;

and from the attributes of God, his infinite wisdom, goodness and power, concluded that nothing could possibly be wrong in the world, and that vice and virtue were empty distinctions, no such things existing, appear'd now not so clever a performance as I once thought it; and I doubted whether some error had not insinuated itself unperceiv'd into my argument, so as to infect all that follow'd, as is common in metaphysical reasonings.

I grew convinc'd that *truth*, *sincerity* and *integrity* in dealings between man and man were of the utmost importance to the felicity of life; and I form'd written resolutions, which still remain in my journal book, to practice them ever while I lived. Revelation had indeed no weight with me, as such; but I entertain'd an opinion that, though certain actions might not be bad *because* they were forbidden by it, or good *because* it commanded them, yet probably these actions might be forbidden *because* they were bad for us, or commanded *because* they were beneficial to us, in their own natures, all the circumstances of things considered. And this persuasion, with the kind hand of Providence, or some guardian angel, or accidental favourable circumstances and situations, or all together, preserved me, thro' this dangerous time of youth, and the hazardous situations I was sometimes in among strangers, remote from the eye and advice of my father, without any wilful gross immorality or injustice, that might have been expected from my want of religion. I say wilful, because the instances I have mentioned had something of *necessity* in them, from my youth, inexperience, and the knavery of others. I had therefore a tolerable character to begin the world with; I valued it properly, and determin'd to preserve it.

We had not been long return'd to Philadelphia before the new types arriv'd from London. We settled with Keimer, and left him by his consent before he heard of it. We found a house to hire near the market, and took it. To lessen the rent, which was then but twenty-four pounds a year, tho' I have since known it to let for seventy, we took in Thomas Godfrey, a glazier, and his family, who were to pay a considerable part of it to us, and we to board with them. We had scarce opened our letters and put our press in order, before George House, an acquaintance of mine, brought a countryman to us, whom he had met in the street inquiring for a printer. All our cash was now expended in the variety of particulars we had been obliged to procure, and this countryman's five shillings, being our first-fruits, and coming so seasonably, gave me more pleasure than any crown I have since earned; and the gratitude I felt toward House has made me often more ready than perhaps I should otherwise have been to assist young beginners.

There are croakers in every country, always boding its ruin. Such a one then lived in Philadelphia; a person of note, an elderly man, with a wise look and a very grave manner of speaking; his name was Samuel Mickle. This gentleman, a stranger to me, stopped one day at my door, and asked me if I was the young man who had lately opened a new printing-house. Being answered in the affirmative, he said he was sorry for me, because it was an expensive undertaking, and the expense would be lost; for Philadelphia was a sinking place, the people already half-bankrupts, or near being so; all appearances to the contrary, such as new buildings and the rise of rents, being to his certain knowledge fallacious; for they were, in fact, among the things that would soon ruin us. And he gave me such a detail of misfortunes now existing, or that were soon to exist, that he left me half melancholy. Had I known him before I engaged in this business, probably I never should have done it. This man continued to live in this decaying place, and to declaim in the same strain, refusing for many years to buy a house there, because all was going to destruction; and at last I had the pleasure of seeing him give five times as much for one as he might have bought it for when he first began his croaking.

I should have mentioned before, that, in the autumn of the preceding year, I had form'd most of my ingenious acquaintance into a club of mutual improvement, which we called the JUNTO; we met on Friday evenings. The rules that I drew up required that every member, in his turn, should produce one or more queries on any point of Morals, Politics, or Natural Philosophy, to be discuss'd by the company; and once in three months produce and read an essay of his own writing, on any subject he pleased. Our debates were to be under the direction of a president, and to be conducted in the sincere spirit of inquiry after truth, without fondness for dispute, or desire of victory; and, to prevent warmth, all expressions of positiveness in opinions, or direct contradiction, were after some time made contraband, and prohibited under small pecuniary penalties.

The first members were Joseph Breintnal, a copyer of deeds for the scriveners, a good-natur'd, friendly, middle-ag'd man, a great lover of poetry, reading all he could meet with, and writing some that was tolerable; very ingenious in many little Nicknackeries, and of sensible conversation.

Thomas Godfrey, a self-taught mathematician, great in his way, and afterwards inventor of what is now called Hadley's Quadrant. But he knew little out of his way, and was not a pleasing companion; as, like most great mathematicians I have met with, he expected universal precision in everything said, or was for ever denying or distinguishing upon trifles, to the disturbance of all conversation. He soon left us.

Nicholas Scull, a surveyor, afterwards surveyor-general, who lov'd books, and sometimes made a few verses.

William Parsons, bred a shoemaker, but, loving reading, had acquir'd a considerable share of mathematics, which he first studied with a view to astrology, that he afterwards laughed at it. He also became surveyor-general.

William Maugridge, a joiner, a most exquisite mechanic, and a solid, sensible man.

Hugh Meredith, Stephen Potts, and George Webb I have characteris'd before.

Robert Grace, a young gentleman of some fortune, generous, lively, and witty; a lover of punning and of his friends.

And William Coleman, then a merchant's clerk, about my age, who had the coolest, clearest head, the best heart, and the exactest morals of almost any man I ever met with. He became afterwards a merchant of great note, and one of our provincial judges. Our friendship continued without interruption to his death, upwards of forty years; and the club continued almost as long, and was the best school of philosophy, morality, and politics that then existed in the province; for our queries, which were read the week preceding their discussion, put us upon reading with attention upon the several subjects, that we might speak more to the purpose; and here, too, we acquired better habits of conversation, everything being studied in our rules which might prevent our disgusting each other. From hence the long continuance of the club, which I shall have frequent occasion to speak further of hereafter.

But my giving this account of it here to show something of the interest I had, everyone of these exerting themselves in recommending business to us. Breintnal particularly procur'd us from the Quakers the printing forty sheets of their history, the rest being to be done by Keimer; and upon this we work'd exceedingly hard, for the price was low. It was a folio, pro patria size, in pica, with long primer notes. I compos'd of it a sheet a day, and Meredith worked it off at press; it was often eleven at night, and sometimes later, before I had finished my distribution for the next day's work, for the little jobs sent in by our other friends now and then put us back. But so determin'd I was to continue doing a sheet a day of the folio, that one night, when, having impos'd my forms, I thought my day's work over, one of them by accident was broken, and two pages reduced to pi, I immediately distributed and compos'd it over again before I went to bed; and this industry, visible to our neighbours, began to give us character and credit; particularly, I was told, that mention being made of the new printing-office at the merchants' Every-night club, the general opinion was that it must fail, there being already two printers in the place, Keimer and Bradford; but Dr Baird (whom you and I saw many years after at his native place, St Andrew's in Scotland) gave a contrary opinion: 'For the industry of that Franklin,' says he, 'is superior to anything I ever saw of the kind; I see him still at work when I go home from club, and he is at work again before his neighbours are out of bed.' This struck the rest, and we soon after had offers from one of them to supply us with stationery; but as yet we did not choose to engage in shop business.

I mention this industry the more particularly and the more freely, tho' it seems to be talking in my own praise, that those of my posterity, who shall read it, may know the use of that virtue, when they see its effects in my favour throughout this relation.

George Webb, who had found a female friend that lent him wherewith to purchase his time of Keimer, now came to offer himself as a journeyman to us. We could not then employ him; but I foolishly let him know as a secret that I soon intended to begin a newspaper, and might then have work for him. My hopes of success, as I told him, were founded on this, that the then only newspaper, printed by Bradford, was a paltry thing, wretchedly manag'd, no way entertaining, and yet was profitable to him; I therefore thought a good paper would scarcely fail of good encouragement. I requested Webb not to mention it; but he told it to Keimer, who immediately, to be beforehand with me, published proposals for printing one himself, on which Webb was to be employed. I resented this; and, to counteract them, as I could not yet begin our paper, I wrote several pieces of entertainment for Bradford's paper, under the title of the BUSY BODY, which Breintnal continu'd some months. By this means the attention of the public was fixed on that paper, and Keimer's proposals, which we burlesqu'd and ridicul'd, were disregarded. He began his paper, however, and, after carrying it on three quarters of a year, with at most only ninety subscribers, he offered it me for a trifle; and I, having been ready some time to go on with it, took it in hand directly; and it prov'd in a few years extremely profitable to me.

I perceive that I am apt to speak in the singular number, though our partnership still continu'd; the reason may be that, in fact, the whole management of the business lay upon me. Meredith was no compositor, a poor pressman, and seldom sober. My friends lamented my connection with him, but I was to make the best of it.

Our first papers made a quite different appearance from any before in the province; a better type, and better printed; but some spirited remarks of my writing, on the dispute then going on between Governor Burnet and the Massachusetts Assembly, struck the principal people, occasioned the paper and the manager of it to be much talk'd of, and in a few weeks brought them all to be our subscribers.

Their example was follow'd by many, and our number went on growing continually. This was one of the first good effects of my having learnt a little to scribble; another was, that the leading men, seeing a newspaper now in the hands of one who could also handle a pen, thought it convenient to oblige and encourage me. Bradford still printed the votes, and laws, and other public business. He had printed an address of the House to the governor, in a coarse, blundering manner, we reprinted it elegantly and correctly, and sent one to every member. They were sensible of the difference: it strengthened the hands of our friends in the House, and they voted us their printers for the year ensuing.

Among my friends in the House I must not forget Mr Hamilton, before mentioned, who was then returned from England, and had a seat in it. He interested himself for me strongly in that instance, as he did in many others afterward, continuing his patronage till his death.*

Mr Vernon, about this time, put me in mind of the debt I ow'd him, but did not press me. I wrote him an ingenuous letter of acknowledgement, crav'd his forbearance a little longer, which he allow'd me, and as soon as I was able, I paid the principal with interest, and many thanks; so that erratum was in some degree corrected.

But now another difficulty came upon me which I had never the least reason to expect. Mr Meredith's father, who was to have paid for our printing-house, according to the expectations given me, was able to advance only one hundred pounds currency, which had been paid; and a hundred more was due to the merchant, who grew impatient, and su'd us all. We gave bail, but saw that, if the money could not be rais'd in time, the suit must soon come to a judgement and execution, and our hopeful prospects must, with us, be ruined, as the press and letters must be sold for payment, perhaps at half price.

In this distress two true friends, whose kindness I have never forgotten, nor ever shall forget while I can remember anything, came to me separately, unknown to each other, and, without any application from me, offering each of them to advance me all the money that should be necessary to enable me to take the whole business upon myself, if that should be practicable; but they did not like my continuing the partnership with Meredith, who, as they said, was often seen drunk in the streets, and playing at low games in alehouses, much to our discredit. These two friends were William Coleman and Robert Grace. I told them I could not propose a separation while any prospect remain'd of the Meredith's fulfilling their part of our agreement, because I thought myself under great obligations to them for what they

* I got his son once £500

had done, and would do if they could; but, if they finally fail'd in their performance, and our partnership must be dissolv'd, I should then think myself at liberty to accept the assistance of my friends.

Thus the matter rested for some time, when I said to my partner, 'Perhaps your father is dissatisfied at the part you have undertaken in this affair of ours, and is unwilling to advance for you and me what he would for you alone. If that is the case, tell me, and I will resign the whole to you, and go about my business.' 'No,' said he, 'my father has really been disappointed, and is really unable; and I am unwilling to distress him farther. I see this is a business I am not fit for. I was bred a farmer, and it was a folly in me to come to town, and put myself, at thirty years of age, an apprentice to learn a new trade. Many of our Welsh people are going to settle in North Carolina, where land is cheap. I am inclin'd to go with them, and follow my old employment. You may find friends to assist you. If you will take the debts of the company upon you; return to my father the hundred pound he has advanced; pay my little personal debts, and give me thirty pounds and a new saddle, I will relinquish the partnership, and leave the whole in your hands.' I agreed to this proposal: it was drawn up in writing, sign'd, and seal'd immediately. I gave him what he demanded, and he went soon after to Carolina, from whence he sent me next year two long letters, containing the best account that had been given of that country, the climate, the soil, husbandry, etc., for in those matters he was very judicious. I printed them in the papers, and they gave great satisfaction to the public.

As soon as he was gone, I recurr'd to my two friends; and because I would not give an unkind preference to either, I took half of what each had offered and I wanted of one, and half of the other; paid off the company's debts, and went on with the business in my own name, advertising that the partnership was dissolved. I think this was in or about the year 1729.

About this time there was a cry among the people for more paper money, only fifteen thousand pounds being extant in the province, and that soon to be sunk. The wealthy inhabitants oppos'd any addition, being against all paper currency, from an apprehension that it would depreciate, as it had done in New England, to the prejudice of all creditors. We had discuss'd this point in our Junto, where I was on the side of an addition, being persuaded that the first small sum struck in 1723 had done much good by increasing the trade, employment, and number of inhabitants in the province, since I now saw all the old houses inhabited, and many new ones building: whereas I remembered well, that when I first walk'd about the streets of Philadelphia, eating my roll, I saw most of the houses in Walnut Street, between Second and Front Streets, with bills on their doors, 'To be let'; and many likewise in Chestnut Street and other streets, which made me then think the inhabitants of the city were deserting it one after another.

Our debates possess'd me so fully of the subject, that I wrote and printed an anonymous pamphlet on it, entitled *The Nature and Necessity of a Paper Currency*. It was well receiv'd by the common people in general; but the rich men dislik'd it, for it increas'd and strengthen'd the clamour for more money, and they happening to have no writers among them that were able to answer it, their opposition slacken'd, and the point was carried by a majority in the House. My friends there, who conceiv'd I had been of some service, thought fit to reward me by employing me in printing the money; a very profitable job and a great help to me. This was another advantage gain'd by my being able to write.

The utility of this currency became by time and experience so evident as never afterwards to be much disputed; so that it grew soon to fifty-five thousand pounds, and in 1739 to eighty thousand pounds, since which it arose during war to upwards of three hundred and fifty thousand pounds, trade, building, and inhabitants all the while increasing, tho' I now think there are limits beyond which the quantity may be hurtful.

I soon after obtain'd, thro' my friend Hamilton, the printing of the Newcastle paper money, another profitable job as I then thought it; small things appearing great to those in small circumstances; and these, to me, were really great advantages, as they were great encouragements. He procured for me, also, the printing of the laws and votes of that government, which continu'd in my hands as long as I follow'd the business.

I now open'd a little stationer's shop. I had in it blanks of all sorts, the correctest that ever appear'd among us, being assisted in that by my friend Breintnal. I had also paper, parchment, chapmen's books, etc. One Whitemash, a compositor I had known in London, an excellent workman, now came to me, and work'd with me constantly and diligently; and I took an apprentice, the son of Aquila Rose.

I began now gradually to pay off the debt I was under for the printing-house. In order to secure my credit and character as a tradesman, I took care not only to be in *reality* industrious and frugal, but to avoid all appearances to the contrary. I dressed plainly; I was seen at no places of idle diversion. I never went out a fishing or shooting; a book, indeed, sometimes debauch'd me from my work, but that was seldom, snug, and gave no scandal; and, to show that I was not above my business, I sometimes brought home the paper I purchas'd at the stores thro' the streets on a wheelbarrow. Thus being esteem'd an industrious, thriving young man, and paying duly for what I bought, the merchants who imported stationery solicited my custom; others proposed supplying me with books, and I went on swimmingly. In the meantime, Keimer's credit and business declining daily, he was at last forc'd to sell his printing-house to satisfy his creditors. He went to Barbados, and there lived some years in very poor circumstances.

His apprentice, David Harry, whom I had instructed while I work'd with him, set up in his place at Philadelphia, having bought his materials. I was at first apprehensive of a powerful rival in Harry, as his friends were very able, and had a good deal of interest. I therefore propos'd a partnership to him, which he, fortunately for me, rejected with scorn. He was very proud, dress'd like a gentleman, liv'd expensively, took much diversion and pleasure abroad, ran in debt, and neglected his business; upon which, all business left him; and, finding nothing to do, he followed Keimer to Barbados, taking the printing-house with him. There this apprentice employ'd his former master as a journeyman; they quarrel'd often; Harry went continually behindhand, and at length was forc'd to sell his types and return to his country work in Pennsylvania. The person that bought them employ'd Keimer to use them, but in a few years he died.

There remained now no competitor with me at Philadelphia but the old one, Bradford; who was rich and easy, did a little printing now and then by straggling hands, but was not very anxious about the business. However, as he kept the post-office, it was imagined he had better opportunities of obtaining news; his paper was thought a better distributer of advertisements than mine, and therefore had many more, which was a profitable thing to him, and a disadvantage to me; for, tho' I did indeed receive and send papers by the post, yet the public opinion was otherwise, for what I did send was by bribing the riders, who took them privately, Bradford being unkind enough to forbid it, which occasion'd some resentment on my part; and I thought so meanly of him for it, that, when I afterward came into his situation, I took care never to imitate it.

I had hitherto continu'd to board with Godfrey, who lived in part of my house with his wife and children, and had one side of the shop for his glazier's business, tho' he worked little, being always absorbed in his mathematics. Mrs Godfrey projected a match for me with a relation's daughter, took opportunities of bringing us often together, till a serious courtship on my part ensu'd, the girl being in herself very deserving. The old folks encourag'd me by continual invitations to supper, and by leaving us together, till at length it was time to explain. Mrs Godfrey manag'd our little treaty. I let her know that I expected as much money with their daughter as would pay off my remaining debt for the printing-house, which I believe was not then above a hundred pounds. She brought me word they had no such sum to spare; I said they might mortgage their house in the loan-office. The answer to this, after some days, was, that they did not approve the match; that, on inquiry of Bradford, they had been informed the printing business was not a profitable one; the types would soon be worn out, and more wanted; that S. Keimer and D. Harry had failed one after the other, and I should probably soon follow them; and, therefore, I was forbidden the house, and the daughter shut up.

Whether this was a real change of sentiment or only artifice, on a supposition of our being too far engaged in affection to retract, and therefore that we should steal a marriage, which would leave them at liberty to give or withhold what they pleas'd, I know not; but I suspected the latter, resented it, and went no more. Mrs Godfrey brought me afterward some more favourable accounts of their disposition, and would have drawn me on again; but I declared absolutely my resolution to have nothing more to do with that family. This was resented by the Godfreys; we differ'd, and they removed, leaving me the whole house, and I resolved to take no more inmates.

But this affair having turned my thoughts to marriage, I look'd around me and made overtures of acquaintance in other places; but soon found that, the business of a printer being generally thought a poor one, I was not to expect money with a wife, unless with such a one as I should not otherwise think agreeable. In the meantime, that hard-to-be-governed passion of youth hurried me frequently into intrigues with low women that fell in my way, which were attended with some expense and great inconvenience, besides a continual risk to my health by a distemper which of all things I dreaded, though by great good luck I escaped it. A friendly correspondence as neighbours and old acquaintances had continued between me and Mrs Read's family, who all had a regard for me from the time of my first lodging in their house. I was often invited there and consulted in their affairs, wherein I sometimes was of service. I piti'd poor Miss Read's unfortunate situation, who was generally dejected, seldom cheerful, and avoided company. I considered my giddiness and inconstancy when in London as in a great degree the cause of her unhappiness, tho' the mother was good enough to think the fault more her own than mine, as she had prevented our marrying before I went thither, and persuaded the other match in my absence. Our mutual affection was revived, but there were now great objections to our union. The match was indeed looked upon as invalid, a preceding wife being said to be living in England; but this could not easily be prov'd, because of the distance; and, tho' there was a report of his death, it was not certain. Then, tho' it should be true, he had left many debts, which his successor might be call'd upon to pay. We ventured, however, over all these difficulties, and I took her to wife, September 1st, 1730. None of the inconveniences happened that we had apprehended; she proved a good and faithful helpmate, assisted me much by attending the shop; we throve together, and have ever mutually endeavour'd to make each other happy. Thus I corrected that great *erratum* as well as I could.

About this time, our club meeting, not at a tavern, but in a little room of Mr Grace's, set apart for that purpose, a proposition was made by me, that, since our books were often referr'd to in our disquisitions upon the queries, it might be convenient to us to have them altogether where we met, that upon occasion they might be consulted; and by thus clubbing our books to a common library, we should, while we lik'd to keep them together, have each of us the advantage of using the books of all the other members, which would be nearly as beneficial as if each owned the whole. It was lik'd and agreed to, and we fill'd one end of the room with such books as we could best spare. The number was not so great as we expected; and tho' they had been of great use, yet some inconveniences occurring for want of due care of them, the collection, after about a year, was separated, and each took his books home again.

And now I set on foot my first project of a public nature, that for a subscription library. I drew up the proposals, got them put into form by our great scrivener, Brockden, and, by the help of my friends in the Junto, procured fifty subscribers of forty shillings each to begin with, and ten shillings a year for fifty years, the term our company was to continue. We afterwards obtain'd a charter, the company being increased to one hundred: this was the mother of all the North American subscription libraries, now so numerous. It is become a great thing itself, and continually increasing. These libraries have improved the general conversation of the Americans, made the common tradesmen and farmers as intelligent as most gentlemen from other countries, and perhaps have contributed in some degree to the stand so generally made throughout the colonies in defence of their privileges.

Mem°. Thus far was written with the intention express'd in the beginning and therefore contains several little family anecdotes of no importance to others. What follows was written many years after in compliance with the advice contain'd in these letters, and accordingly intended for the public. The affairs of the Revolution occasion'd the interruption.

Letter from Mr Abel James, with Notes of my Life
(received in Paris)

MY DEAR AND HONOURED FRIEND – I have often been desirous of writing to thee, but could not be reconciled to the thought, that the letter might fall into the hands of the British, lest some printer or busy-body should publish some part of the contents, and give our friend pain, and myself censure.

Some time since there fell into my hands, to my great joy, about twenty-three sheets in thy own handwriting, containing an account of the parentage and life of thyself, directed to thy son, ending in the year 1730, with which there were notes, likewise in thy writing; a copy of which I enclose, in hopes it may be a means, if thou continued it up to a later period, that the first and latter part may be put together; and if it is not yet continued, I hope thee will not delay it. Life is uncertain, as the preacher tells us; and what will the world say if kind, humane, and benevolent Ben. Franklin should leave his friends and the world deprived of so pleasing and profitable a work; a work which would be useful and entertaining not only to a few, but to millions? The influence writings under that class have on the minds of youth is very great, and has nowhere appeared to me so plain, as in our public friend's journals. It almost insensibly leads the youth into the resolution of endeavouring to become as good and eminent as the journalist. Should thine, for instance, when published (and I think it could not fail of it), lead the youth to equal the industry and temperance of thy early youth, what a blessing with that class would such a work be! I know of no character living, nor many of them put together, who has so much in his power as thyself to promote a greater spirit of industry and early attention to business, frugality, and temperance with the American youth. Not that I think the work would have no other merit and use in the world, far from it; but the first is of such vast importance that I know nothing that can equal it.

The foregoing letter and the minutes accompanying it being shown to a friend, I received from him the following:

Letter from Mr Benjamin Vaughan

Paris, January 31st, 1783

MY DEAREST SIR – When I had read over your sheets of minutes of the principal incidents of your life, recovered for you by your Quaker acquaintance, I told you I would send you a letter expressing my reasons why I thought it would be useful to complete and publish it as he desired. Various concerns have for some time past prevented this letter being written, and I do not know whether it was worth any expectation; happening to be at leisure, however, at present, I shall by writing, at least interest and instruct myself; but as the terms I am inclined to use may tend to offend a person of your manners, I shall only tell you how I would address any other person, who was as good and as great as yourself, but less diffident. I would say to him, Sir, I solicit the history of your life from the following motives: Your history is so remarkable, that if you do not give it, somebody else will certainly give it; and perhaps so as nearly to do as much harm, as your own management of the thing might do good. It will moreover present a table of the internal circumstances of your country, which will very much tend to invite to it settlers of virtuous and manly minds. And considering the eagerness with which such information is sought by them, and the extent of your reputation, I do not know of a more efficacious advertisement than your biography would give. All that has happened to you is also connected with the detail of the manners and situation of a rising people; and in this respect I do not think that the writings of Cæsar and Tacitus can be more interesting to a true judge of human nature and society. But these, sir, are small reasons, in my opinion, compared with the chance which your life will give for the forming of future great men; and in conjunction with your Art of Virtue (which you design to publish) of improving the features of private character, and consequently of aiding all happiness, both public and domestic. The two works I allude to, sir, will in particular give a noble rule and example of self-education. School and other education constantly proceed upon false principles, and show a clumsy apparatus pointed at a false mark; but your apparatus is simple, and the mark a true one; and while parents and young persons are left destitute of other just means of estimating and becoming prepared for a reasonable course in life, your discovery that the thing is in many a man's private power, will be invaluable! Influence upon the private character, late in life, is not only an influence late in life, but a weak influence. It is in youth that we plant our chief habits and prejudices; it is in youth that we take our party as to profession, pursuits and matrimony. In youth, therefore, the turn is given; in youth the education even of the next generation is given; in youth the private and public character is determined; and the term of life extending but from youth to age, life ought to begin well from youth, and more especially before we take our party as to our principal objects. But your biography will not merely teach self-education, but the education of a wise man; and the wisest man will receive lights and improve his progress, by seeing detailed the conduct of another wise man. And why are weaker men to be deprived of such helps, when we see our race has been blundering on in the dark, almost without a guide in this particular, from the farthest trace of time? Show then, sir, how much is to be done, both to sons and fathers; and invite all wise men to become like yourself, and other men to become wise. When we see how cruel statesmen and warriors can be to the human race, and how absurd distinguished men can be to their acquaintance, it will be instructive to observe the instances multiply of pacific, acquiescing manners; and to find how compatible it is to be great and domestic, enviable and yet good-humoured.

The little private incidents which you will also have to relate, will have considerable use, as we want, above all things, rules of prudence in ordinary affairs; and it will be curious to see how you have acted in these. It will be so far a sort of key to life, and explain many things that all men ought to have once explained to them, to give them a chance of becoming wise by foresight. The nearest thing to having experience of one's own, is to have other people's affairs brought before us in a shape that is interesting; this is sure to happen from your pen; our affairs and management will have an air of simplicity or importance that will not fail to strike; and I am convinced you have conducted them with as much originality as if you had been conducting discussions in politics or philosophy; and what more worthy of experiments and system (its importance and its errors considered) than human life?

Some men have been virtuous blindly, others have speculated fantastically, and others have been shrewd to bad purposes; but you, sir, I am sure, will give under your hand, nothing but what is at the same moment, wise, practical and good. Your account of yourself (for I suppose the parallel I am drawing for Dr Franklin, will hold not only in point of character, but of private history) will show that you are ashamed of no origin; a thing the more important, as you prove how little necessary all origin is to happiness, virtue, or greatness. As no end likewise happens without a means, so we shall find, sir, that even you yourself framed a plan by which you became considerable; but at the same time we may see that though the event is flattering, the means are as simple as wisdom could make them; that is, depending upon nature, virtue, thought and habit. Another thing demonstrated will be the propriety of every man's waiting for his time for appearing upon the stage of the world. Our sensations being very much fixed to the moment, we are apt to forget that more moments are to follow the first, and consequently that man should arrange his conduct so as to suit the whole of a life. Your attribution appears to have been applied to your life, and the passing moments of it have been enlivened with content and enjoyment, instead of being tormented with foolish impatience or regrets. Such a conduct is easy for those who make virtue and themselves in countenance by examples of other truly great men, of whom patience is so often the characteristic. Your Quaker correspondent, sir (for here again I will suppose the subject of my letter resembling Dr Franklin), praised your frugality, diligence and temperance, which is considered as a pattern for all youth; but it is singular that he should have forgotten your modesty and your disinterestedness, without which you never could have waited for your advancement, or found your situation in the meantime comfortable; which is a strong lesson to show the poverty of glory and the importance of regulating our minds. If this correspondent had known the nature of your reputation as well as I do, he would have said, Your former writings and measures would secure attention to your Biography, and Art of Virtue; and your Biography and Art of Virtue, in return, would secure attention to them. This is an advantage attendant upon a various character, and which brings all that belongs to it into greater play; and it is the more useful, as perhaps more persons are at a loss for the means of improving their minds and characters, than they are for the time or the inclination to do it. But there is one concluding reflection, sir, that will show the use of your life as a mere piece of biography. This style of writing seems a little gone out of vogue, and yet it is a very useful one; and your specimen of it may be particularly serviceable, as it will make a subject of comparison with the lives of various public cutthroats and intriguers, and with absurd monastic self-tormentors or vain literary triflers. If it encourages more writings of the same kind with your own, and induces more men to spend lives fit to be written, it will be worth all Plutarch's Lives put together. But being tired of figuring to myself a character of which every feature suits only one man in the world, without giving him the praise of it, I shall end my letter, my dear Dr Franklin, with a personal application to your proper self. I am earnestly desirous, then, my dear sir, that you should let the world into the traits of your genuine character, as civil broils may otherwise tend to disguise or traduce it. Considering your great age, the caution of your character, and your peculiar style of thinking, it is not likely that anyone besides yourself can be sufficiently master of the facts of your life, or the intentions of your mind. Besides all this, the immense revolution of the present period, will necessarily turn our attention towards the author of it, and when virtuous principles have been pretended in it, it will be highly important to show that such have really influenced; and, as your own character will be the principal one to receive a scrutiny, it is proper (even for its effects upon your vast and rising country, as well as upon England and upon Europe) that it should stand respectable and eternal. For the furtherance of human happiness, I have always maintained that it is necessary to prove that man is not even at present a vicious and detestable animal; and still more to prove that good management may greatly amend him; and it is for much the same reason, that I am anxious to see the opinion established, that there are fair characters existing among the individuals of the race; for the moment that all men, without exception, shall be conceived abandoned, good people will cease efforts deemed to be hopeless, and perhaps think of taking their share in the scramble of life, or at least of making it comfortable principally for themselves. Take then, my dear sir, this work most speedily into hand: show yourself good as you are good; temperate as you are temperate; and above all things, prove yourself as one, who from your infancy have loved justice, liberty and concord, in a way that has made it natural and consistent for you to have acted, as we have seen you act in the last seventeen years of your life. Let Englishmen be made not only to respect, but even to love you. When they think well of individuals in your native country, they will go nearer to thinking well of your country; and when your countrymen see themselves well thought of by Englishmen, they will go nearer to thinking well of England. Extend your views even further; do not stop at those who speak the English tongue, but after having settled so many points in nature and politics, think of bettering the whole race of men. As I have not read any part of the life in question, but know only the character that lived it, I write somewhat at hazard. I am sure, however, that the life and the treatise I allude to (on the Art of Virtue) will necessarily fulfil the chief of my expectations; and still more so if you take up the measure of suiting these performances to the several views above stated. Should they even prove unsuccessful in all that a sanguine admirer of yours hopes from them, you will at least have framed pieces to interest the human mind; and whoever gives a feeling of pleasure that is innocent to man, has added so much to the fair side of a life otherwise too much darkened by anxiety and too much injured by pain. In the hope, therefore, that you will listen to the prayer addressed to you in this letter, I beg to subscribe myself, my dearest sir, etc., etc.,

Signed,

BENJAMIN VAUGHAN

Continuation of the Account of my Life, begun at
Passy, near Paris, 1784

It is some time since I receiv'd the above letters, but I have been too busy till now to think of complying with the request they contain. It might, too, be much better done if I were at home among my papers, which would aid my memory, and help to ascertain dates; but my return being uncertain, and having just now a little leisure, I will endeavour to recollect and write what I can; if I live to get home, it may there be corrected and improv'd.

Not having any copy here of what is already written, I know not whether an account is given of the means I used to establish the Philadelphia public library, which, from a small beginning, is now become so considerable, though I remember to have come down to near the time of that transaction (1730). I will therefore begin here with an account of it, which may be struck out if found to have been already given.

At the time I establish'd myself in Pennsylvania, there was not a good bookseller's shop in any of the colonies to the southward of Boston. In New York and Philad'a the printers were indeed stationers; they sold only paper, etc., almanacs, ballads, and a few common school-books. Those who lov'd reading were oblig'd to send for their books from England; the members of the Junto had each a few. We had left the alehouse, where we first met, and hired a room to hold our club in. I propos'd that we should all of us bring our books to that room, where they would not only be ready to consult in our conferences, but become a common benefit, each of us being at liberty to borrow such as he wish'd to read at home. This was accordingly done, and for some time contented us.

Finding the advantage of this little collection, I propos'd to render the benefit from books more common, by commencing a public subscription library. I drew a sketch of the plan and rules that would be necessary, and got a skilful conveyancer, Mr Charles Brockden, to put the whole in form of articles of agreement to be subscribed, by which each subscriber engag'd to pay a certain sum down for the first purchase of books, and an annual contribution for increasing them. So few were the readers at that time in Philadelphia, and the majority of us so poor, that I was not able, with great industry, to find more than fifty persons, mostly young tradesmen, willing to pay down for this purpose forty shillings each, and ten shillings per annum. On this little fund we began. The books were imported; the library was opened one day in the week for lending to the subscribers, on their promissory notes to pay double the value if not duly returned. The institution soon manifested its utility, was imitated by other towns, and in other provinces. The libraries were augmented by donations; reading became fashionable; and our people, having no public amusements to divert their attention from study, became better acquainted with books, and in a few years were observ'd by strangers to be better instructed and more intelligent than people of the same rank generally are in other countries.

When we were about to sign the above-mentioned articles, which were to be binding on us, our heirs, etc., for fifty years, Mr Brockden, the scrivener, said to us, 'You are young men, but it is scarcely probable that any of you will live to see the expiration of the term fix'd in the instrument.' A number of us, however, are yet living; but the instrument was after a few years rendered null by a charter that incorporated and gave perpetuity to the company.

The objections and reluctances I met with in soliciting the subscriptions, made me soon feel the impropriety of presenting one's self as the proposer of any useful project, that might be suppos'd to raise one's reputation in the smallest degree above that of one's neighbours, when one has need of their assistance to accomplish that project. I therefore put myself as much as I could out of sight, and stated it as a scheme of a *number of friends*, who had requested me to go about and propose it to such as they thought lovers of reading. In this way my affair went on more smoothly, and I ever after practis'd it on such occasions; and, from my frequent successes, can heartily recommend it. The present little sacrifice of your vanity will afterwards be amply repaid. If it remains a while uncertain to whom the merit belongs, someone more vain than yourself will be encouraged to claim it, and then even envy will be disposed to do you justice by plucking those assumed feathers, and restoring them to their right owner.

This library afforded me the means of improvement by constant study, for which I set apart an hour or two each day, and thus repair'd in some degree the loss of the learned education my father once intended for me. Reading was the only amusement I allow'd myself. I spent no time in taverns, games, or frolics of any kind; and my industry in my business continu'd as indefatigable as it was necessary. I was indebted for my printing-house; I had a young family coming on to be educated, and I had to contend with for business two printers, who were established in the place before me. My circumstances, however, grew daily easier. My original habits of frugality continuing, and my father having, among his instructions to me when a boy, frequently repeated a proverb of Solomon, 'Seest thou a man diligent in his calling, he shall stand before kings, he shall not stand before mean men,' I from thence considered industry as a means of obtaining wealth and distinction, which encourag'd me, tho' I did not think that I should ever literally *stand before kings*, which, however, has since happened; for I have stood before *five*, and even had the honour of sitting down with one, the King of Denmark, to dinner.

We have an English proverb that says, '*He that would thrive, must ask his wife.*' It was lucky for me that I had one as much dispos'd to industry and frugality as myself. She assisted me cheerfully in my business, folding and stitching pamphlets, tending shop, purchasing old linen rags for the paper-makers, etc., etc. We kept no idle servants, our table was plain and simple, our furniture of the cheapest. For instance, my breakfast was a long time bread and milk (no tea), and I ate it out of a twopenny earthen porringer, with a pewter spoon. But mark how luxury will enter families, and make a progress, in spite of principle: being call'd one morning to breakfast, I found it in a China bowl, with a spoon of silver! They had been bought for me without my knowledge by my wife, and had cost her the enormous sum of three-and-twenty shillings, for which she had no other excuse or apology to make, but that she thought *her* husband deserv'd a silver spoon and China bowl as well as any of his neighbours. This was the first appearance of plate and

China in our house, which afterward, in a course of years, as our wealth increas'd, augmented gradually to several hundred pounds in value.

I had been religiously educated as a Presbyterian; and tho' some of the dogmas of that persuasion, such as *the eternal decrees of God, election, reprobation, etc.*, appeared to me unintelligible, others doubtful, and I early absented myself from the public assemblies of the sect, Sunday being my studying day, I never was without some religious principles. I never doubted, for instance, the existence of the Deity; that he made the world, and govern'd it by his Providence; that the most acceptable service of God was the doing good to man; that our souls are immortal; and that all crime will be punished, and virtue rewarded, either here or hereafter. These I esteem'd the essentials of every religion; and, being to be found in all the religions we had in our country, I respected them all, tho' with different degrees of respect, as I found them more or less mix'd with other articles, which, without any tendency to inspire, promote, or confirm morality, serv'd principally to divide us, and make us unfriendly to one another. This respect to all, with an opinion that the worst had some good effects, induc'd me to avoid all discourse that might tend to lessen the good opinion another might have of his own religion; and as our province increas'd in people, and new places of worship were continually wanted, and generally erected by voluntary contribution, my mite for such purpose, whatever might be the sect, was never refused.

Tho' I seldom attended any public worship, I had still an opinion of its propriety, and of its utility when rightly conducted, and I regularly paid my annual subscription for the support of the only Presbyterian minister or meeting we had in Philadelphia. He us'd to visit me sometimes as a friend, and admonish me to attend his administrations, and I was now and then prevail'd on to do so, once for five Sundays successively. Had he been in my opinion a good preacher, perhaps I might have continued, notwithstanding the occasion I had for the Sunday's leisure in my course of study; but his discourses were chiefly either polemic arguments, or explications of the peculiar doctrines of our sect, and were all to me very dry, uninteresting, and unedifying, since not a single moral principle was inculcated or enforc'd, their aim seeming to be rather to make us Presbyterians than good citizens.

At length he took for his text that verse of the fourth chapter of Philippians, '*Finally, brethren, whatsoever things are true, honest, just, pure, lovely, or of good report, if there be any virtue, or any praise, think on these things.*' And I imagin'd, in a sermon on such a text, we could not miss of having some morality. But he confin'd himself to five points only, as meant by the apostle, viz.: 1. Keeping holy the Sabbath day. 2. Being diligent in reading the holy Scriptures. 3. Attending duly the public worship. 4. Partaking of the Sacrament. 5. Paying a due respect to God's ministers. These might be all good things; but, as they were not the kind of good things that I expected from that text, I despaired of ever meeting with them from any other, was disgusted, and attended his preaching no more. I had some years before compos'd a little Liturgy, or form of prayer, for my own private use (viz., in 1728), entitled, *Articles of Belief and Acts of Religion.* I return'd to the use of this, and went no more to the public assemblies. My conduct might be blameable, but I leave it, without attempting further to excuse it; my present purpose being to relate facts, and not to make apologies for them.

It was about this time I conceiv'd the bold and arduous project of arriving at moral perfection. I wish'd to live without committing any fault at any time; I would conquer all that either natural inclination, custom, or company might lead me into. As I knew, or thought I knew, what was right and wrong, I did not see why I might not always do the one and avoid the other. But I soon found I had undertaken a task of more difficulty than I had imagined. While my care was employ'd in guarding against one fault, I was often surprised by another; habit took the advantage of inattention; inclination was sometimes too strong for reason. I concluded, at length, that the mere speculative conviction that it was our interest to be completely virtuous, was not sufficient to prevent our slipping; and that the contrary habits must be broken, and good ones acquired and established, before we can have any dependence on a steady, uniform rectitude of conduct. For this purpose I therefore contrived the following method.

In the various enumerations of the moral virtues I had met with in my reading, I found the catalogue more or less numerous, as different writers included more or fewer ideas under the same name. Temperance, for example, was by some confined to eating and drinking, while by others it was extended to mean the moderating every other pleasure, appetite, inclination, or passion, bodily or mental, even to our avarice and ambition. I propos'd to myself, for the sake of clearness, to use rather more names, with fewer ideas annex'd to each, than a few names with more ideas; and I included under thirteen names of virtues all that at that time occurr'd to me as necessary or desirable, and annexed to each a short precept, which fully express'd the extent I gave to its meaning.

These names of virtues, with their precepts, were:

1. TEMPERANCE

Eat not to dullness; drink not to elevation.

2. SILENCE

Speak not but what may benefit others or yourself; avoid trifling conversation.

3. ORDER

Let all your things have their places; let each part of your business have its time.

4. RESOLUTION

Resolve to perform what you ought; perform without fail what you resolve.

5. FRUGALITY

Make no expense but to do good to others or yourself; i.e., waste nothing.

6. INDUSTRY

Lose no time; be always employ'd in something useful; cut off all unnecessary actions.

7. SINCERITY

Use no hurtful deceit; think innocently and justly, and, if you speak, speak accordingly.

8. JUSTICE

Wrong none by doing injuries, or omitting the benefits that are your duty.

9. MODERATION

Avoid extremes; forbear resenting injuries so much as you think they deserve.

10. CLEANLINESS

Tolerate no uncleanliness in body, clothes, or habitation.

11. TRANQUILLITY

Be not disturbed at trifles, or at accidents common or unavoidable.

12. CHASTITY

Rarely use venery but for health or offspring, never to dullness, weakness, or the injury of your own or another's peace or reputation.

13. HUMILITY

Imitate Jesus and Socrates.

My intention being to acquire the *habitude* of all these virtues, I judg'd it would be well not to distract my attention by attempting the whole at once, but to fix it on one of them at a time; and, when I should be master of that, then to proceed to another, and so on, till I should have gone thro' the thirteen; and, as the previous acquisition of some might facilitate the acquisition of certain others, I arrang'd them with that view, as they stand above. Temperance first, as it tends to procure that coolness and clearness of head, which is so necessary where constant vigilance was to be kept up, and guard maintained against the unremitting attraction of ancient habits, and the force of perpetual temptations. This being acquir'd and establish'd, Silence would be more easy; and my desire being to gain knowledge at the same time that I improv'd in virtue, and considering that in conversation it was obtain'd rather by the use of the ears than of the tongue, and therefore wishing to break a habit I was getting into of prattling, punning, and joking, which only made me acceptable to trifling company, I gave *Silence* the second place. This and the next, *Order*, I expected would allow me more time for attending to my project and my studies. *Resolution*, once become habitual, would keep me firm in my endeavours to obtain all the subsequent virtues; *Frugality* and Industry freeing me from my remaining debt, and producing affluence and independence, would make more easy the practice of Sincerity and Justice, etc., etc. Conceiving then, that, agreeably to the advice of Pythagoras in his Golden Verses, daily examination would be necessary, I contrived the following method for conducting that examination.

I made a little book, in which I allotted a page for each of the virtues. I rul'd each page with red ink, so as to have seven columns, one for each day of the week, marking each column with a letter for the day. I cross'd these columns with thirteen red lines, marking the beginning of each line with the first letter of one of the virtues, on which line, and in its proper column, I might mark, by a little black spot, every fault I found upon examination to have been committed respecting that virtue upon that day.

I determined to give a week's strict attention to each of the virtues successively. Thus, in the first week, my great guard was to avoid every the least offence against *Temperance*, leaving the other virtues to their ordinary chance, only marking every evening the faults of the day. Thus, if in the first week I could keep my first line, marked T, clear of spots, I suppos'd the habit of that virtue so much strengthen'd, and its opposite weaken'd, that I might venture extending my attention to include the next, and for the following week keep both

TEMPERANCE

Eat not to dullness; drink not to elevation

	Sun	Mon	Tues	Wed	Thurs	Fri	Sat
T							
S	*	*		*		*	
O	**	*	*		*	*	*
R			*			*	
F		*			*		
I			*				
S							
J							
M							
C							
T							
C							
H							

lines clear of spots. Proceeding thus to the last, I could go thro' a course complete in thirteen weeks, and four courses in a year. And like him who, having a garden to weed, does not attempt to eradicate all the bad herbs at once, which would exceed his reach and his strength, but works on one of the beds at a time, and, having accomplish'd the first, proceeds to a second, so I should have, I hoped, the encouraging pleasure of seeing on my pages the progress I made in virtue, by clearing successively my lines of their spots, till in the end, by a number of courses, I should be happy in viewing a clean book, after a thirteen weeks' daily examination.

This my little book had for its motto these lines from Addison's *Cato:*

> Here will I hold. If there's a power above us
> (And that there is, all nature cries aloud
> Thro' all her works), He must delight in virtue;
> And that which he delights in must be happy.

Another from Cicero,

O vitæ Philosophia dux! O virtutum indagatrix expultrixque vitiorum! Unus dies, bene et ex præceptis tuis actus, peccanti immortalitati est anteponendus.

Another from the Proverbs of Solomon, speaking of wisdom or virtue:

Length of days is in her right hand, and in her left hand riches and honour. Her ways are ways of pleasantness, and all her paths are peace. iii. 16, 17.

And conceiving God to be the fountain of wisdom, I thought it right and necessary to solicit his assistance for obtaining it; to this end I formed the following little prayer, which was prefix'd to my tables of examination, for daily use.

O powerful Goodness! bountiful Father! merciful Guide! Increase in me that wisdom which discovers my truest interest. Strengthen my resolutions to perform what that wisdom dictates. Accept my kind offices to thy other children as the only return in my power for thy continual favours to me.

I used also sometimes a little prayer which I took from Thomson's *Poems*, viz.:

Father of light and life, thou Good Supreme!
O teach me what is good; teach me Thyself!
Save me from folly, vanity, and vice,
From every low pursuit; and fill my soul
With knowledge, conscious peace, and virtue pure;
Sacred, substantial, never-fading bliss!

The precept of *Order* requiring that *every part of my business should have its allotted time*, one page in my little book contain'd the following scheme of employment for the twenty-four hours of a natural day.

I enter'd upon the execution of this plan for self-examination, and continu'd it with occasional intermissions for some time. I was surpris'd to find myself so much fuller of faults than I had imagined; but I had the satisfaction of seeing them diminish. To avoid the trouble of renewing now and then my little book, which, by scraping out the marks on the paper of old faults to make room for new ones in a new course, became full of holes, I transferr'd my tables and precepts to the ivory leaves of a memorandum book, on which the lines were drawn with red ink, that made a durable stain, and on those lines I mark'd my faults with a black-lead pencil, which marks I could easily wipe out with a wet sponge.

THE	5	Rise, wash and address Powerful Goodness!
MORNING	6	Contrive day's business, and take the resolution
Question	7	of the day; prosecute the present study, and
What good	8	breakfast.
shall		
I do this	9	Work
day?	10	
	11	
NOON	12	
	1	Read, or overlook my accounts, and dine.
	2	
	3	Work
	4	
	5	
EVENING	6	
Question	7	
What good	8	Put things in their places. Supper.
have I done	9	Music or diversion, or conversation.
today?	10	Examination of the day.
NIGHT	11	
	12	
	1	Sleep
	2	
	3	
	4	

After a while I went thro' one course only in a year, and afterward only one in several years, till at length I omitted them entirely, being employ'd in voyages and business abroad, with a multiplicity of affairs that interfered; but I always carried my little book with me.

My scheme of ORDER gave me the most trouble; and I found that, tho' it might be practicable where a man's business was such as to leave him the disposition of his time, that of a journeyman printer, for instance, it was not possible to be exactly observed by a master, who must mix with the world, and often receive people of business at their own hours. *Order*, too, with regard to places for things, papers, etc., I found extremely difficult to acquire. I had not been early accustomed to it, and, having an exceeding good memory, I was not so sensible of the inconvenience attending want of method. This article, therefore, cost me so much painful attention, and my faults in it vexed me so much, and I made so little progress in amendment, and had such frequent relapses, that I was almost ready to give up the attempt, and content myself with a faulty character in that respect, like the man who, in buying an axe of a smith, my neighbour, desired to have the whole of its surface as bright as the edge. The smith consented to grind it bright for him if he would turn the wheel; he turn'd, while the smith press'd the broad face of the axe hard and heavily on the stone, which made the turning of it very fatiguing. The man came every now and then from the wheel to see how the work went on, and at length would take his axe as it was, without farther grinding. 'No,' said the smith, 'turn on, turn on; we shall have it bright by and by; as yet, it is only speckled.' 'Yes,' says the man, '*but I think I like a speckled axe best*.' And I believe this may have been the case with many, who, having, for want of some such means as I employ'd, found the difficulty of obtaining good and breaking bad habits in other points of vice and virtue, have given up the struggle, and concluded that '*a speckled axe was best*'; for something, that pretended to be reason, was every now and then suggesting to me that such extreme nicety as I exacted of myself might be a kind of foppery in morals, which, if it were known, would make me ridiculous; that a perfect character might be attended with the inconvenience of being envied and hated; and that a benevolent man should allow a few faults in himself, to keep his friends in countenance.

In truth, I found myself incorrigible with respect to Order; and now I am grown old, and my memory bad, I feel very sensibly the want of it. But, on the whole, tho' I never arrived at the perfection I had been so ambitious of obtaining, but fell far short of it, yet I was, by the endeavour, a better and a happier man than I otherwise should have been if I had not attempted it; as those who aim at perfect writing by imitating the engraved copies, tho' they never reach the wish'd-for excellence of those copies, their hand is mended by the endeavour, and is tolerable while it continues fair and legible.

It may be well my posterity should be informed that to this little artifice, with the blessing of God, their ancestor ow'd the constant felicity of his life, down to his 79th year, in which this is written. What reverses may attend the remainder is in the hand of Providence; but, if they arrive, the reflection on past happiness enjoy'd ought to help his bearing them with more resignation. To Temperance he ascribes his long-continued health, and what is still left to him of a good constitution; to Industry and Frugality, the early easiness of his circumstances and acquisition of his fortune, with all that knowledge that enabled him to be a useful citizen, and obtained for him some degree of reputation among the learned; to Sincerity and Justice, the confidence of his country, and the honourable employs it conferred upon him; and to the joint influence of the whole mass of the virtues, even in the imperfect state he was able to acquire them, all that evenness of temper, and that cheerfulness in conversation, which makes his company still sought for, and agreeable even to his younger acquaintance. I hope, therefore, that some of my descendants may follow the example and reap the benefit.

It will be remark'd that, tho' my scheme was not wholly without religion, there was in it no mark of any of the distinguishing tenets of any particular sect. I had purposely avoided them; for, being fully persuaded of the utility and excellency of my method, and that it might be serviceable to people in all religions, and intending sometime or other to publish it, I would not have anything in it that should prejudice anyone, of any sect, against it. I purposed writing a little comment on each virtue, in which I would have shown the advantages of possessing it, and the mischiefs attending its opposite vice; and I should have called my book THE ART OF VIRTUE,* because it would have shown the means and manner of obtaining virtue, which would have distinguished it from the mere exhortation to be good, that does not instruct and indicate the means, but is like the apostle's man of verbal charity, who only without showing to the naked and hungry how or where they might get clothes or victuals, exhorted them to be fed and clothed. – JAMES II. 15, 16.

But it so happened that my intention of writing and publishing this comment was never fulfilled. I did, indeed, from time to time, put down short hints of the sentiments, reasonings, etc., to be made use of in it, some of which I have still by me; but the necessary close attention to private business in the earlier part of my life, and public business since, have occasioned my postponing it; for, it being connected in my mind with *a great and extensive project*, that required the whole man to execute, and which an unforeseen succession of employs prevented my attending to, it has hitherto remain'd unfinish'd.

In this piece it was my design to explain and enforce this doctrine, that vicious actions are not hurtful because they are forbidden, but forbidden because they are hurtful, the nature of man alone considered; that it was, therefore, everyone's interest to be virtuous who wish'd to be happy even in this world; and I should, from this circumstance (there being always in the world a number of rich merchants, nobility, states,

---

* Nothing so likely to make a man's fortune as virtue.

and princes, who have need of honest instruments for the management of their affairs, and such being so rare), have endeavoured to convince young persons that no qualities were so likely to make a poor man's fortune as those of probity and integrity.

My list of virtues contain'd at first but twelve; but a Quaker friend having kindly informed me that I was generally thought proud; that my pride show'd itself frequently in conversation; that I was not content with being in the right when discussing any point, but was overbearing, and rather insolent, of which he convinc'd me by mentioning several instances; I determined endeavouring to cure myself, if I could, of this vice or folly among the rest, and I added *Humility* to my list, giving an extensive meaning to the word.

I cannot boast of much success in acquiring the *reality* of this virtue, but I had a good deal with regard to the *appearance* of it. I made it a rule to forbear all direct contradiction to the sentiments of others, and all positive assertion of my own. I even forbid myself, agreeably to the old laws of our Junto, the use of every word or expression in the language that imported a fix'd opinion, such as *certainly*, *undoubtedly*, etc., and I adopted, instead of them, *I conceive*, *I apprehend*, or I imagine a thing to be so or so; or it *so appears to me at present*. When another asserted something that I thought an error, I deny'd myself the pleasure of contradicting him abruptly, and of showing immediately some absurdity in his proposition; and in answering I began by observing that in certain cases or circumstances his opinion would be right, but in the present case there *appear'd* or *seem'd* to me some difference, etc. I soon found the advantage of this change in my manner; the conversations I engag'd in went on more pleasantly. The modest way in which I propos'd my opinions procur'd them a readier reception and less contradiction; I had less mortification when I was found to be in the wrong, and I more easily prevail'd with others to give up their mistakes and join with me when I happened to be in the right.

And this mode, which I at first put on with some violence to natural inclination, became at length so easy, and so habitual to me, that perhaps for these fifty years past no one has ever heard a dogmatical expression escape me. And to this habit (after my character of integrity) I think it principally owing that I had early so much weight with my fellow-citizens when I proposed new institutions, or alterations in the old, and so much influence in public councils when I became a member; for I was but a bad speaker, never eloquent, subject to much hesitation in my choice of words, hardly correct in language, and yet I generally carried my points.

In reality, there is, perhaps, no one of our national passions so hard to subdue *as pride*. Disguise it, struggle with it, beat it down, stifle it, mortify it as much as one pleases, it is still alive, and will every now and then peep out and show itself; you will see it, perhaps, often in this history; for, even if I could conceive that I had completely overcome it, I should probably be proud of my humility.

Thus far written at Passy, 1784.

*I am now about to write at home, August, 1788, but cannot have the help expected from my papers, many of them being lost in the war. I have, however, found the following:**

Having mentioned a *great and extensive project* which I had conceiv'd, it seems proper that some account should be here given of that project and its object. Its first rise in my mind appears in the following little paper, accidentally preserv'd, viz.:

Observations on my reading history, in Library, May 19th, 1731.

That the great affairs of the world, the wars, revolutions, etc., are carried on and affected by parties.

That the view of these parties is their present general interest, or what they take to be such.

That the different views of these different parties occasion all confusion.

That while a party is carrying on a general design, each man has his particular private interest in view.

That as soon as a party has gain'd its general point, each member becomes intent upon his particular interest; which, thwarting others, breaks that party into divisions, and occasions more confusion.

That few in public affairs act from a mere view of the good of their country, whatever they may pretend; and, tho' their actings bring real good to their country, yet men primarily considered that their own and their country's interest was united, and did not act from a principle of benevolence.

That fewer still, in public affairs, act with a view to the good of mankind.

There seems to me at present to be great occasion for raising a United Party for Virtue, by forming the virtuous and good men of all nations into a regular body, to be govern'd by suitable good and wise rules, which good and wise men may probably be more

* This is a marginal memorandum. – B.

unanimous in their obedience to, than common people are to common laws.

I at present think that whoever attempts this aright, and is well qualified, cannot fail of pleasing God, and of meeting with success.

B. F.

Revolving this project in my mind, as to be undertaken hereafter, when my circumstances should afford me the necessary leisure, I put down from time to time, on pieces of paper, such thoughts as occurr'd to me respecting it. Most of these are lost; but I find one purporting to be the substance of an intended creed, containing, as I thought, the essentials of every known religion, and being free of everything that might shock the professors of any religion. It is express'd in these words, viz.:

That there is one God, who made all things.

That he governs the world by his providence.

That he ought to be worshipped by adoration, prayer, and thanksgiving.

But that the most acceptable service of God is doing good to man.

That the soul is immortal.

And that God will certainly reward virtue and punish vice, either here or hereafter.

My ideas at that time were, that the sect should be begun and spread at first among young and single men only; that each person to be initiated should not only declare his assent to such creed, but should have exercised himself with the thirteen weeks' examination and practice of the virtues, as in the before-mention'd model; that the existence of such a society should be kept a secret, till it was become considerable, to prevent solicitations for the admission of improper persons, but that the members should each of them search among his acquaintance for ingenuous, well-disposed youths, to whom, with prudent caution, the scheme should be gradually communicated; that the members should engage to afford their advice, assistance, and support to each other in promoting one another's interests, business, and advancement in life; that, for distinction, we should be call'd *The Society of the Free end Easy:* free, as being, by the general practice and habit of the virtues, free from the dominion of vice; and particularly by the practice of industry and frugality, free from debt, which exposes a man to confinement, and a species of slavery to his creditors.

This is as much as I can now recollect of the project, except that I communicated it in part to two young men, who adopted it with some enthusiasm; but my then narrow circumstances, and the necessity I was under of sticking close to my business, occasion'd my postponing the further prosecution of it at that time; and my multifarious occupations, public and private, induc'd me to continue postponing, so that it has been omitted till I have no longer strength or activity left sufficient for such an enterprise; tho' I am still of opinion that it was a practicable scheme, and might have been very useful, by forming a great number of good citizens; and I was not discourag'd by the seeming magnitude of the undertaking, as I have always thought that one man of tolerable abilities may work great changes, and accomplish great affairs among mankind, if he first forms a good plan, and, cutting off all amusements or other employments that would divert his attention, makes the execution of that same plan his sole study and business.

In 1732 I first publish'd my Almanac, under the name of *Richard Saunders*; it was continu'd by me about twenty-five years, commonly call'd *Poor Richard's Almanac*. I endeavour'd to make it both entertaining and useful, and it accordingly came to be in such demand, that I reap'd considerable profit from it, vending annually near ten thousand. And observing that it was generally read, scarce any neighbourhood in the province being without it, I consider'd it as a proper vehicle for conveying instruction among the common people, who bought scarcely any other books; I therefore filled all the little spaces that occurr'd between the remarkable days in the calendar with proverbial sentences, chiefly such as inculcated industry and frugality, as the means of procuring wealth, and thereby securing virtue; it being more difficult for a man in want, to act always honestly, as, to use here one of those proverbs, *it is hard for an empty sack to stand upright*.

These proverbs, which contained the wisdom of many ages and nations, I assembled and form'd into a connected discourse prefix'd to the Almanac of 1757, as the harangue of a wise old man to the people attending an auction. The bringing all these scatter'd counsels thus into a focus enabled them to make greater impression. The piece, being universally approved, was copied in all the newspapers of the Continent; reprinted in Britain on a broad side, to be stuck up in houses; two translations were made of it in French, and great numbers bought by the clergy and gentry, to distribute gratis among their poor parishioners and tenants. In Pennsylvania, as it discouraged useless expense in foreign superfluities, some thought it had its share of influence in producing that growing plenty of money which was observable for several years after its publication.

I considered my newspaper, also, as another means of communicating instruction, and in that view frequently reprinted in it extracts from the *Spectator*, and other moral writers; and sometimes publish'd little pieces of my own, which had been first compos'd for reading in our Junto. Of these are a Socratic dialogue, tending to prove that, whatever might be his parts and abilities, a vicious man could not properly be called a man of sense; and a discourse on self-denial, showing that virtue was not secure till its practice became a habitude, and was free from the opposition of contrary inclinations. These may be found in the papers about the beginning of 1735.

In the conduct of my newspaper, I carefully excluded all libelling and personal abuse, which is of late years become so disgraceful to our country. Whenever I was solicited to insert anything of that kind, and the writers pleaded, as they generally did, the liberty of the press, and that a newspaper was like a stage-coach, in which anyone who would pay had a right to a place, my answer was, that I would print the piece separately if desired, and the author might have as many copies as he pleased to distribute himself, but that I would not take upon me to spread his detraction; and that, having contracted with my subscribers to furnish them with what might be either useful or entertaining, I could not fill their papers with private altercation, in which they had no concern, without doing them manifest injustice. Now, many of our printers make no scruple of gratifying the malice of individuals by false accusations of the fairest characters among ourselves, augmenting animosity even to the producing of duels; and are, moreover, so indiscreet as to print scurrilous reflections on the government of neighbouring states, and even on the conduct of our best national allies, which may be attended with the most pernicious consequences. These things I mention as a caution to young printers, and that they may be encouraged not to pollute their presses and disgrace their profession by such infamous practices, but refuse steadily, as they may see by my example that such a course of conduct will not, on the whole, be injurious to their interests.

In 1733 I sent one of my journeymen to Charleston, South Carolina, where a printer was wanting. I furnish'd him with a press and letters, on an agreement of partnership, by which I was to receive one-third of the profits of the business, paying one-third of the expense. He was a man of learning, and honest but ignorant in matters of account; and, tho' he sometimes made me remittances, I could get no account from him, nor any satisfactory state of our partnership while he lived. On his decease, the business was continued by his widow, who, being born and bred in Holland, where, as I have been inform'd, the knowledge of accounts makes a part of female education, she not only sent me as clear a state as she could find of the transactions past, but continued to account with the greatest regularity and exactness every quarter afterwards, and managed the business with such success, that she not only brought up reputably a family of children, but, at the expiration of the term, was able to purchase of me the printing-house, and establish her son in it.

I mention this affair chiefly for the sake of recommending that branch of education for our young females, as likely to be of more use to them and their children, in case of widowhood, than either music or dancing, by preserving them from losses by imposition of crafty men, and enabling them to continue, perhaps, a profitable mercantile house, with establish'd correspondence, till a son is grown up fit to undertake and go on with it, to the lasting advantage and enriching of the family.

About the year 1734 there arrived among us from Ireland a young Presbyterian preacher, named Hemphill, who delivered with a good voice, and apparently extempore, most excellent discourses, which drew together considerable numbers of different persuasions, who join'd in admiring them. Among the rest, I became one of his constant hearers, his sermons pleasing me, as they had little of the dogmatical kind, but inculcated strongly the practice of virtue, or what in the religious style are called good works. Those, however, of our congregation, who considered themselves as orthodox Presbyterians, disapprov'd his doctrine, and were join'd by most of the old clergy, who arraign'd him of heterodoxy before the synod, in order to have him silenc'd. I became his zealous partisan, and contributed all I could to raise a party in his favour, and we combated for him a while with some hopes of success. There was much scribbling pro and con upon the occasion; and finding that, tho' an elegant preacher, he was but a poor writer, I lent him my pen and wrote for him two or three pamphlets, and one piece in the *Gazette* of April, 1735. Those pamphlets, as is generally the case with controversial writings, tho' eagerly read at the time, were soon out of vogue, and I question whether a single copy of them now exists.

During the contest an unlucky occurrence hurt his cause exceedingly. One of our adversaries having heard him preach a sermon that was much admired, thought he had somewhere read the sermon before, or at least a part of it. On search, he found that part quoted at length, in one of the British Reviews, from a discourse of Dr Foster's. This detection gave many of our party disgust, who accordingly abandoned his cause, and occasion'd our more speedy discomfiture in the synod. I stuck by him, however, as I rather approv'd his giving us good sermons compos'd by others, than bad ones of his own manufacture, tho' the latter was the practice of our common teachers. He afterward acknowledg'd to me that none of those he preach'd were his own; adding, that his memory was such as enabled him to retain and repeat any sermon after one reading only. On our defeat, he left us in search elsewhere of better fortune, and I quitted the congregation, never joining it after, tho' I continu'd many years my subscription for the support of its ministers.

I had begun in 1733 to study languages; I soon made myself so much a master of the French as to be able to read the books with ease. I then undertook the Italian. An acquaintance, who was also learning it, us'd often to tempt me to play chess with him. Finding this took up too much of the time I had to spare for study, I at length refus'd to play any more, unless on this condition, that the victor in every game should have a right to impose a task, either in parts of the grammar to be got by heart, or in translations, etc., which tasks the vanquish'd was to perform upon honour, before our next meeting. As we play'd pretty equally, we thus beat one another into that language. I afterwards with a little painstaking, acquir'd as much of the Spanish as to read their books also.

I have already mention'd that I had only one year's instruction in a Latin school, and that when very young, after which I neglected that language entirely. But, when I had attained an acquaintance with the French, Italian, and Spanish, I was surpris'd to find, on looking over a Latin Testament, that I understood so much more of that language than I had imagined, which encouraged me to apply myself again to the study of it, and I met with more success, as those preceding languages had greatly smooth'd my way.

From these circumstances, I have thought that there is some inconsistency in our common mode of teaching languages. We are told that it is proper to begin first with the Latin, and, having acquir'd that, it will be more easy to attain those modern languages which are deriv'd from it; and yet we do not begin with the Greek, in order more easily to acquire the Latin. It is true that, if you can clamber and get to the top of a staircase without using the steps, you will more easily gain them in descending; but certainly, if you begin with the lowest you will with more ease ascend to the top; and I would therefore offer it to the consideration of those who superintend the education of our youth, whether, since many of those who begin with the Latin quit the same after spending some years without having made any great proficiency, and what they have learnt becomes almost useless, so that their time has been lost, it would not have been better to have begun with the French, proceeding to the Italian, etc.; for, tho', after spending the same time, they should quit the study of languages and never arrive at the Latin, they would, however, have acquired another tongue or two, that, being in modern use, might be serviceable to them in common life.

After ten years' absence from Boston, and having become easy in my circumstances, I made a journey thither to visit my relations, which I could not sooner well afford. In returning, I call'd at Newport to see my brother, then settled there with his printing-house. Our former differences were forgotten, and our meeting was very cordial and affectionate. He was fast declining in his health, and requested of me that, in case of his death, which he apprehended not far distant, I would take home his son, then but ten years of age, and bring him up to the printing business. This I accordingly perform'd, sending him a few years to school before I took him into the office. His mother carried on the business till he was grown up, when I assisted him with an assortment of new types, those of his father being in a manner worn out. Thus it was that I made my brother ample amends for the service I had depriv'd him of by leaving him so early.

In 1736 I lost one of my sons, a fine boy of four years old, by the small-pox, taken in the common way. I long regretted bitterly, and still regret that I had not given it to him by inoculation. This I mention for the sake of parents who omit that operation, on the supposition that they should never forgive themselves if a child died under it; my example showing that the regret may be the same either way, and that, therefore, the safer should be chosen.

Our club, the Junto, was found so useful, and afforded such satisfaction to the members, that several were desirous of introducing their friends, which could not well be done without exceeding what we had settled as a convenient number, viz., twelve. We had from the beginning made it a rule to keep our institution a secret, which was pretty well observ'd; the intention was to avoid applications of improper persons for admittance, some of whom, perhaps, we might find it difficult to refuse. I was one of those who were against any addition to our number, but, instead of it, made in writing a proposal, that every member separately should endeavour to form a subordinate club, with the same rules respecting queries, etc., and without informing them of the connection with the Junto. The advantages proposed were, the improvement of so many more young citizens by the use of our institutions; our better acquaintance with the general sentiments of the inhabitants on any occasion, as the Junto member might propose what queries we should desire, and was to report to the Junto what pass'd in his separate club; the promotion of our particular interests in business by more extensive recommendation, and the increase of our influence in public affairs, and our power of doing good by spreading thro' the several clubs the sentiments of the Junto.

The project was approv'd, and every member undertook to form his club, but they did not all succeed. Five or six only were completed, which were called by different names, as the Vine, the Union, the Band, etc. They were useful to themselves, and afforded us a good deal of amusement, information, and instruction, besides answering, in some considerable degree, our views of influencing the public opinion on particular occasions, of which I shall give some instances in course of time as they happened.

My first promotion was my being chosen, in 1736, clerk of the General Assembly. The choice was made that year without opposition; but the year following, when I was again propos'd (the choice, like that of the members, being annual), a new member made a long speech against me, in order to favour some other candidate. I was, however, chosen, which was the more agreeable to me, as, besides the pay for the immediate service as clerk, the place gave me a better opportunity of keeping up an interest among the members, which secur'd to me the business of printing the votes, laws, paper money, and other occasional jobs for the public, that, on the whole, were very profitable.

I therefore did not like the opposition of this new member, who was a gentleman of fortune and education, with talents that were likely to give him, in time, great influence in the House, which, indeed, afterwards happened. I did not, however, aim at gaining his favour by paying any servile respect to him, but, after some time, took this other method. Having heard that he had in his library a certain very scarce and curious book, I wrote a note to him, expressing my desire of perusing that book, and requesting he would do me the favour of lending it to me for a few days. He sent it immediately, and I return'd it in about a week with another note, expressing strongly my sense of the favour. When we next met in the House, he spoke to me (which he had never done before), and with great civility; and he ever after manifested a readiness to serve me on all occasions, so that we became great friends, and our friendship continued to his death. This is another instance of the truth of an old maxim I had learned, which says, '*He that has once done you a kindness will be more ready to do you another, than he whom you yourself have obliged.*' And it shows how much more profitable it is prudently to remove, than to resent, return, and continue inimical proceedings.

In 1737, Colonel Spotswood, late governor of Virginia, and then postmaster-general, being dissatisfied with the conduct of his deputy at Philadelphia, respecting some negligence in rendering, and inexactitude of his accounts, took from him the commission and offered it to me. I accepted it readily, and found it of great advantage; for, tho' the salary was small, it facilitated the correspondence that improv'd my newspaper, increas'd the number demanded, as well as the advertisements to be inserted, so that it came to afford me a considerable income. My old competitor's newspaper declin'd proportionably, and I was satisfy'd without retaliating his refusal, while postmaster, to permit my papers being carried by the riders. Thus he suffer'd greatly from his neglect in due accounting; and I mention it as a lesson to those young men who may be employ'd in managing affairs for others, that they should always render accounts, and make remittances, with great clearness and punctuality. The character of observing such a conduct is the most powerful of all recommendations to new employments and increase of business.

I began now to turn my thoughts a little to public affairs, beginning, however, with small matters. The city watch was one of the first things that I conceiv'd to want regulation. It was managed by the constables of the respective wards in turn; the constable warned a number of housekeepers to attend him for the night. Those who chose never to attend, paid him six shillings a year to be excus'd, which was suppos'd to be for hiring substitutes, but was, in reality, much more than was necessary for that purpose, and made the constableship a place of profit; and the constable, for a little drink, often got such ragamuffins about him as a watch, that respectable housekeepers did not choose to mix with. Walking the rounds, too, was often neglected, and most of the nights spent in tippling. I thereupon wrote a paper to be read in Junto, representing these irregularities, but insisting more particularly on the inequality of this six-shilling tax of the constables, respecting the circumstances of those who paid it, since a poor widow housekeeper, all whose property to be guarded by the watch did not perhaps exceed the value of fifty pounds, paid as much as the wealthiest merchant, who had thousands of pounds' worth of goods in his stores.

On the whole, I proposed as a more effectual watch, the hiring of proper men to serve constantly in that business; and as a more equitable way of supporting the charge, the levying a tax that should be proportion'd to the property. This idea, being approv'd by the Junto, was communicated to the other clubs, but as arising in each of them; and though the plan was not immediately carried into execution, yet, by preparing the minds of people for the change, it paved the way for the law obtained a few years after, when the members of our clubs were grown into more influence.

About this time I wrote a paper (first to be read in Junto, but it was afterward publish'd) on the different accidents and carelessnesses by which houses were set on fire, with cautions against them, and means proposed of avoiding them. This was much spoken of as a useful piece, and gave rise to a project, which soon followed it, of forming a company for the more ready extinguishing of fires, and mutual assistance in removing and securing of goods when in danger. Associates in this scheme were presently found, amounting to thirty. Our articles of agreement oblig'd every member to keep always in good order, and fit for use, a certain number of leather buckets, with strong bags and baskets (for packing and transporting of goods), which were to be brought to every fire; and we agreed to meet once a month to spend a social evening together, in discoursing and communicating such ideas as occurred to us upon the subject of fires, as might be useful in our conduct on such occasions.

The utility of this institution soon appeared, and many more desiring to be admitted than we thought convenient for one company, they were advised to form another, which was accordingly done; and this went on, one new company being formed after another, till they became so numerous as to include most of the inhabitants who were men of property; and now, at the time of my writing this, tho' upward of fifty years since its establishment, that which I first formed, called the Union Fire Company, still subsists and flourishes, tho' the first members are all deceas'd but myself and one, who is older by a year than I am. The small fines that have been paid by members for absence at the monthly meetings have been apply'd to the purchase of fire-engines, ladders, firehooks, and other useful implements for each company, so that I question whether there is a city in the world better provided with the means of putting a stop to beginning conflagrations; and, in fact, since these institutions, the city has never lost by fire more than one or two houses at a time, and the flames have often been extinguished before the house in which they began has been half consumed.

In 1739 arrived among us from Ireland the Reverend Mr Whitefield, who had made himself remarkable there as an itinerant preacher. He was at first permitted to preach in some of our churches; but the clergy, taking a dislike to him, soon refus'd him their pulpits, and he was oblig'd to preach in the fields. The multitudes of all sects and denominations that attended his sermons were enormous, and it was matter of speculation to me, who was one of the number, to observe the extraordinary influence of his oratory on his hearers, and how much they admir'd and respected him, notwithstanding his common abuse of them, by assuring them they were naturally *half beasts and half devils*. It was wonderful to see the change soon made in the manners of our inhabitants. From being thoughtless or indifferent about religion, it seem'd as if all the world were growing religious, so that one could not walk thro' the town in an evening without hearing psalms sung in different families of every street.

And it being found inconvenient to assemble in the open air, subject to its inclemencies, the building of a house to meet in was no sooner propos'd, and persons appointed to receive contributions, but sufficient sums were soon receiv'd to procure the ground and erect the building, which was one hundred feet long and seventy broad, about the size of Westminster Hall; and the work was carried on with such spirit as to be finished in a much shorter time than could have been expected. Both house and ground were vested in trustees, expressly for the use of any preacher of any religious persuasion who might desire to say something to the people at Philadelphia; the design in building not being to accommodate any particular sect, but the inhabitants in general; so that even if the Mufti of Constantinople were to send a missionary to preach Mohammedanism to us, he would find a pulpit at his service.

Mr Whitefield, in leaving us, went preaching all the way thro' the colonies to Georgia. The settlement of that province had lately been begun, but, instead of being made with hardy, industrious husbandmen, accustomed to labour, the only people fit for such an enterprise, it was with families of broken shop-keepers and other insolvent debtors, many of indolent and idle habits, taken out of the jails, who, being set down in the woods, unqualified for clearing land, and unable to endure the hardships of a new settlement, perished in numbers, leaving many helpless children unprovided for. The sight of their miserable situation inspir'd the benevolent heart of Mr Whitefield with the idea of building an Orphan House there, in which they might be supported and educated. Returning northward, he preach'd up this charity, and made large collections, for his eloquence had a wonderful power over the hearts and purses of his hearers, of which I myself was an instance.

I did not disapprove of the design, but, as Georgia was then destitute of materials and workmen, and it was proposed to send them from

Philadelphia at a great expense, I thought it would have been better to have built the house there, and brought the children to it. This I advis'd; but he was resolute in his first project, rejected my counsel, and I therefore refus'd to contribute. I happened soon after to attend one of his sermons, in the course of which I perceived he intended to finish with a collection, and I silently resolved he should get nothing from me. I had in my pocket a handful of copper money, three or four silver dollars, and five pistoles in gold. As he proceeded I began to soften, and concluded to give the coppers. Another stroke of his oratory made me asham'd of that, and determin'd me to give the silver; and he finish'd so admirably, that I empty'd my pocket wholly into the collector's dish, gold and all. At this sermon there was also one of our club, who, being of my sentiments respecting the building in Georgia, and suspecting a collection might be intended, had, by precaution, emptied his pockets before he came from home. Towards the conclusion of the discourse, however, he felt a strong desire to give, and apply'd to a neighbour, who stood near him, to borrow some money for the purpose. The application was unfortunately [made] to perhaps the only man in the company who had the firmness not to be affected by the preacher. His answer was, 'At any other time, Friend Hopkinson, I would lend to thee freely; but not now, for thee seems to be out of thy right senses.'

Some of Mr Whitefield's enemies affected to suppose that he would apply these collections to his own private emolument; but I, who was intimately acquainted with him (being employed in printing his Sermons and Journals, etc.), never had the least suspicion of his integrity, but am to this day decidedly of opinion that he was in all his conduct a perfectly *honest man*; and methinks my testimony in his favour ought to have the more weight, as we had no religious connection. He us'd, indeed, sometimes to pray for my conversion, but never had the satisfaction of believing that his prayers were heard. Ours was a mere civil friendship, sincere on both sides, and lasted to his death.

The following instance will show something of the terms on which we stood. Upon one of his arrivals from England at Boston, he wrote to me that he should come soon to Philadelphia, but knew not where he could lodge when there, as he understood his old friend and host, Mr Benezet, was removed to Germantown. My answer was, 'You know my house; if you can make shift with its scanty accommodations, you will be most heartily welcome.' He reply'd, that if I made that kind offer for Christ's sake, I should not miss of a reward. And I returned, 'Don't let me be mistaken; it was not for Christ's sake, but for your sake.' One of our common acquaintance jocosely remark'd, that, knowing it to be the custom of the saints, when they received any favour, to shift the burden of the obligation from off their own shoulders, and place it in heaven, I had contriv'd to fix it on earth.

The last time I saw Mr Whitefield was in London, when he consulted me about his Orphan House concern, and his purpose of appropriating it to the establishment of a college.

He had a loud and clear voice, and articulated his words and sentences so perfectly, that he might be heard and understood at a great distance, especially as his auditories, however numerous, observ'd the most exact silence. He preach'd one evening from the top of the Court-house steps, which are in the middle of Market Street, and on the west side of Second Street, which crosses it at right angles. Both streets were fill'd with his hearers to a considerable distance. Being among the hindmost in Market Street, I had the curiosity to learn how far he could be heard, by retiring backwards down the street towards the river; and I found his voice distinct till I came near Front Street, when some noise in that street obscur'd it. Imagining then a semi-circle, of which my distance should be the radius, and that it were fill'd with auditors, to each of whom I allow'd two square feet, I computed that he might well be heard by more than thirty thousand. This reconcil'd me to the newspaper accounts of his having preach'd to twenty-five thousand people in the fields, and to the ancient histories of generals haranguing whole armies, of which I had sometimes doubted.

By hearing him often, I came to distinguish easily between sermons newly compos'd, and those which he had often preach'd in the course of his travels. His delivery of the latter was so improv'd by frequent repetitions that every accent, every emphasis, every modulation of voice, was so perfectly well turn'd and well plac'd, that, without being interested in the subject, one could not help being pleas'd with the discourse; a pleasure of much the same kind with that receiv'd from an excellent piece of music. This is an advantage itinerant preachers have over those who are stationary, as the latter cannot well improve their delivery of a sermon by so many rehearsals.

His writing and printing from time to time gave great advantage to his enemies; unguarded expressions, and even erroneous opinions, delivered in preaching, might have been afterwards explain'd or qualifi'd by supposing others that might have accompani'd them, or they might have been deny'd; but *litera scripta manet*. Critics attack'd his writing violently, and with no such appearance of reason as to diminish the number of his votaries and prevent their increase; so that I am of opinion if he had never written anything, he would have left behind him a much more numerous and important sect, and his reputation might in that case have been still growing, even after his death, as there being nothing of his writing on which to found a censure and give him a lower character, his proselytes would be left at liberty to feign for him as great a variety of excellences as their enthusiastic admiration might wish him to have possessed.

My business was now continually augmenting, and my circumstances growing daily easier, my newspaper having become very profitable, as being for a time almost the only one in this and the neighbouring provinces. I experienced, too, the truth of the observation, 'that after getting the first hundred pound, it is more easy to get the second', money itself being of a prolific nature.

The partnership at Carolina having succeeded, I was encourag'd to engage in others, and to promote several of my workmen, who had behaved well, by establishing them with printing-houses in different colonies, on the same terms with that in Carolina. Most of them did well, being enabled at the end of our term, six years, to purchase the types of me and go on working for themselves, by which means several families were raised. Partnerships often finish in quarrels; but I was happy in this, that mine were all carried on and ended amicably, owing, I think, a good deal to the precaution of having very explicitly settled, in our articles, everything to be done by or expected from each partner, so that there was nothing to dispute, which precaution I would therefore recommend to all who enter into partnerships; for, whatever esteem partners may have for, and confidence in each other at the time of the contract, little jealousies and disgusts may arise, with ideas of inequality in the care and burden of the business, etc., which are attended often with breach of friendship and of the connection, perhaps with lawsuits and other disagreeable consequences.

I had, on the whole, abundant reason to be satisfied with my being established in Pennsylvania. There were, however, two things that I regretted, there being no provision for defence, nor for a complete education of youth; no militia, nor any college. I therefore, in 1743, drew up a proposal for establishing an academy; and at that time, thinking the Reverend Mr Peters, who was out of employ, a fit person to superintend such an institution, I communicated the project to him; but he, having more profitable views in the service of the proprietaries, which succeeded, declin'd the undertaking; and, not knowing another at that time suitable for such a trust, I let the scheme lie a while dormant. I succeeded better the next year, 1744, in proposing and establishing a Philosophical Society. The paper I wrote for that purpose will be found among my writings, when collected.

With respect to defence, Spain having been several years at war against Great Britain, and being at length join'd by France, which brought us into great danger; and the laboured and long-continued endeavour of our governor, Thomas, to prevail with our Quaker Assembly to pass a militia law, and make other provisions for the security of the province, having proved abortive, I determined to try what might be done by a voluntary association of the people. To promote this, I first wrote and published a pamphlet, entitled PLAIN TRUTH, in which I stated our defenceless situation in strong lights, with the necessity of union and discipline for our defence, and promis'd to propose in a few days an association, to be generally signed for that purpose. The pamphlet had a sudden and surprising effect. I was call'd upon for the instrument of association, and having settled the draft of it with a few friends, I appointed a meeting of the citizens in the large building before mentioned. The house was pretty full; I had prepared a number of printed copies, and provided pens and ink dispers'd all over the room. I harangued them a little on the subject, read the paper, and explained it, and then distributed the copies, which were eagerly signed, not the least objection being made.

When the company separated, and the papers were collected, we found above twelve hundred hands; and, other copies being dispersed in the country, the subscribers amounted at length to upward of ten thousand. These all furnished themselves as soon as they could with arms, formed themselves into companies and regiments, chose their own officers, and met every week to be instructed in the manual exercise, and other parts of military discipline. The women, by subscriptions among themselves, provided silk colours, which they presented to the companies, painted with different devices and mottoes, which I supplied.

The officers of the companies composing the Philadelphia regiment, being met, chose me for their colonel; but, conceiving myself unfit, I declin'd that station, and recommended Mr Lawrence, a fine person, and man of influence, who was accordingly appointed. I then propos'd a lottery to defray the expense of building a battery below the town, and furnishing it with cannon. It filled expeditiously, and the battery was soon erected, the merlons being fram'd of logs and fill'd with earth. We bought some old cannon from Boston, but, these not being sufficient, we wrote to England for more, soliciting, at the same time, our proprietaries for some assistance, tho' without much expectation of obtaining it.

Meanwhile, Colonel Lawrence, William Allen, Abram Taylor, Esqr., and myself were sent to New York by the associators, commission'd to borrow some cannon of Governor Clinton. He at first refus'd us peremptorily; but at dinner with his council, where there was great drinking of Madeira wine, as the custom of that place then was, he softened by degrees, and said he would lend us six. After a few more bumpers he advanc'd to ten; and at length he very good-naturedly conceded eighteen. They were fine cannon, eighteen-pounders, with their carriages, which we soon transported and mounted on our battery, where the associators kept a nightly guard while the war lasted, and among the rest I regularly took my turn of duty there as a common soldier.

My activity in these operations was agreeable to the governor and council; they took me into confidence, and I was consulted by them in every measure wherein their concurrence was thought useful to the association. Calling in the aid of religion, I propos'd to them the proclaiming a fast, to promote reformation, and implore the blessing of Heaven on our undertaking. They embrac'd the motion; but, as it was the first fast ever thought of in the province, the secretary had no precedent from which to draw the proclamation. My education in New England, where a fast is proclaimed every year, was here of some advantage: I drew it in the accustomed style, it was translated into German, printed in both languages, and divulg'd thro' the province. This gave the clergy of the different sects an opportunity of influencing their congregations to join in the association, and it would probably have been general among all but Quakers if the peace had not soon interven'd.

It was thought by some of my friends that, by my activity in these affairs, I should offend that sect, and thereby lose my interest in the Assembly of the province, where they formed a great majority. A young gentleman who had likewise some friends in the House, and wished to succeed me as their clerk, acquainted me that it was decided to displace me at the next election; and he, therefore, in good will, advis'd me to resign, as more consistent with my honour than being turn'd out. My answer to him was, that I had read or heard of some public man who made it a rule never to ask for an office, and never to refuse one when offer'd to him. 'I approve,' says I, 'of his rule, and will practice it with a small addition; I shall never *ask*, never *refuse*, nor ever *resign* an office. If they will have my office of clerk to dispose of to another, they shall take it from me. I will not, by giving it up, lose my right of sometime or other making reprisals on my adversaries.' I heard, however, no more of this; I was chosen again unanimously as usual at the next election. Possibly, as they dislik'd my late intimacy with the members of council, who had join'd the governors in all the disputes about military preparations, with which the House had long been harass'd, they might have been pleas'd if I would voluntarily have left them; but they did not care to displace me on account merely of my zeal for the association, and they could not well give another reason.

Indeed I had some cause to believe that the defence of the country was not disagreeable to any of them, provided they were not requir'd to assist in it. And I found that a much greater number of them than I could have imagined, tho' against offensive war, were clearly for the defensive. Many pamphlets *pro and con* were publish'd on the subject, and some by good Quakers, in favour of defence, which I believe convinc'd most of their younger people.

A transaction in our fire company gave me some insight into their prevailing sentiments. It had been propos'd that we should encourage the scheme for building a battery by laying out the present stock, then about sixty pounds, in tickets of the lottery. By our rules, no money could be dispos'd of till the next meeting after the proposal. The company consisted of thirty members, of which twenty-two were Quakers, and eight only of other persuasions. We eight punctually attended the meeting; but, tho' we thought that some of the Quakers would join us, we were by no means sure of a majority. Only one Quaker, Mr James Morris, appear'd to oppose the measure. He expressed much sorrow that it had ever been propos'd, as he said *Friends* were all against it, and it would create such discord as might break up the company. We told him that we saw no reason for that; we were the minority, and if *Friends* were against the measure, and outvoted us, we must and should, agreeably to the usage of all societies, submit. When the hour for business arriv'd it was mov'd to put the vote; he allow'd we might then do it by the rules, but, as he could assure us that a number of members intended to be present for the purpose of opposing it, it would be but candid to allow a little time for their appearing.

While we were disputing this, a waiter came to tell me two gentlemen below desir'd to speak with me. I went down, and found they were two of our Quaker members. They told me there were eight of them assembled at a tavern just by; that they were determin'd to come and vote with us if there should be occasion, which they hop'd would not be the case, and desir'd we would not call for their assistance if we could do without it, as their voting for such a measure might embroil them with their elders and friends. Being thus secure of a majority, I went up, and after a little seeming hesitation, agreed to a delay of another hour. This Mr Morris allow'd to be extremely fair. Not one of his opposing friends appear'd, at which he express'd great surprise; and, at the expiration of the hour, we carry'd the resolution eight to one; and as, of the twenty-two Quakers, eight were ready to vote with us, and thirteen, by their absence, manifested that they were not inclin'd to oppose the measure, I afterward estimated the proportion of Quakers sincerely against defence as one to twenty-one only; for these were all regular members of that society, and in good reputation among them, and had due notice of what was propos'd at that meeting.

The honourable and learned Mr Logan, who had always been of that sect, was one who wrote an address to them, declaring his approbation of defensive war, and supporting his opinion by many strong arguments. He put into my hands sixty pounds to be laid out in lottery tickets for the battery, with direction to apply what prizes might be drawn wholly to that service. He told me the following anecdote of his old master, William Penn, respecting defence. He came over from England, when a young man, with that proprietary, and as his secretary. It was war-time, and their ship was chas'd by an armed vessel, suppos'd to be an enemy. Their captain prepar'd for defence; but told William Penn, and his company of Quakers, that he did not expect their assistance, and they might retire into the cabin, which they did, except James Logan, who chose to stay upon deck, and was quarter'd to a gun. The suppos'd enemy prov'd a friend, so there was no fighting; but when the secretary went down to communicate the intelligence, William Penn rebuk'd him severely for staying upon deck, and undertaking to assist in defending the vessel, contrary to the principles of *Friends*, especially as it had not been required by the captain. This reproof, being before all the company, piqu'd the secretary who answer'd, 'I being thy servant, why did thee not order me to come down? But thee was willing enough that I should stay and help to fight the ship when thee thought there was danger.'

My being many years in the Assembly, the majority of which were constantly Quakers, gave me frequent opportunities of seeing the embarrassment given them by their principle against war, whenever application was made to them, by order of the crown, to grant aids for military purposes. They were unwilling to offend government, on the one hand, by a direct refusal; and their friends, the body of the Quakers, on the other, by a compliance contrary to their principles; hence a variety of evasions to avoid complying, and modes of disguising the compliance when it became unavoidable. The common mode at last was, to grant money under the phrase of its being *for the king's use*, and never to inquire how it was applied.

But, if the demand was not directly from the crown, that phrase was found not so proper, and some other was to be invented. As, when powder was wanting (I think it was for the garrison at Louisburg), and the government of New England solicited a grant of some from Pennsylvania, which was much urg'd on the House by Governor Thomas, they could not grant money to buy powder, because that was an ingredient of war; but they voted an aid to New England of three thousand pounds, to be put into the hands of the governor, and appropriated it for the purchasing of bread, flour, wheat, or *other grain*. Some of the council, desirous of giving the House still further embarrassment, advis'd the governor not to accept provision, as not being the thing he had demanded; but he reply'd, 'I shall take the money, for I understand very well their meaning; other grain is gunpowder', which he accordingly bought, and they never objected to it.

It was in allusion to this fact that, when in our fire company we feared the success of our proposal in favour of the lottery, and I had said to my friend Mr Syng, one of our members, 'If we fail, let us move the purchase of a fire-engine with the money; the Quakers can have no objection to that; and then, if you nominate me and I you as a committee for that purpose, we will buy a great gun, which is certainly a *fire-engine*.' 'I see,' says he, 'you have improv'd by being so long in the Assembly; your equivocal project would be just a match for their wheat or *other grain*.'

These embarrassments that the Quakers suffer'd from having establish'd and published it as one of their principles that no kind of war was lawful, and which, being once published, they could not afterwards, however they might change their minds, easily get rid of, reminds me of what I think a more prudent conduct in another sect among us, that of the Dunkers. I was acquainted with one of its founders, Michael Welfare, soon after it appear'd. He complain'd to me that they were grievously calumniated by the zealots of other persuasions, and charg'd with abominable principles and practices, to which they were utter strangers. I told him this had always been the case with new sects, and that, to put a stop to such abuse, I imagin'd it might be well to publish the articles of their belief, and the rules of their discipline. He said that it had been propos'd among them, but not agreed to, for this reason: 'When we were first drawn together as a society,' says he, 'it had pleased God to enlighten our minds so far as to see that some doctrines, which we once esteemed truths, were errors; and that others, which we had esteemed errors, were real truths. From time to time He has been pleased to afford us farther light, and our principles have been improving, and our errors diminishing. Now we are not sure that we are arrived at the end of this progression, and at the perfection of spiritual or theological knowledge; and we fear that, if we should once print our confession of faith, we should feel ourselves as if bound and confin'd by it, and perhaps be unwilling to receive further improvement, and our successors still more so, as conceiving what we their elders and founders had done, to be something sacred, never to be departed from.'

This modesty in a sect is perhaps a singular instance in the history of mankind, every other sect supposing itself in possession of all truth, and that those who differ are so far in the wrong; like a man travelling in foggy weather, those at some distance before him on the road he sees wrapped up in the fog, as well as those behind him, and also the people in the fields on each side, but near him all appears clear, tho' in truth he is as much in the fog as any of them. To avoid this kind of embarrassment, the Quakers have of late years been gradually declining the public service in the Assembly and in the magistracy, choosing rather to quit their power than their principle.

In order of time, I should have mentioned before, that having, in 1742, invented an open stove for the better warming of rooms, and at the same time saving fuel, as the fresh air admitted was warmed in entering, I made a present of the model to Mr Robert Grace, one of my early friends, who, having an iron-furnace, found the casting of the plates for these stoves a profitable thing, as they were growing in demand. To promote that demand, I wrote and published a pamphlet, entitled '*An Account of the new-invented Pennsylvania Fireplaces; wherein their Construction and Manner of Operation is particularly explained; their Advantages above every other Method of warming Rooms demonstrated; and all Objections that have been raised against the Use of them answered and obviated*', etc. This pamphlet had a good effect. Gov'r Thomas was so pleas'd with the construction of this stove, as described in it, that he offered to give me a patent for the sole vending of them for a term of years; but I declin'd it from a principle which has ever weighed with me on such occasions, viz., That, as we enjoy great advantages from the inventions of others, we should be glad of an opportunity to serve others by any invention of ours; and this we should do freely and generously.

An ironmonger in London however, assuming a good deal of my pamphlet, and working it up into his own, and making some small changes in the machine, which rather hurt its operation, got a patent for it there, and made, as I was told, a little fortune by it. And this is not the only instance of patents taken out for my inventions by others, tho' not always with the same success, which I never contested, as having no desire of profiting by patents myself, and hating disputes. The use of these fireplaces in very many houses, both of this and the neighbouring colonies, has been, and is, a great saving of wood to the inhabitants.

Peace being concluded, and the association business therefore at an end, I turn'd my thoughts again to the affair of establishing an academy. The first step I took was to associate in the design a number of active friends, of whom the Junto furnished a good part; the next was to write and publish a pamphlet, entitled *Proposals Relating to the Education of Youth in Pennsylvania*. This I distributed among the principal inhabitants gratis; and as soon as I could suppose their minds a little prepared by the perusal of it, I set on foot a subscription for opening and supporting an academy; it was to be paid in quotas yearly for five years; by so dividing it, I judg'd the subscription might be larger, and I believed it was so, amounting to no less, if I remember right, than five thousand pounds.

In the introduction to these proposals, I stated their publication, not as an act of mine, but of some *public-spirited gentlemen*, avoiding as much as I could, according to my usual rule, the presenting myself to the public as the author of any scheme for their benefit.

The subscribers, to carry the project into immediate execution, chose out of their number twenty-four trustees, and appointed Mr Francis, then attorney-general, and myself to draw up constitutions for the government of the academy; which being done and signed, a house was hired, masters engag'd, and the schools opened, I think, in the same year, 1749.

The scholars increasing fast, the house was soon found too small, and we were looking out for a piece of ground, properly situated, with intention to build, when Providence threw into our way a large house ready built, which, with a few alterations, might well serve our purpose. This was the building before mentioned, erected by the hearers of Mr Whitefield, and was obtained for us in the following manner.

It is to be noted that the contributions to this building being made by people of different sects, care was taken in the nomination of trustees, in whom the building and ground was to be vested, that a predominancy should not be given to any sect, lest in time that predominancy might be a means of appropriating the whole to the use of such sect, contrary to the original intention. It was therefore that one of each sect was appointed, viz., one Church-of-England man, one Presbyterian, one Baptist, one Moravian, etc., those, in case of vacancy by death, were to fill it by election from among the contributors. The Moravian happen'd not to please his colleagues, and on his death they resolved to have no other of that sect. The difficulty then was, how to avoid having two of some other sect, by means of the new choice.

Several persons were named, and for that reason not agreed to. At length one mention'd me, with the observation that I was merely an honest man, and of no sect at all, which prevail'd with them to choose me. The enthusiasm which existed when the house was built had long since abated, and its trustees had not been able to procure fresh contributions for paying the ground-rent, and discharging some other debts the building had occasion'd, which embarrass'd them greatly. Being now a member of both sets of trustees, that for the building and that for the Academy, I had a good opportunity of negotiating with both, and brought them finally to an agreement, by which the trustees for the building were to cede it to those of the academy, the latter undertaking to discharge the debt, to keep forever open in the building a large hall for occasional preachers, according to the original intention, and maintain a free-school for the instruction of poor children. Writings were accordingly drawn, and on paying the debts the trustees of the academy were put in possession of the premises; and by dividing the great and lofty hall into stories, and different rooms above and below for the several schools, and purchasing some additional ground, the whole was soon made fit for our purpose, and the scholars remov'd into the building. The care and trouble of agreeing with the workmen, purchasing materials, and superintending the work, fell upon me; and I went thro' it the more cheerfully, as it did not then interfere with my private business, having the year before taken a very able, industrious, and honest partner, Mr David Hall, with whose character I was well acquainted, as he had work'd for me four years. He took off my hands all care of the printing-office, paying me punctually my share of the profits. The partnership continued eighteen years, successfully for us both.

The trustees of the academy, after a while, were incorporated by a charter from the governor; their funds were increas'd by contributions in Britain and grants of land from the proprietaries, to which the Assembly has since made considerable addition; and thus was established the present University of Philadelphia. I have been continued one of its trustees from the beginning, now near forty years, and have had the very great pleasure of seeing a number of the youth who have receiv'd their education in it, distinguish'd by their improv'd abilities, serviceable in public stations, and ornaments to their country.

When I disengaged myself, as above mentioned, from private business, I flatter'd myself that, by the sufficient tho' moderate fortune I had acquir'd, I had secured leisure during the rest of my life for philosophical studies and amusements. I purchased all Dr Spence's apparatus, who had come from England to lecture here, and I proceeded in my electrical experiments with great alacrity; but the public, now considering me as a man of leisure, laid hold of me for their purposes, every part of our civil government, and almost at the same time, imposing some duty upon me. The governor put me into the commission of the peace; the corporation of the city chose me of the common council, and soon after an alderman; and the citizens at large chose me a burgess to represent them in Assembly. This latter station was the more agreeable to me, as I was at length tired with sitting there to hear debates, in which, as clerk, I could take no part, and which were often so unentertaining that I was induc'd to amuse myself with making magic squares or circles, or anything to avoid weariness; and I conceiv'd my becoming a member would enlarge my power of doing good. I would not, however, insinuate that my ambition was not flatter'd by all these promotions; it certainly was; for, considering my low beginning, they were great things to me; and they were still more pleasing, as being so many spontaneous testimonies of the public good opinion, and by me entirely unsolicited.

The office of justice of the peace I try'd a little, by attending a few courts, and sitting on the bench to hear causes; but finding that more knowledge of the common law than I possess'd was necessary to act in that station with credit, I gradually withdrew from it, excusing myself by my being oblig'd to attend the higher duties of a legislator in the Assembly. My election to this trust was repeated every year for ten years, without my ever asking any elector for his vote, or signifying, either directly or indirectly, any desire of being chosen. On taking my seat in the House, my son was appointed their clerk.

The year following, a treaty being to be held with the Indians at Carlisle, the governor sent a message to the House, proposing that they should nominate some of their members, to be join'd with some members of council, as commissioners for that purpose. The House named the speaker (Mr Norris) and myself; and, being commission'd, we went to Carlisle, and met the Indians accordingly.

As those people are extremely apt to get drunk, and, when so, are very quarrelsome and disorderly, we strictly forbad the selling any liquor to them; and when they complain'd of this restriction, we told them that if they would continue sober during the treaty, we would give them plenty of rum when business was over. They promis'd this, and they kept their promise, because they could get no liquor, and the treaty was conducted very orderly, and concluded to mutual satisfaction. They then claim'd and receiv'd the rum; this was in the afternoon: they were near one hundred men, women, and children, and were lodg'd in temporary cabins, built in the form of a square, just without the town. In the evening, hearing a great noise among them, the commissioners walk'd out to see what was the matter. We found they had made a great bonfire in the middle of the square; they were all drunk, men and women, quarrelling and fighting. Their dark-colour'd bodies, half naked, seen only by the gloomy light of the bonfire, running after and beating one another with firebrands, accompanied by their horrid yellings, form'd a scene the most resembling our ideas of hell that could well be imagin'd; there was no appeasing the tumult, and we retired to our lodging. At midnight a number of them came thundering at our door, demanding more rum, of which we took no notice.

The next day, sensible they had misbehav'd in giving us that disturbance, they sent three of their old counsellors to make their apology. The orator acknowledg'd the fault, but laid it upon the rum; and then endeavoured to excuse the rum by saying, 'The Great Spirit, who made all things, made everything for some use, and whatever use he design'd anything for, that use it should always be put to. Now, when he made rum, he said, "Let this be for the Indians to get drunk with," and it must be so.' And, indeed, if it be the design of Providence to extirpate these savages in order to make room for cultivators of the earth, it seems not improbable that rum may be the appointed means. It has already annihilated all the tribes who formerly inhabited the seacoast.

In 1751, Dr Thomas Bond, a particular friend of mine, conceived the idea of establishing a hospital in Philadelphia (a very beneficent design, which has been ascrib'd to me, but was originally his), for the reception and cure of poor sick persons, whether inhabitants of the province or strangers. He was zealous and active in endeavouring to procure subscriptions for it, but the proposal being a novelty in America, and at first not well understood, he met with but small success.

At length he came to me with the compliment that he found there was no such thing as carrying a public-spirited project through without my being concern'd in it. 'For,' says he, 'I am often ask'd by those to whom I propose subscribing, Have you consulted Franklin upon this business? And what does he think of it? And when I tell them that I have not (supposing it rather out of your line), they do not subscribe, but say they will consider of it.' I enquired into the nature and probable utility of his scheme, and receiving from him a very satisfactory explanation, I not only subscrib'd to it myself, but engag'd heartily in the design of procuring subscriptions from others. Previously, however, to the solicitation, I endeavoured to prepare the minds of the people by writing on the subject in the newspapers, which was my usual custom in such cases, but which he had omitted.

The subscriptions afterwards were more free and generous; but, beginning to flag, I saw they would be insufficient without some assistance from the Assembly, and therefore propos'd to petition for it, which was done. The country members did not at first relish the project; they objected that it could only be serviceable to the city, and therefore the citizens alone should be at the expense of it; and they doubted whether the citizens themselves generally approv'd of it. My allegation on the contrary, that it met with such approbation as to leave no doubt of our being able to raise two thousand pounds by voluntary donations, they considered as a most extravagant supposition, and utterly impossible.

On this I form'd my plan; and, asking leave to bring in a bill for incorporating the contributors according to the prayer of their petition, and granting them a blank sum of money, which leave was obtained chiefly on the consideration that the House could throw the bill out if they did not like it, I drew it so as to make the important clause a conditional one, viz., 'And be it enacted, by the authority aforesaid, that when the said contributors shall have met and chosen their managers and treasurer, *and shall have raised by their contributions a capital stock of — value* (the yearly interest of which is to be applied to the accommodating of the sick poor in the said hospital, free of charge for diet, attendance, advice, and medicines), *and shall make the same appear to the satisfaction of the speaker of the Assembly for the time being,* that *then* it shall and may be lawful for the said speaker, and he is hereby required, to sign an order on the provincial treasurer for the payment of two thousand pounds, in two yearly payments, to the treasurer of the said hospital, to be applied to the founding, building, and finishing of the same.'

This condition carried the bill through; for the members, who had oppos'd the grant, and now conceiv'd they might have the credit of being charitable without the expense, agreed to its passage; and then, in soliciting subscriptions among the people, we urg'd the conditional promise of the law as an additional motive to give, since every man's donation would be doubled; thus the clause work'd both ways. The subscriptions accordingly soon exceeded the requisite sum, and we claim'd and receiv'd the public gift, which enabled us to carry the design into execution. A convenient and handsome building was soon erected; the institution has by constant experience been found useful, and flourishes to this day; and I do not remember any of my political manoeuvres, the success of which gave me at the time more pleasure, or wherein, after thinking of it, I more easily excus'd myself for having made some use of cunning.

It was about this time that another projector, the Revd Gilbert Tennent, came to me with a request that I would assist him in procuring a subscription for erecting a new meeting-house. It was to be for the use of a congregation he had gathered among the Presbyterians, who were originally disciples of Mr Whitefield. Unwilling to make myself disagreeable to my fellow-citizens by too frequently soliciting their contributions, I absolutely refus'd. He then desired I would furnish him with a list of names of persons I knew by experience to be generous and public-spirited. I thought it would be unbecoming in me, after their kind compliance with my solicitations, to mark them out to be worried by other beggars, and therefore refus'd also to give such a list. He then desir'd I would at least give him my advice. 'That I will readily do,' said I; 'and, in the first place, I advise you to apply to all those whom you know will give something; next, to those whom you are uncertain whether they will give anything or not, and show them the list of those who have given; and, lastly, do not neglect those who you are sure will give nothing, for in some of them you may be mistaken.' He laugh'd and thank'd me, and said he would take my advice. He did so, for he ask'd of *everybody*, and he obtain'd a much larger sum than he expected, with which he erected the capacious and very elegant meeting-house that stands in Arch Street.

Our city, tho' laid out with a beautiful regularity, the streets large, straight, and crossing each other at right angles, had the disgrace of suffering those streets to remain long unpav'd, and in wet weather the wheels of heavy carriages plough'd them into a quagmire, so that it was difficult to cross them; and in dry weather the dust was offensive. I had liv'd near what was call'd the Jersey Market, and saw with pain the inhabitants wading in mud while purchasing their provisions. A strip of ground down the middle of that market was at length pav'd with brick, so that, being once in the market, they had firm footing, but were often over shoes in dirt to get there. By talking and writing on the subject, I was at length instrumental in getting the street pav'd with stone between the market and the brick'd foot-pavement, that was on each side next the houses. This, for some time, gave an easy access to the market dry-shod; but, the rest of the street not being pav'd, whenever a carriage came out of the mud upon this pavement, it shook off and left its dirt upon it, and it was soon cover'd with mire, which was not remov'd, the city as yet having no scavengers.

After some inquiry, I found a poor, industrious man, who was willing to undertake keeping the pavement clean, by sweeping it twice a week, carrying off the dirt from before all the neighbours' doors, for the sum of sixpence per month, to be paid by each house. I then wrote and printed a paper setting forth the advantages to the neighbourhood that might be obtain'd by this small expense; the greater ease in keeping our houses clean, so much dirt not being brought in by people's feet; the benefit to the shops by more custom, etc., etc., as buyers could more easily get at them; and by not having, in windy weather, the dust blown in upon their goods, etc., etc. I sent one of these papers to each house, and in a day or two went round to see who would subscribe an agreement to pay these sixpences; it was unanimously sign'd, and for a time well executed. All the inhabitants of the city were delighted with the cleanliness of the pavement that surrounded the market, it being a convenience to all, and this rais'd a general desire to have all the streets paved, and made the people more willing to submit to a tax for that purpose.

After some time I drew a bill for paving the city, and brought it into the Assembly. It was just before I went to England, in 1757, and did not pass till I was gone,* and then with an alteration in the mode of assessment, which I thought not for the better, but with an additional provision for lighting as well as paving the streets, which was a great improvement. It was by a private person, the late Mr John Clifton, his giving a sample of the utility of lamps, by placing one at his door, that the people were first impress'd with the idea of enlighting all the city. The honour of this public benefit has also been ascrib'd to me, but it belongs truly to that gentleman. I did but follow his example, and have only some merit to claim respecting the form of our lamps, as differing from the globe lamps we were at first supply'd with from London. Those we found inconvenient in these respects: they admitted no air

* See votes.

below; the smoke, therefore, did not readily go out above, but circulated in the globe, lodg'd on its inside, and soon obstructed the light they were intended to afford; giving, besides, the daily trouble of wiping them clean; and an accidental stroke on one of them would demolish it, and render it totally useless. I therefore suggested the composing them of four flat panes, with a long funnel above to draw up the smoke, and crevices admitting air below, to facilitate the ascent of the smoke; by this means they were kept clean, and did not grow dark in a few hours, as the London lamps do, but continu'd bright till morning, and an accidental stroke would generally break but a single pane, easily repair'd.

I have sometimes wonder'd that the Londoners did not, from the effect holes in the bottom of the globe lamps us'd at Vauxhall have in keeping them clean, learn to have such 135 holes in their street lamps. But, these holes being made for another purpose, viz., to communicate flame more suddenly to the wick by a little flax hanging down thro' them, the other use, of letting in air, seems not to have been thought of; and therefore, after the lamps have been lit a few hours, the streets of London are very poorly illuminated.

The mention of these improvements puts me in mind of one I propos'd, when in London, to Dr Fothergill, who was among the best men I have known, and a great promoter of useful projects. I had observ'd that the streets, when dry, were never swept, and the light dust carried away; but it was suffer'd to accumulate till wet weather reduc'd it to mud, and then, after lying some days so deep on the pavement that there was no crossing but in paths kept clean by poor people with brooms, it was with great labour rak'd together and thrown up into carts open above, the sides of which suffer'd some of the slush at every jolt on the pavement to shake out and fall, sometimes to the annoyance of foot-passengers. The reason given for not sweeping the dusty streets was, that the dust would fly into the windows of shops and houses.

An accidental occurrence had instructed me how much sweeping might be done in a little time. I found at my door in Craven Street, one morning, a poor woman sweeping my pavement with a birch broom; she appeared very pale and feeble, as just come out of a fit of sickness. I ask'd who employ'd her to sweep there; she said, 'Nobody, but I am very poor and in distress, and I sweeps before gentlefolkses doors, and hopes they will give me something.' I bid her sweep the whole street clean, and I would give her a shilling; this was at nine o'clock; at 12 she came for the shilling. From the slowness I saw at first in her working, I could scarce believe that the work was done so soon, and sent my servant to examine it, who reported that the whole street was swept perfectly clean, and all the dust plac'd in the gutter, which was in the middle; and the next rain wash'd it quite away, so that the pavement and even the kennel were perfectly clean.

I then judg'd that, if that feeble woman could sweep such a street in three hours, a strong, active man might have done it in half the time. And here let me remark the convenience of having but one gutter in such a narrow street, running down its middle, instead of two, one on each side, near the footway; for where all the rain that falls on a street runs from the sides and meets in the middle, it forms there a current strong enough to wash away all the mud it meets with; but when divided into two channels, it is often too weak to cleanse either, and only makes the mud it finds more fluid, so that the wheels of carriages and feet of horses throw and dash it upon the foot-pavement, which is thereby rendered foul and slippery, and sometimes splash it upon those who are walking. My proposal, communicated to the good doctor, was as follows:

> For the more effectual cleaning and keeping clean the streets of London and Westminster, it is proposed that the several watchmen be contracted with to have the dust swept up in dry seasons, and the mud rak'd up at other times, each in the several streets and lanes of his round; that they be furnish'd with brooms and other proper instruments for these purposes, to be kept at their respective stands, ready to furnish the poor people they may employ in the service.
>
> That in the dry summer months the dust be all swept up into heaps at proper distances, before the shops and windows of houses are usually opened, when the scavengers, with close-covered carts, shall also carry it all away.
>
> That the mud, when rak'd up, be not left in heaps to be spread abroad again by the wheels of carriages and trampling of horses, but that the scavengers be provided with bodies of carts, not plac'd high upon wheels, but low upon sliders, with lattice bottoms, which, being cover'd with straw, will retain the mud thrown into them, and permit the water to drain from it, whereby it will become much lighter, water making the greatest part of its weight; these bodies of carts to be plac'd at convenient distances, and the mud brought to them in wheelbarrows; they remaining where plac'd till the mud is drain'd, and then horses brought to draw them away.

I have since had doubts of the practicability of the latter part of this proposal, on account of the narrowness of some streets, and the difficulty of placing the draining-sleds so as not to encumber too much the passage; but I am still of opinion that the former, requiring the dust to be swept up and carry'd away before the shops are open, is very practicable in the summer, when the days are long; for, in walking thro' the Strand and Fleet Street one morning at seven o'clock, I observ'd there was not one shop open, tho' it had been daylight and the sun up above three hours; the inhabitant of London choosing voluntarily to live much by candlelight, and sleep by sunshine, and yet often complain, a little absurdly, of the duty on candles, and the high price of tallow.

Some may think these trifling matters not worth minding or relating; but when they consider that tho' dust blown into the eyes of a single person, or into a single shop on a windy day, is but of small importance, yet the great number of the instances in a populous city, and its frequent repetitions give it weight and consequence, perhaps they will not censure very severely those who bestow some attention to affairs of this seemingly low nature. Human felicity is produc'd not so much by great pieces of good fortune that seldom happen, as by little advantages that occur every day. Thus, if you teach a poor young man to shave himself, and keep his razor in order, you may contribute more to the happiness of his life than in giving him a thousand guineas. The money may be soon spent, the regret only remaining of having foolishly consumed it; but in the other case, he escapes the frequent vexation of waiting for barbers, and of their sometimes dirty fingers, offensive breaths, and dull razors; he shaves when most convenient to him, and enjoys daily the pleasure of its being done with a good instrument. With these sentiments I have hazarded the few preceding pages, hoping they may afford hints which sometime or other may be useful to a city I love, having lived many years in it very happily, and perhaps to some of our towns in America.

Having been for sometime employed by the postmaster-general of America as his comptroller in regulating several offices, and bringing the officers to account, I was, upon his death in 1753, appointed, jointly with Mr William Hunter, to succeed him, by a commission from the postmaster-general in England. The American office never had hitherto paid anything to that of Britain. We were to have six hundred pounds a year between us, if we could make that sum out of the profits of the office. To do this, a variety of improvements were necessary; some of these were inevitably at first expensive, so that in the first four years the office became above nine hundred pounds in debt to us. But it soon after began to repay us; and before I was displac'd by a freak of the ministers, of which I shall speak hereafter, we had brought it to yield *three times* as much clear revenue to the crown as the post-office of Ireland. Since that imprudent transaction, they have receiv'd from it – not one farthing!

The business of the post-office occasion'd my taking a journey this year to New England, where the College of Cambridge, of their own motion, presented me with the degree of Master of Arts. Yale College, in Connecticut, had before made me a similar compliment. Thus, without studying in any college, I came to partake of their honours. They were conferr'd in consideration of my improvements and discoveries in the electric branch of natural philosophy.

In 1754, war with France being again apprehended, a congress of commissioners from the different colonies was, by order of the Lord of Trade, to be assembled at Albany, there to confer with the chiefs of the Six Nations concerning the means of defending both their country and ours. Governor Hamilton, having receiv'd this order, acquainted the House with it, requesting they would furnish proper presents for the Indians, to be given on this occasion; and naming the speaker (Mr Norris) and myself to join Mr Thomas Penn and Mr Secretary Peters as commissioners to act for Pennsylvania. The House approv'd the nomination, and provided the goods for the present, and tho' they did not much like treating out of the provinces; and we met the other commissioners at Albany about the middle of June.

In our way thither, I projected and drew a plan for the union of all the colonies under one government, so far as might be necessary for defence, and other important general purposes. As we pass'd thro' New York, I had there shown my project to Mr James Alexander and Mr Kennedy, two gentlemen of great knowledge in public affairs, and, being fortified by their approbation, I ventur'd to lay it before the Congress. It then appeared that several of the commissioners had form'd plans of the same kind. A previous question was first taken, whether a union should be established, which pass'd in the affirmative unanimously. A committee was then appointed, one member from each colony, to consider the several plans and report. Mine happen'd to be preferr'd, and, with a few amendments, was accordingly reported.

By this plan the general government was to be administered by a president-general, appointed and supported by the crown, and a grand council was to be chosen by the representatives of the people of the several colonies, met in their respective assemblies. The debates upon it in Congress went on daily, hand in hand with the Indian business. Many objections and difficulties were started, but at length they were all overcome, and the plan was unanimously agreed to, and copies ordered to be transmitted to the Board of Trade and to the assemblies of the several provinces. Its fate was singular: the assemblies did not adopt it, as they all thought there was too much *prerogative* in it, and in England it was judg'd to have too much of the *democratic*. The Board of Trade therefore did not approve of it, nor recommend it for the approbation of his majesty; but another scheme was form'd, supposed to answer the same purpose better, whereby the governors of the provinces, with some members of their respective councils, were to meet and order the raising of troops, building of forts, etc., and to draw on the treasury of Great Britain for the expense; which was afterwards to be refunded by an act of Parliament laying a tax on America. My plan, with my reasons in support of it, is to be found among my political papers that are printed.

Being the winter following in Boston, I had much conversation with Governor Shirley upon both the plans. Part of what passed between us on the occasion may also be seen among those papers. The different and contrary reasons of dislike to my plan makes me suspect that it was really the true medium; and I am still of opinion it would have been happy for both sides the water if it had been adopted. The colonies, so united, would have been sufficiently strong to have defended themselves; there would then have been no need of troops from England; of course, the subsequent pretence for taxing America, and the bloody contest it occasioned, would have been avoided. But such mistakes are not new; history is full of the errors of states and princes.

> Look around the habitable world, how few
> Know their own good, or, knowing it, pursue!

Those who govern, having much business on their hands, do not generally like to take the trouble of considering and carrying into execution new projects. The best public measures are therefore seldom *adopted from previous wisdom, but forc'd by the occasion.*

The Governor of Pennsylvania, in sending it down to the Assembly, express'd his approbation of the plan, 'as appearing to him to be drawn up with great clearness and strength of judgement, and therefore recommended it as well worthy of their closest and most serious attention.' The House, however, by the management of a certain member, took it up when I happen'd to be absent, which I thought not very fair, and reprobated it without paying any attention to it at all, to my no small mortification.

In my journey to Boston this year, I met at New York with our new governor, Mr Morris, just arrived there from England, with whom I had been before intimately acquainted. He brought a commission to supersede Mr Hamilton, who, tir'd with the disputes his proprietary instructions subjected him to, had resign'd. Mr Morris ask'd me if I thought he must expect as uncomfortable an administration. I said, 'No; you may, on the contrary, have a very comfortable one, if you will only take care not to enter into any dispute with the Assembly.' 'My dear friend,' says he, pleasantly, 'how can you advise my avoiding disputes? You know I love disputing; it is one of my greatest pleasures; however, to show the regard I have for your counsel, I promise you I will, if possible, avoid them.' He had some reason for loving to dispute, being eloquent, an acute sophister, and, therefore, generally successful in argumentative conversation. He had been brought up to it from a boy, his father, as I have heard, accustoming his children to dispute with one another for his diversion, while sitting at table after dinner; but I think the practice was not wise; for, in the course of my observation, these disputing, contradicting, and confuting people are generally unfortunate in their affairs. They get victory sometimes, but they never get good will, which would be of more use to them. We parted, he going to Philadelphia, and I to Boston.

In returning, I met at New York with the votes of the Assembly, by which it appear'd that, notwithstanding his promise to me, he and the House were already in high contention; and it was a continual battle between them as long as he retain'd the government. I had my share of it; for, as soon as I got back to my seat in the Assembly, I was put on every committee for answering his speeches and messages, and by the committees always desired to make the drafts. Our answers, as well as his messages, were often tart, and sometimes indecently abusive; and, as he knew I wrote for the Assembly, one might have imagined that, when we met, we could hardly avoid cutting throats; but he was so good-natur'd a man that no personal difference between him and me was occasion'd by the contest, and we often din'd together.

One afternoon, in the height of this public quarrel, we met in the street. 'Franklin,' says he, 'you must go home with me and spend the evening; I am to have some company that you will like'; and, taking me by the arm, he led me to his house. In gay conversation, over our wine, after supper, he told us, jokingly, that he much admir'd the idea of Sancho Panza, who, when it was proposed to give him a government, requested it might be a government of *blacks*, as then, if he could not agree with his people, he might sell them. One of his friends, who sat next to me, says, 'Franklin, why do you continue to side with these damn'd Quakers? Had not you better sell them? The proprietor would give you a good price.' 'The governor,' says I, 'has not yet *blacked* them enough.' He, indeed, had laboured hard to blacken the Assembly in all his messages, but they wip'd off his colouring as fast as he laid it on, and plac'd it, in return, thick upon his own face; so that, finding he was likely to be negrofied himself, he, as well as Mr Hamilton, grew tir'd of the contest, and quitted the government.

*These public quarrels were all at bottom owing to the proprietaries, our hereditary governors, who, when any expense was to be incurred for the defence of their province, with incredible meanness instructed their deputies to pass no act for levying the necessary taxes, unless their vast estates were in the same act expressly excused; and they had even taken bonds of these deputies to observe such instructions. The Assemblies for three years held out against this injustice, tho' constrained to bend at last. At length Captain Denny, who was Governor Morris's successor, ventured to disobey those instructions; how that was brought about I shall show hereafter.

But I am got forward too fast with my story: there are still some transactions to be mention'd that happened during the administration of Governor Morris.

War being in a manner commenced with France, the government of Massachusetts Bay projected an attack upon Crown Point, and sent Mr Quincy to Pennsylvania, and Mr Pownall, afterward Governor Pownall, to New York, to solicit assistance. As I was in the Assembly, knew its temper, and was Mr Quincy's countryman, he appli'd to me for my influence and assistance. I dictated his address to them, which was well receiv'd. They voted an aid of ten thousand pounds, to be laid out in provisions. But the governor refusing his assent to their bill (which included this with other sums granted for the use of the crown), unless a clause were inserted exempting the proprietary estate from bearing any part of the tax that would be necessary, the Assembly, tho' very desirous of making their grant to New England effectual, were at a loss how to accomplish it. Mr Quincy laboured hard with the governor to obtain his assent, but he was obstinate.

I then suggested a method of doing the business without the governor, by orders on the trustees of the Loan Office, which, by law, the Assembly had the right of drawing. There was, indeed, little or no money at that time in the office, and therefore I propos'd that the orders should be payable in a year, and to bear an interest of five per

* My acts in Morris's time, military, etc. – Marg. note.

cent. With these orders I suppos'd the provisions might easily be purchas'd. The Assembly, with very little hesitation, adopted the proposal. The orders were immediately printed, and I was one of the committee directed to sign and dispose of them. The fund for paying them was the interest of all the paper currency then extant in the province upon loan, together with the revenue arising from the excise, which being known to be more than sufficient, they obtain'd instant credit, and were not only receiv'd in payment for the provisions, but many money'd people, who had cash lying by them, vested it in those orders, which they found advantageous, as they bore interest while upon hand, and might on any occasion be used as money; so that they were eagerly all bought up, and in a few weeks none of them were to be seen. Thus this important affair was by my means completed. Mr Quincy return'd thanks to the Assembly in a handsome memorial, went home highly pleas'd with the success of his embassy, and ever after bore for me the most cordial and affectionate friendship.

The British government, not choosing to permit the union of the colonies as propos'd at Albany, and to trust that union with their defence, lest they should thereby grow too military, and feel their own strength, suspicions and jealousies at this time being entertain'd of them, sent over General Braddock with two regiments of regular English troops for that purpose. He landed at Alexandria, in Virginia, and thence march'd to Frederictown, in Maryland, where he halted for carriages. Our Assembly apprehending, from some information, that he had conceived violent prejudices against them, as averse to the service, wish'd me to wait upon him, not as from them, but as postmaster-general, under the guise of proposing to settle with him the mode of conducting with most celerity and certainty the dispatches between him and the governors of the several provinces, with whom he must necessarily have continual correspondence, and of which they propos'd to pay the expense. My son accompanied me on this journey.

We found the general at Frederictown, waiting impatiently for the return of those he had sent thro' the back parts of Maryland and Virginia to collect waggons. I stayed with him several days, din'd with him daily, and had full opportunity of removing all his prejudices, by the information of what the Assembly had before his arrival actually done, and were still willing to do, to facilitate his operations. When I was about to depart, the returns of waggons to be obtained were brought in, by which it appear'd that they amounted only to twenty-five, and not all of those were in serviceable condition. The general and all the officers were surpris'd, declar'd the expedition was then at an

end, being impossible, and exclaim'd against the ministers for igno-
rantly landing them in a country destitute of the means of conveying
their stores, baggage, etc., not less than one hundred and fifty waggons
being necessary.

I happen'd to say I thought it was pity they had not been landed
rather in Pennsylvania, as in that country almost every farmer had his
waggon. The general eagerly laid hold of my words, and said, 'Then
you, sir, who are a man of interest there, can probably procure them for
us; and I beg you will undertake it.' I ask'd what terms were to be
offer'd the owners of the waggons; and I was desir'd to put on paper the
terms that appeared to me necessary. This I did, and they were agreed
to, and a commission and instructions accordingly prepar'd immediately. What those terms were will appear in the advertisement I
publish'd as soon as I arriv'd at Lancaster, which being, from the great
and sudden effect it produc'd, a piece of some curiosity, I shall insert it
at length, as follows:

Advertisement

Lancaster, April 26th, 1755

Whereas, one hundred and fifty waggons, with four horses to each
waggon, and fifteen hundred saddle or pack horses, are wanted for the
service of his majesty's forces now about to rendezvous at Will's Creek,
and his excellency General Braddock having been pleased to empower
me to contract for the hire of the same, I hereby give notice that I shall
attend for that purpose at Lancaster from this day to next Wednesday
evening, and at York from next Thursday morning till Friday evening,
where I shall be ready to agree for waggons and teams, or single horses,
on the following terms, viz.: 1. That there shall be paid for each
waggon, with four good horses and a driver, fifteen shillings per diem;
and for each able horse with a pack-saddle, or other saddle and
furniture, two shillings per diem; and for each able horse without a
saddle, eighteen pence per diem. 2. That the pay commence from the
time of their joining the forces at Will's Creek, which must be on or
before the 20th of May ensuing, and that a reasonable allowance be
paid over and above for the time necessary for their travelling to Will's
Creek and home again after their discharge. 3. Each waggon and team,
and every saddle or pack horse, is to be valued by indifferent persons
chosen between me and the owner; and in case of the loss of any
waggon, team, or other horse in the service, the price according to such
valuation is to be allowed and paid. 4. Seven days' pay is to be advanced

and paid in hand by me to the owner of each waggon and team, or horse, at the time of contracting, if required, and the remainder to be paid by General Braddock, or by the paymaster of the army, at the time of their discharge, or from time to time, as it shall be demanded. 5. No drivers of waggons, or persons taking care of the hired horses, are on any account to be called upon to do the duty of soldiers, or be otherwise employed than in conducting or taking care of their carriages or horses. 6. All oats, Indian corn, or other forage that waggons or horses bring to the camp, more than is necessary for the subsistence of the horses, is to be taken for the use of the army, and a reasonable price paid for the same.

Note. – My son, William Franklin, is empowered to enter into like contracts with any person in Cumberland county.

B. FRANKLIN

To the inhabitants of the Counties of Lancaster, York and Cumberland

FRIENDS AND COUNTRYMEN – Being occasionally at the camp at Frederic a few days since, I found the general and officers extremely exasperated on account of their not being supplied with horses and carriages, which had been expected from this province, as most able to furnish them; but, through the dissensions between our governor and Assembly, money had not been provided, nor any steps taken for that purpose.

It was proposed to send an armed force immediately into these counties, to seize as many of the best carriages and horses as should be wanted, and compel as many persons into the service as would be necessary to drive and take care of them.

I apprehended that the progress of British soldiers through these counties on such an occasion, especially considering the temper they are in, and their resentment against us, would be attended with many and great inconveniences to the inhabitants, and therefore more willingly took the trouble of trying first what might be done by fair and equitable means. The people of these back counties have lately complained to the Assembly that a sufficient currency was wanting; you have an opportunity of receiving and dividing among you a very considerable sum; for, if the service of this expedition should continue, as it is more than probable it will, for one hundred and twenty days, the hire of these waggons and horses will amount to upward of thirty thousand pounds, which will be paid you in silver and gold of the king's money.

The service will be light and easy, for the army will scarce march above twelve miles per day, and the waggons and baggage-horses, as they carry those things that are absolutely necessary to the welfare of the army, must march with the army, and no faster; and are, for the army's sake, always placed where they can be most secure, whether in a march or in a camp.

If you are really, as I believe you are, good and loyal subjects to his majesty, you may now do a most acceptable service, and make it easy to yourselves; for three or four of such as cannot separately spare from the business of their plantations a waggon and four horses and a driver, may do it together, one furnishing the waggon, another one or two horses, and another the driver, and divide the pay proportionably between you; but if you do not this service to your king and country voluntarily, when such good pay and reasonable terms are offered to you, your loyalty will be strongly suspected. The king's business must be done; so many brave troops, come so far for your defence, must not stand idle through your backwardness to do what may be reasonably expected from you; waggons and horses must be had; violent measures will probably be used, and you will be left to seek for a recompense where you can find it, and your case, perhaps, be little pitied or regarded.

I have no particular interest in this affair, as, except the satisfaction of endeavouring to do good, I shall have only my labour for my pains. If this method of obtaining the waggons and horses is not likely to succeed, I am obliged to send word to the general in fourteen days; and I suppose Sir John St Clair, the hussar, with a body of soldiers, will immediately enter the province for the purpose, which I shall be sorry to hear, because I am very sincerely and truly your friend and well-wisher,

B. FRANKLIN

I received of the general about eight hundred pounds, to be disbursed in advance-money to the waggon owners, etc.; but that sum being insufficient, I advanc'd upward of two hundred pounds more, and in two weeks the one hundred and fifty waggons, with two hundred and fifty-nine carrying horses, were on their march for the camp. The advertisement promised payment according to the valuation, in case any waggon or horse should be lost. The owners, however, alleging they did not know General Braddock, or what dependence might be had on his promise, insisted on my bond for the performance, which I accordingly gave them.

While I was at the camp, supping one evening with the officers of

Colonel Dunbar's regiment, he represented to me his concern for the subalterns, who, he said, were generally not in affluence, and could ill afford, in this dear country, to lay in the stores that might be necessary in so long a march, thro' a wilderness, where nothing was to be purchas'd. I commiserated their case, and resolved to endeavour procuring them some relief. I said nothing, however, to him of my intention, but wrote the next morning to the committee of the Assembly, who had the disposition of some public money, warmly recommending the case of these officers to their consideration, and proposing that a present should be sent them of necessaries and refreshments. My son, who had some experience of a camp life, and of its wants, drew up a list for me, which I enclos'd in my letter. The committee approv'd, and used such diligence that, conducted by my son, the stores arrived at the camp as soon as the waggons. They consisted of twenty parcels, each containing

6 lbs loaf sugar	1 Gloucester cheese
6 lbs good Muscovado do.	1 keg containing 20 lbs good butter
1 lb good green tea	2 dozen old Madeira wine
1 lb good bohea do.	2 gallons Jamaica spirits
6 lbs good ground coffee	1 bottle flour of mustard
6 lbs chocolate	2 well-cur'd hams
½ cwt best white biscuit	½ dozen dry'd tongues
½ lb pepper	6 lbs rice
1 quart best white wine vinegar	6 lbs raisins

These twenty parcels, well pack'd, were placed on as many horses, each parcel, with the horse, being intended as a present for one officer. They were very thankfully receiv'd, and the kindness acknowledg'd by letters to me from the colonels of both regiments, in the most grateful terms. The general, too, was highly satisfied with my conduct in procuring him the waggons, etc., and readily paid my account of disbursements, thanking me repeatedly, and requesting my farther assistance in sending provisions after him. I undertook this also, and was busily employ'd in it till we heard of his defeat, advancing for the service of my own money, upwards of one thousand pounds sterling, of which I sent him an account. It came to his hands, luckily for me, a few days before the battle, and he return'd me immediately an order on the paymaster for the round sum of one thousand pounds, leaving the remainder to the next account. I consider this payment as good luck, having never been able to obtain that remainder, of which more hereafter.

This general was, I think, a brave man, and might probably have made a figure as a good officer in some European war. But he had too much self-confidence, too high an opinion of the validity of regular troops, and too mean a one of both Americans and Indians. George Croghan, our Indian interpreter, join'd him on his march with one hundred of those people, who might have been of great use to his army as guides, scouts, etc., if he had treated them kindly; but he slighted and neglected them, and they gradually left him.

In conversation with him one day, he was giving me some account of his intended progress. 'After taking Fort Duquesne,' says he, 'I am to proceed to Niagara; and, having taken that, to Frontenac, if the season will allow time; and I suppose it will, for Duquesne can hardly detain me above three or four days; and then I see nothing that can obstruct my march to Niagara.' Having before revolv'd in my mind the long line his army must make in their march by a very narrow road, to be cut for them thro' the woods and bushes, and also what I had read of a former defeat of fifteen hundred French, who invaded the Iroquois country, I had conceiv'd some doubts and some fears for the event of the campaign. But I ventur'd only to say, 'To be sure, sir, if you arrive well before Duquesne, with these fine troops, so well provided with artillery, that place not yet completely fortified, and as we hear with no very strong garrison, can probably make but a short resistance. The only danger I apprehend of obstruction to your march is from ambuscades of Indians, who, by constant practice, are dexterous in laying and executing them; and the slender line, near four miles long, which your army must make, may expose it to be attack'd by surprise in its flanks, and to be cut like a thread into several pieces, which, from their distance, cannot come up in time to support each other.'

He smil'd at my ignorance, and reply'd, 'These savages may, indeed, be a formidable enemy to your raw American militia, but upon the king's regular and disciplin'd troops, sir, it is impossible they should make any impression.' I was conscious of an impropriety in my disputing with a military man in matters of his profession, and said no more. The enemy, however, did not take the advantage of his army which I apprehended its long line of march expos'd it to, but let it advance without interruption till within nine miles of the place; and then, when more in a body (for it had just passed a river, where the front had halted till all were come over), and in a more open part of the woods than any it had pass'd, attack'd its advanced guard by a heavy fire from behind trees and bushes, which was the first intelligence the general had of an enemy's being near him. This guard being disordered, the general hurried the troops up to their assistance, which was done in great confusion, thro' waggons, baggage, and cattle; and presently the fire came upon their flank: the officers, being on horseback, were more easily distinguish'd, pick'd out as marks, and fell very fast; and the soldiers were crowded together in a huddle, having or hearing no orders, and standing to be shot at till two-thirds of them were killed; and then, being seiz'd with a panic, the whole fled with precipitation.

The waggoners took each a horse out of his team and scamper'd; their example was immediately followed by others; so that all the waggons, provisions, artillery, and stores were left to the enemy. The general, being wounded, was brought off with difficulty; his secretary, Mr Shirley, was killed by his side; and out of eighty-six officers, sixty-three were killed or wounded, and seven hundred and fourteen men killed out of eleven hundred. These eleven hundred had been picked men from the whole army; the rest had been left behind with Colonel Dunbar, who was to follow with the heavier part of the stores, provisions, and baggage. The flyers, not being pursu'd, arriv'd at Dunbar's camp, and the panic they brought with them instantly seiz'd him and all his people; and, tho' he had now above one thousand men, and the enemy who had beaten Braddock did not at most exceed four hundred Indians and French together, instead of proceeding, and endeavouring to recover some of the lost honour, he ordered all the stores, ammunition, etc., to be destroy'd, that he might have more horses to assist his flight towards the settlements, and less lumber to remove. He was there met with requests from the governors of Virginia, Maryland, and Pennsylvania, that he would post his troops on the frontier, so as to afford some protection to the inhabitants; but he continu'd his hasty march thro' all the country, not thinking himself safe till he arriv'd at Philadelphia, where the inhabitants could protect him. This whole transaction gave us Americans the first suspicion that our exalted ideas of the prowess of British regulars had not been well founded.

In their first march, too, from their landing till they got beyond the settlements, they had plundered and stripped the inhabitants, totally ruining some poor families, besides insulting, abusing, and confining the people if they remonstrated. This was enough to put us out of conceit of such defenders, if we had really wanted any. How different was the conduct of our French friends in 1781, who, during a march thro' the most inhabited part of our country from Rhode Island to Virginia, near seven hundred miles, occasioned not the smallest complaint for the loss of a pig, a chicken, or even an apple.

Captain Orme, who was one of the general's aides-de-camp, and, being grievously wounded, was brought off with him, and continu'd with him to his death, which happen'd in a few days, told me that he was totally silent all the first day, and at night only said, 'Who would have thought it?' That he was silent again the following day, saying only at last, 'We shall better know how to deal with them another time'; and dy'd in a few minutes after.

The secretary's papers, with all the general's orders, instructions, and correspondence, falling into the enemy's hands, they selected and translated into French a number of the articles, which they printed, to prove the hostile intentions of the British court before the declaration of war. Among these I saw some letters of the general to the ministry, speaking highly of the great service I had rendered the army, and recommending me to their notice. David Hume, too, who was some years after secretary to Lord Hertford, when minister in France, and afterward to General Conway, when secretary of state, told me he had seen among the papers in that office, letters from Braddock highly recommending me. But, the expedition having been unfortunate, my service, it seems, was not thought of much value, for those recommendations were never of any use to me.

As to rewards from himself, I ask'd only one, which was, that he would give orders to his officers not to enlist any more of our bought servants, and that he would discharge such as had been already enlisted. This he readily granted, and several were accordingly return'd to their masters, on my application. Dunbar, when the command devolv'd on him, was not so generous. He being at Philadelphia, on his retreat, or rather flight, I apply'd to him for the discharge of the servants of three poor farmers of Lancaster county that he had enlisted, reminding him of the late general's orders on that head. He promised me that, if the masters would come to him at Trenton, where he should be in a few days on his march to New York, he would there deliver their men to them. They accordingly were at the expense and trouble of going to Trenton, and there he refus'd to perform his promise, to their great loss and disappointment.

As soon as the loss of the waggons and horses was generally known, all the owners came upon me for the valuation which I had given bond to pay. Their demands gave me a great deal of trouble, my acquainting them that the money was ready in the paymaster's hands, but that orders for paying it must first be obtained from General Shirley, and my assuring them that I had apply'd to that general by letter; but, he being at a distance, an answer could not soon be receiv'd, and they must have patience, all this was not sufficient to satisfy, and some began to sue me. General Shirley at length relieved me from this terrible situation by appointing commissioners to examine the claims, and ordering payment. They amounted to near twenty thousand pound, which to pay would have ruined me.

Before we had the news of this defeat, the two Doctors Bond came to me with a subscription paper for raising money to defray the expense of a grand firework, which it was intended to exhibit at a rejoicing on receipt of the news of our taking Fort Duquesne. I looked grave, and said it would, I thought, be time enough to prepare for the rejoicing when we knew we should have occasion to rejoice. They seem'd surpris'd that I did not immediately comply with their proposal. 'Why the devil!' say one of them, 'you surely don't suppose that the fort will not be taken?' 'I don't know that it will not be taken, but I know that the events of war are subject to great uncertainty.' I gave them the reasons of my doubting; the subscription was dropped, and the projectors thereby missed the mortification they would have undergone if the firework had been prepared. Dr Bond, on some other occasion afterward, said that he did not like Franklin's forebodings.

Governor Morris, who had continually worried the Assembly with message after message before the defeat of Braddock, to beat them into the making of acts to raise money for the defence of the province, without taxing, among others, the proprietary estates, and had rejected all their bills for not having such an exempting clause, now redoubled his attacks with more hope of success, the danger and necessity being greater. The Assembly, however, continu'd firm, believing they had justice on their side, and that it would be giving up an essential right if they suffered the governor to amend their money-bills. In one of the last, indeed, which was for granting fifty thousand pounds, his propos'd amendment was only of a single word. The bill express'd 'that all estates, real and personal, were to be taxed, those of the proprietaries *not* excepted.' His amendment was, for *not* read *only:* a small, but very material alteration. However, when the news of this disaster reached England, our friends there, whom we had taken care to furnish with all the Assembly's answers to the governor's messages, rais'd a clamour against the proprietaries for their meanness and injustice in giving their governor such instructions; some going so far as to say that, by obstructing the defence of their province, they forfeited their right to it. They were intimidated by this, and sent orders to their receiver-general to add five thousand pounds of their money to whatever sum might be given by the Assembly for such purpose.

This, being notified to the House, was accepted in lieu of their share of a general tax, and a new bill was form'd, with an exempting clause, which passed accordingly. By this act I was appointed one of the commissioners for disposing of the money, sixty thousand pounds. I had been active in modelling the bill and procuring its passage, and had, at the same time, drawn a bill for establishing and disciplining a voluntary militia, which I carried thro' the House without much difficulty, as care was taken in it to leave the Quakers at their liberty. To promote the association necessary to form the militia, I wrote a dialogue, stating and answering all the objections I could think of to such a militia, which was printed, and had, as I thought, great effect.

While the several companies in the city and country were forming, and learning their exercise, the governor prevail'd with me to take charge of our North-western frontier, which was infested by the enemy, and provide for the defence of the inhabitants by raising troops and building a line of forts. I undertook this military business, tho' I did not conceive myself well qualified for it. He gave me a commission with full powers, and a parcel of blank commissions for officers, to be given to whom I thought fit. I had but little difficulty in raising men, having soon five hundred and sixty under my command. My son, who had in the preceding war been an officer in the army rais'd against Canada, was my aide-de-camp, and of great use to me. The Indians had burned Gnadenhut, a village settled by the Moravians, and massacred the inhabitants; but the place was thought a good situation for one of the forts.

In order to march thither, I assembled the companies at Bethlehem, the chief establishment of those people. I was surprised to find it in so good a posture of defence; the destruction of Gnadenhut had made them apprehend danger. The principal buildings were defended by a stockade; they had purchased a quantity of arms and ammunition from New York, and had even plac'd quantities of small paving stones between the windows of their high stone houses, for their women to throw down upon the heads of any Indians that should attempt to force into them. The armed brethren, too, kept watch, and reliev'd as methodically as in any garrison town. In conversation with the bishop, Spangenberg, I mention'd this my surprise; for, knowing they had obtained an act of Parliament exempting them from military duties in the colonies, I had suppos'd they were conscientiously scrupulous of bearing arms. He answer'd me that it was not one of their established principles, but that, at the time of their obtaining that act, it was thought to be a principle with many of their people. On this occasion, however, they, to their surprise, found it adopted by but a few. It seems they were either deceiv'd in themselves, or deceiv'd the Parliament; but common sense, aided by present danger, will sometimes be too strong for whimsical opinions.

It was the beginning of January when we set out upon this business of building forts. I sent one detachment toward the Minisink, with instructions to erect one for the security of that upper part of the country, and another to the lower part, with similar instructions; and I concluded to go myself with the rest of my force to Gnadenhut, where a fort was tho't more immediately necessary. The Moravians procur'd me five waggons for our tools, stores, baggage, etc.

Just before we left Bethlehem, eleven farmers, who had been driven from their plantations by the Indians, came to me requesting a supply of firearms, that they might go back and fetch off their cattle. I gave them each a gun with suitable ammunition. We had not march'd many miles before it began to rain, and it continued raining all day; there were no habitations on the road to shelter us, till we arriv'd near night at the house of a German, where, and in his barn, we were all huddled together, as wet as water could make us. It was well we were not attack'd in our march, for our arms were of the most ordinary sort, and our men could not keep their gun locks dry. The Indians are dextrous in contrivances for that purpose, which we had not. They met that day the eleven poor farmers above mentioned, and killed ten of them. The one who escap'd inform'd that his and his companions' guns would not go off, the priming being wet with the rain.

The next day being fair, we continu'd our march, and arriv'd at the desolated Gnadenhut. There was a saw-mill near, round which were left several piles of boards, with which we soon hutted ourselves; an operation the more necessary at that inclement season, as we had no tents. Our first work was to bury more effectually the dead we found there, who had been half interr'd by the country people.

The next morning our fort was plann'd and mark'd out, the circumference measuring four hundred and fifty-five feet, which would require as many palisades to be made of trees, one with another, of a foot diameter each. Our axes, of which we had seventy, were immediately set to work to cut down trees, and, our men being dextrous in the use of them, great dispatch was made. Seeing the trees fall so fast, I had the curiosity to look at my watch when two men began to cut at a pine; in six minutes they had it upon the ground, and I found it of fourteen inches diameter. Each pine made three palisades of eighteen feet long, pointed at one end. While these were preparing, our other men dug a trench all round, of three feet deep, in which the palisades were to be planted; and, our waggons, the bodys being taken off, and the fore and hind wheels separated by taking out the pin which united the two parts of the perch, we had ten carriages, with two horses each, to bring the palisades from the woods to the spot. When they were set up, our carpenters built a stage of boards all round within, about six feet high, for the men to stand on when to fire thro' the loopholes. We had one swivel gun, which we mounted on one of the angles, and fir'd it as soon as fix'd, to let the Indians know, if any were within hearing, that we had such pieces; and thus our fort, if such a magnificent name may be given to so miserable a stockade, was finish'd in a week, though it rain'd so hard every other day that men could not work.

This gave me occasion to observe, that, when men are employed, they are best content'd; for on the days they worked they were good-natur'd and cheerful, and, with the consciousness of having done a good day's work, they spent the evening jollily; but on our idle days they were mutinous and quarrelsome, finding fault with their pork, the bread, etc., and in continual ill-humour, which put me in mind of a sea-captain, whose rule it was to keep his men constantly at work; and, when his mate once told him that they had done everything, and there was nothing further to employ them about, 'Oh,' says he, 'make them scour the anchor.'

This kind of fort, however contemptible, is a sufficient defence against Indians, who have no cannon. Finding ourselves now posted securely, and having a place to retreat to on occasion, we ventur'd out in parties to scour the adjacent country. We met with no Indians, but we found the places on the neighbouring hills where they had lain to watch our proceedings. There was an art in their contrivance of those places that seems worth mention. It being winter, a fire was necessary for them; but a common fire on the surface of the ground would by its light have discover'd their position at a distance. They had therefore dug holes in the ground about three feet diameter, and somewhat deeper; we saw where they had with their hatchets cut off the charcoal from the sides of burnt logs lying in the woods. With these coals they had made small fires in the bottom of the holes, and we observ'd among the weeds and grass the prints of their bodies, made by their laying all round, with their legs hanging down in the holes to keep their feet warm, which, with them, is an essential point. This kind of fire, so manag'd, could not discover them, either by its light, flame, sparks, or even smoke: it appear'd that their number was not great, and it seems they saw we were too many to be attacked by them with prospect of advantage.

We had for our chaplain a zealous Presbyterian minister, Mr Beatty, who complained to me that the men did not generally attend his prayers and exhortations. When they enlisted, they were promised, besides pay and provisions, a gill of rum a day, which was punctually serv'd out to them, half in the morning, and the other half in the evening; and I observ'd they were as punctual in attending to receive it; upon which I said to Mr Beatty, 'It is, perhaps, below the dignity of your profession to act as steward of the rum, but if you were to deal it out and only just after prayers, you would have them all about you.' He liked the tho't, undertook the office, and, with the help of a few hands to measure out the liquor, executed it to satisfaction, and never were prayers more generally and more punctually attended; so that I thought this method preferable to the punishment inflicted by some military laws for non-attendance on divine service.

I had hardly finish'd this business, and got my fort well stor'd with provisions, when I receiv'd a letter from the governor, acquainting me that he had call'd the Assembly, and wished my attendance there, if the posture of affairs on the frontiers was such that my remaining there was no longer necessary. My friends, too, of the Assembly, pressing me by their letters to be, if possible, at the meeting, and my three intended forts being now completed, and the inhabitants contented to remain on their farms under that protection, I resolved to return; the more willingly, as a New England officer, Colonel Clapham, experienced in Indian war, being on a visit to our establishment, consented to accept the command. I gave him a commission, and, parading the garrison, had it read before them, and introduc'd him to them as an officer who, from his skill in military affairs, was much more fit to command them than myself; and, giving them a little exhortation, took my leave. I was escorted as far as Bethlehem, where I rested a few days to recover from the fatigue I had undergone. The first night, being in a good bed, I could hardly sleep, it was so different from my hard lodging on the floor of our hut at Gnaden wrapped only in a blanket or two.

While at Bethlehem, I inquir'd a little into the practice of the Moravians: some of them had accompanied me, and all were very kind to me. I found they work'd for a common stock, eat at common tables, and slept in common dormitories, great numbers together. In the dormitories I observed loopholes, at certain distances all along just under the ceiling, which I thought judiciously placed for change of air. I was at their church, where I was entertain'd with good music, the organ being accompanied with violins, hautboys, flutes, clarinets, etc. I understood that their sermons were not usually preached to mixed congregations of men, women, and children, as is our common practice, but that they assembled sometimes the married men, at other times their wives, then the young men, the young women, and the little children, each division by itself. The sermon I heard was to the latter, who came in and were plac'd in rows on benches; the boys under the conduct of a young man, their tutor, and the girls conducted by a young woman. The discourse seem'd well adapted to their capacities, and was deliver'd in a pleasing, familiar manner, coaxing them, as it were, to be good. They behav'd very orderly, but looked pale and unhealthy, which made me suspect they were kept too much within doors, or not allow'd sufficient exercise.

I inquir'd concerning the Moravian marriages, whether the report was true that they were by lot. I was told that lots were us'd only in particular cases; that generally, when a young man found himself dispos'd to marry, he inform'd the elders of his class, who consulted the elder ladies that govern'd the young women. As these elders of the different sexes were well acquainted with the tempers and dispositions of their respective pupils, they could best judge what matches were suitable, and their judgements were generally acquiesc'd in; but if, for example, it should happen that two or three young women were found to be equally proper for the young man, the lot was then recurred to. I objected, if the matches are not made by the mutual choice of the parties, some of them may chance to be very unhappy. 'And so they may,' answer'd my informer, 'if you let the parties choose for themselves'; which, indeed, I could not deny.

Being returned to Philadelphia, I found the association went on swimmingly, the inhabitants that were not Quakers having pretty generally come into it, formed themselves into companies, and chose their captains, lieutenants, and ensigns, according to the new law. Dr B. visited me, and gave me an account of the pains he had taken to spread a general good liking to the law, and ascribed much to those endeavours. I had had the vanity to ascribe all to my *Dialogue*; however, not knowing but that he might be in the right, I let him enjoy his opinion, which I take to be generally the best way in such cases. The officers, meeting, chose me to be colonel of the regiment, which I this time accepted. I forget how many companies we had, but we paraded about twelve hundred well-looking men, with a company of artillery, who had been furnished with six brass field-pieces, which they had become so expert in the use of as to fire twelve times in a minute. The first time

I reviewed my regiment they accompanied me to my house, and would salute me with some rounds fired before my door, which shook down and broke several glasses of my electrical apparatus. And my new honour proved not much less brittle; for all our commissions were soon after broken by a repeal of the law in England.

During this short time of my colonelship, being about to set out on a journey to Virginia, the officers of my regiment took it into their heads that it would be proper for them to escort me out of town, as far as the Lower Ferry. Just as I was getting on horseback they came to my door, between thirty and forty, mounted, and all in their uniforms. I had not been previously acquainted with the project, or I should have prevented it, being naturally averse to the assuming of state on any occasion; and I was a good deal chagrin'd at their appearance, as I could not avoid their accompanying me. What made it worse was, that, as soon as we began to move, they drew their swords and rode with them naked all the way. Somebody wrote an account of this to the proprietor, and it gave him great offence. No such honour had been paid him when in the province, nor to any of his governors; and he said it was only proper to princes of the blood royal, which may be true for aught I know, who was, and still am, ignorant of the etiquette in such cases.

This silly affair, however, greatly increased his rancour against me, which was before not a little, on account of my conduct in the Assembly respecting the exemption of his estate from taxation, which I had always oppos'd very warmly, and not without severe reflections on his meanness and injustice of contending for it. He accused me to the ministry as being the great obstacle to the king's service, preventing, by my influence in the House, the proper form of the bills for raising money, and he instanced this parade with my officers as a proof of my having an intention to take the government of the province out of his hands by force. He also applied to Sir Everard Fawkener, the postmaster-general, to deprive me of my office; but it had no other effect than to procure from Sir Everard a gentle admonition.

Notwithstanding the continued wrangle between the governor and the House, in which I, as a member, had so large a share, there still subsisted a civil intercourse between that gentleman and myself, and we never had any personal difference. I have sometimes since thought that his little or no resentment against me, for the answers it was known I drew up to his messages, might be the effect of professional habit, and that, being bred a lawyer, he might consider us both as merely advocates for contending clients in a suit, he for the proprietaries and I for the Assembly. He would, therefore, sometimes call in a friendly way to advise with me on difficult points, and sometimes, tho' not often, take my advice.

We acted in concert to supply Braddock's army with provisions; and, when the shocking news arrived of his defeat, the governor sent in haste for me, to consult with him on measures for preventing the desertion of the back counties. I forget now the advice I gave; but I think it was, that Dunbar should be written to, and prevail'd with, if possible, to post his troops on the frontiers for their protection, till, by re-enforcements from the colonies, he might be able to proceed on the expedition. And after my return from the frontier, he would have had me undertake the conduct of such an expedition with provincial troops, for the reduction of Fort Duquesne, Dunbar and his men being otherwise employed; and he proposed to commission me as general. I had not so good an opinion of my military abilities as he profess'd to have, and I believe his professions must have exceeded his real sentiments; but probably he might think that my popularity would facilitate the raising of the men, and my influence in Assembly, the grant of money to pay them, and that, perhaps, without taxing the proprietary estate. Finding me not so forward to engage as he had expected, the project was dropped, and he soon after left the government, being superseded by Captain Denny.

Before I proceed in relating the part I had in public affairs under this new governor's administration, it may not be amiss here to give some account of the rise and progress of my philosophical reputation.

In 1746, being at Boston, I met there with a Dr Spence, who was lately arrived from Scotland, and show'd me some electric experiments. They were imperfectly perform'd, as he was not very expert; but, being on a subject quite new to me, they equally surpris'd and pleased me. Soon after my return to Philadelphia, our library company receiv'd from Mr P. Collinson, Fellow of the Royal Society of London, a present of a glass tube, with some account of the use of it in making such experiments. I eagerly seized the opportunity of repeating what I had seen at Boston; and, by much practice, acquir'd great readiness in performing those, also, which we had an account of from England, adding a number of new ones. I say much practice, for my house was continually full, for some time, with people who came to see these new wonders.

To divide a little this incumbrance among my friends, I caused a number of similar tubes to be blown at our glass-house, with which they furnish'd themselves, so that we had at length several performers. Among these, the principal was Mr Kinnersley, an ingenious neighbour, who, being out of business, I encouraged to undertake showing the experiments for money, and drew up for him two lectures, in which the experiments were rang'd in such order, and accompanied with such explanations in such method, as that the foregoing should assist in comprehending the following. He procur'd an elegant apparatus for the purpose, in which all the little machines that I had roughly made for myself were nicely form'd by instrument-makers. His lectures were well attended, and gave great satisfaction; and after some time he went thro' the colonies, exhibiting them in every capital town, and pick'd up some money. In the West India islands, indeed, it was with difficulty the experiments could be made, from the general moisture of the air.

Oblig'd as we were to Mr Collinson for his present of the tube, etc., I thought it right he should be inform'd of our success in using it, and wrote him several letters containing accounts of our experiments. He got them read in the Royal Society, where they were not at first thought worth so much notice as to be printed in their Transactions. One paper, which I wrote for Mr Kinnersley, on the sameness of lightning with electricity, I sent to Dr Mitchel, an acquaintance of mine, and one of the members also of that society, who wrote me word that it had been read, but was laughed at by the connoisseurs. The papers, however, being shown to Dr Fothergill, he thought them of too much value to be stifled, and advis'd the printing of them. Mr Collinson then gave them to *Cave* for publication in his Gentleman's Magazine; but he chose to print them separately in a pamphlet, and Dr Fothergill wrote the preface. Cave, it seems, judged rightly for his profit, for by the additions that arrived afterward they swell'd, to a quarto volume, which has had five editions, and cost him nothing for copy-money.

It was, however, some time before those papers were much taken notice of in England. A copy of them happening to fall into the hands of the Count de Buffon, a philosopher deservedly of great reputation in France, and, indeed, all over Europe, he prevailed with M. Dalibard to translate them into French, and they were printed at Paris. The publication offended the Abbé Nollet, preceptor in Natural Philosophy to the royal family, and an able experimenter, who had form'd and publish'd a theory of electricity, which then had the general vogue. He could not at first believe that such a work came from America, and said it must have been fabricated by his enemies at Paris, to decry his system. Afterwards, having been assur'd that there really existed such a person as Franklin at Philadelphia, which he had doubted, he wrote and published a volume of Letters, chiefly address'd to me, defending his theory, and denying the verity of my experiments, and of the positions deduc'd from them.

I once purpos'd answering the abbé, and actually began the answer; but, on consideration that my writings contain'd a description of experiments which anyone might repeat and verify, and if not to be verifi'd, could not be defended; or of observations offer'd as conjectures, and not delivered dogmatically, therefore not laying me under any obligation to defend them; and reflecting that a dispute between two persons, writing in different languages, might be lengthened greatly by mistranslations, and thence misconceptions of one another's meaning, much of one of the abbé's letters being founded on an error in the translation, I concluded to let my papers shift for themselves, believing it was better to spend what time I could spare from public business in making new experiments, than in disputing about those already made. I therefore never answered M. Nollet, and the event gave me no cause to repent my silence; for my friend M. le Roy, of the Royal Academy of Sciences, took up my cause and refuted him; my book was translated into the Italian, German, and Latin languages; and the doctrine it contain'd was by degrees universally adopted by the philosophers of Europe, in preference to that of the abbé; so that he lived to see himself the last of his sect, except Monsieur B—, of Paris, his *élève* and immediate disciple.

What gave my book the more sudden and general celebrity, was the success of one of its proposed experiments, made by Messrs Dalibard and De Lor at Marly, for drawing lightning from the clouds. This engag'd the public attention everywhere. M. de Lor, who had an apparatus for experimental philosophy, and lectur'd in that branch of science, undertook to repeat what he called the *Philadelphia Experiments*; and, after they were performed before the king and court, all the curious of Paris flocked to see them. I will not swell this narrative with an account of that capital experiment, nor of the infinite pleasure I receiv'd in the success of a similar one I made soon after with a kite at Philadelphia, as both are to be found in the histories of electricity.

Dr Wright, an English physician, when at Paris, wrote to a friend, who was of the Royal Society, an account of the high esteem my experiments were in among the learned abroad, and of their wonder that my writings had been so little noticed in England. The society, on this, resum'd the consideration of the letters that had been read to them; and the celebrated Dr Watson drew up a summary account of them, and of all I had afterwards sent to England on the subject, which he accompanied with some praise of the writer. This summary was then printed in their Transactions; and some members of the society in London, particularly the very ingenious Mr Canton, having verified the experiment of procuring lightning from the clouds by a pointed rod, and acquainting them with the success, they soon made me more than amends for the slight with which they had before treated me. Without my having made any application for that honour, they chose me a member, and voted that I should be excus'd the customary payments, which would have amounted to twenty-five guineas; and ever since have given me their Transactions gratis. They also presented me with the gold medal of Sir Godfrey Copley for the year 1753, the delivery of which was accompanied by a very handsome speech of the president, Lord Macclesfield, wherein I was highly honoured.

Our new governor, Captain Denny, brought over for me the before-mentioned medal from the Royal Society, which he presented to me at an entertainment given him by the city. He accompanied it with very polite expressions of his esteem for me, having, as he said, been long acquainted with my character. After dinner, when the company, as was customary at that time, were engag'd in drinking, he took me aside into another room, and acquainted me that he had been advis'd by his friends in England to cultivate a friendship with me, as one who was capable of giving him the best advice, and of contributing most effectually to the making his administration easy; that he therefore desired of all things to have a good understanding with me, and he begg'd me to be assur'd of his readiness on all occasions to render me every service that might be in his power. He said much to me, also, of the proprietor's good disposition towards the province, and of the advantage it might be to us all, and to me in particular, if the opposition that had been so long continu'd to his measures was dropped, and harmony restor'd between him and the people; in effecting which, it was thought no one could be more serviceable than myself; and I might depend on adequate acknowledgements and recompenses, etc., etc. The drinkers, finding we did not return immediately to the table, sent us a decanter of Madeira, which the governor made liberal use of, and in proportion became more profuse of his solicitations and promises.

My answers were to this purpose: that my circumstances, thanks to God, were such as to make proprietary favours unnecessary to me; and that, being a member of the Assembly, I could not possibly accept of any; that, however, I had no personal enmity to the proprietary, and that, whenever the public measures he propos'd should appear to be for the good of the people, no one should espouse and forward them more zealously than myself; my past opposition having been founded on this, that the measures which had been urged were evidently intended to serve the proprietary interest, with great prejudice to that of the people; that I was much obliged to him (the governor) for his professions of regard to me, and that he might rely on everything in my power to make his administration as easy as possible, hoping at the same time that he had not brought with him the same unfortunate instruction his predecessor had been hamper'd with.

On this he did not then explain himself; but when he afterwards came to do business with the Assembly, they appear'd again, the disputes were renewed, and I was as active as ever in the opposition, being the penman, first, of the request to have a communication of the instructions, and then of the remarks upon them, which may be found in the votes of the time, and in the Historical Review I afterward publish'd. But between us personally no enmity arose; we were often together; he was a man of letters, had seen much of the world, and was very entertaining and pleasing in conversation. He gave me the first information that my old friend Jas. Ralph was still alive; that he was esteem'd one of the best political writers in England; had been employ'd in the dispute between Prince Frederic and the king, and had obtain'd a pension of three hundred a year; that his reputation was indeed small as a poet, Pope having damned his poetry in the Dunciad; but his prose was thought as good as any man's.

The Assembly finally finding the proprietary obstinately persisted in manacling their deputies with instructions inconsistent not only with the privileges of the people, but with the service of the crown, resolv'd to petition the king against them, and appointed me their agent to go over to England, to present and support the petition. The House had sent up a bill to the governor, granting a sum of sixty thousand pounds for the king's use (ten thousand pounds of which was subjected to the orders of the then general, Lord Loudoun), which the governor absolutely refus'd to pass, in compliance with his instructions.

I had agreed with Captain Morris, of the packet at New York, for my passage, and my stores were put on board, when Lord Loudoun arriv'd at Philadelphia, expressly, as he told me, to endeavour an accommodation between the governor and Assembly, that his majesty's service might not be obstructed by their dissensions. Accordingly, he desir'd the governor and myself to meet him, that he might hear what was to be said on both sides. We met and discuss'd the business. In behalf of the Assembly, I urg'd all the various arguments that may be found in the public papers of that time, which were of my writing, and are printed with the minutes of the Assembly; and the governor pleaded his instructions; the bond he had given to observe them, and his ruin if he disobey'd, yet seemed not unwilling to hazard himself if Lord Loudoun would advise it. This his lordship did not choose to do, though I once thought I had nearly prevail'd with him to do it; but finally he rather chose to urge the compliance of the Assembly; and he entreated me to use my endeavours with them for that purpose, declaring that he would spare none of the king's troops for the defence of our frontiers, and that, if we did not continue to provide for that defence ourselves, they must remain expos'd to the enemy.

I acquainted the House with what had pass'd, and, presenting them with a set of resolutions I had drawn up, declaring our rights, and that we did not relinquish our claim to those rights, but only suspended the exercise of them on this occasion thro' *force*, against which we protested, they at length agreed to drop that bill, and frame another conformable to the proprietary instructions. This of course the governor pass'd, and I was then at liberty to proceed on my voyage. But, in the meantime, the packet had sailed with my sea-stores, which was some loss to me, and my only recompense was his lordship's thanks for my service, all the credit of obtaining the accommodation falling to his share.

He set out for New York before me; and, as the time for dispatching the packet-boats was at his disposition, and there were two then remaining there, one of which, he said, was to sail very soon, I requested to know the precise time, that I might not miss her by any delay of mine. His answer was, 'I have given out that she is to sail on Saturday next; but I may let you know, *entre nous*, that if you are there by Monday morning, you will be in time, but do not delay longer.' By some accidental hindrance at a ferry, it was Monday noon before I arrived, and I was much afraid she might have sailed, as the wind was fair; but I was soon made easy by the information that she was still in the harbour, and would not move till the next day. One would imagine that I was now on the very point of departing for Europe. I thought so; but I was not then so well acquainted with his lordship's character, of which *indecision* was one of the strongest features. I shall give some instances. It was about the beginning of April that I came to New York, and I think it was near the end of June before we sail'd. There were then two of the packet-boats, which had been long in port, but were detained for the general's letters, which were always to be ready tomorrow. Another packet arriv'd; she too was detain'd; and, before we sail'd, a fourth was expected. Ours was the first to be dispatch'd, as having been there longest. Passengers were engag'd in all, and some extremely impatient to be gone, and the merchants uneasy about their letters, and the orders they had given for insurance (it being war time) for fall goods; but their anxiety avail'd nothing; his lordship's letters were not ready; and yet whoever waited on him found him always at his desk, pen in hand, and concluded he must needs write abundantly.

Going myself one morning to pay my respects, I found in his antechamber one Innis, a messenger of Philadelphia, who had come from thence express with a packet from Governor Denny for the General. He delivered to me some letters from my friends there, which occasion'd my inquiring when he was to return, and where he lodg'd, that I might send some letters by him. He told me he was order'd to call tomorrow at nine for the general's answer to the governor, and should set off immediately. I put my letters into his hands the same day. A fortnight after I met him again in the same place. 'So, you are soon return'd, Innis?' '*Return'd*! no, I am not *gone* yet.' 'How so?' 'I have called here by order every morning these two weeks past for his lordship's letter, and it is not yet ready.' 'Is it possible, when he is so great a writer? for I see him constantly at his escritoire.' 'Yes,' says Innis, 'but he is like St George on the signs, *always on horseback, and never rides on*.' This observation of the messenger was, it seems, well founded; for, when in England, I understood that Mr Pitt gave it as one reason for removing this general, and sending Generals Amherst and Wolfe, *that the minister never heard from him, and could not know what he was doing*.

This daily expectation of sailing, and all the three packets going down to Sand Hook, to join the fleet there, the passengers thought it best to be on board, lest by a sudden order the ships should sail, and they be left behind. There, if I remember right, we were about six weeks, consuming our sea-stores, and oblig'd to procure more. At length the fleet sail'd, the General and all his army on board, bound to Louisburg, with intent to besiege and take that fortress; all the packet-boats in company ordered to attend the General's ship, ready to receive his dispatches when they should be ready. We were out five days before we got a letter with leave to part, and then our ship quitted the fleet and steered for England. The other two packets he still detained, carried them with him to Halifax, where he stayed some time to exercise the men in sham attacks upon sham forts, then alter'd his mind as to besieging Louisburg, and return'd to New York, with all his troops, together with the two packets above mentioned, and all their passengers! During his absence the French and savages had taken Fort George, on the frontier of that province, and the savages had massacred many of the garrison after capitulation.

I saw afterwards in London Captain Bonnell, who commanded one of those packets. He told me that, when he had been detain'd a month, he acquainted his lordship that his ship was grown foul, to a degree that must necessarily hinder her fast sailing, a point of consequence for a packet-boat, and requested an allowance of time to heave her down and clean her bottom. He was asked how long time that would require. He answer'd, three days. The general replied, 'If you can do it in one day, I give leave; otherwise not; for you must certainly sail the day after tomorrow.' So he never obtain'd leave, though detained afterwards from day to day during full three months.

I saw also in London one of Bonnell's passengers, who was so enrag'd against his lordship for deceiving and detaining him so long at New York, and then carrying him to Halifax and back again, that he swore he would sue him for damages. Whether he did or not, I never heard; but, as he represented the injury to his affairs, it was very considerable.

On the whole, I wonder'd much how such a man came to be intrusted with so important a business as the conduct of a great army; but, having since seen more of the great world, and the means of obtaining, and motives for giving places, my wonder is diminished. General Shirley, on whom the command of the army devolved upon the death of Braddock, would, in my opinion, if continued in place, have made a much better campaign than that of Loudoun in 1757, which was frivolous, expensive, and disgraceful to our nation beyond conception; for, tho' Shirley was not a bred soldier, he was sensible and sagacious in himself, and attentive to good advice from others, capable of forming judicious plans, and quick and active in carrying them into execution. Loudoun, instead of defending the colonies with his great army, left them totally expos'd while he paraded idly at Halifax, by which means Fort George was lost, besides, he derang'd all our mercantile operations, and distress'd our trade, by a long embargo on the exportation of provisions, on pretence of keeping supplies from being obtain'd by the enemy, but in reality for beating down their price in favour of the contractors, in whose profits, it was said, perhaps from suspicion only, he had a share. And, when at length the embargo was taken off, by neglecting to send notice of it to Charlestown, the Carolina fleet was detain'd near three months longer, whereby their bottoms were so much damaged by the worm that a great part of them foundered in their passage home.

Shirley was, I believe, sincerely glad of being relieved from so burdensome a charge as the conduct of an army must be to a man unacquainted with military business. I was at the entertainment given by the city of New York to Lord Loudoun, on his taking upon him the command. Shirley, tho' thereby superseded, was present also. There was a great company of officers, citizens, and strangers, and, some chairs having been borrowed in the neighbourhood, there was one among them very low, which fell to the lot of Mr Shirley. Perceiving it as I sat by him, I said, 'They have given you, sir, too low a seat.' 'No matter,' says he, 'Mr Franklin, I find *a low seat* the easiest.'

While I was, as afore mention'd, detain'd at New York, I receiv'd all the accounts of the provisions, etc., that I had furnish'd to Braddock, some of which accounts could not sooner be obtain'd from the different persons I had employ'd to assist in the business. I presented them to Lord Loudoun, desiring to be paid the balance. He caus'd them to be regularly examined by the proper officer, who, after comparing every article with its voucher, certified them to be right; and the balance due for which his lordship promis'd to give me an order on the paymaster. This was, however, put off from time to time; and, tho' I call'd often for it by appointment, I did not get it. At length, just before my departure, he told me he had, on better consideration, concluded not to mix his accounts with those of his predecessors. 'And you,' says he, 'when in England, have only to exhibit your accounts at the treasury, and you will be paid immediately.'

I mention'd, but without effect, the great and unexpected expense I had been put to by being detain'd so long at New York, as a reason for my desiring to be presently paid; and on my observing that it was not right I should be put to any further trouble or delay in obtaining the money I had advanc'd, as I charged no commission for my service, 'O, Sir,' says he, 'you must not think of persuading us that you are no gainer; we understand better those affairs, and know that everyone concerned in supplying the army finds means, in the doing it, to fill his own pockets.' I assur'd him that was not my case, and that I had not pocketed a farthing; but he appear'd clearly not to believe me; and, indeed, I have since learnt that immense fortunes are often made in such employments. As to my balance, I am not paid it to this day, of which more hereafter.

Our captain of the packet had boasted much, before we sailed, of the swiftness of his ship; unfortunately, when we came to sea, she proved the dullest of ninety-six sail, to his no small mortification. After many conjectures respecting the cause, when we were near another ship almost as dull as ours, which, however, gain'd upon us, the captain ordered all hands to come aft, and stand as near the ensign staff as possible. We were, passengers included, about forty persons. While we stood there, the ship mended her pace, and soon left her neighbour far behind, which prov'd clearly what our captain suspected, that she was loaded too much by the head. The casks of water, it seems, had been all plac'd forward; these he therefore order'd to be mov'd further aft, on which the ship recover'd her character, and proved the sailer in the fleet.

The captain said she had once gone at the rate of thirteen knots, which is accounted thirteen miles per hour. We had on board, as a passenger, Captain Kennedy, of the Navy, who contended that it was impossible, and that no ship ever sailed so fast, and that there must have been some error in the division of the log-line, or some mistake in heaving the log. A wager ensu'd between the two captains, to be decided when there should be sufficient wind. Kennedy thereupon examin'd rigorously the log-line, and, being satisfi'd with that, he determin'd to throw the log himself. Accordingly some days after, when the wind blew very fair and fresh, and the captain of the packet, Lutwidge, said he believ'd she then went at the rate of thirteen knots, Kennedy made the experiment, and own'd his wager lost.

The above fact I give for the sake of the following observation. It has been remark'd, as an imperfection in the art of ship-building, that it can never be known, till she is tried, whether a new ship will or will not be a good sailer; for that the model of a good-sailing ship has been exactly follow'd in a new one, which has prov'd, on the contrary, remarkably dull. I apprehend that this may partly be occasion'd by the different opinions of seamen respecting the modes of lading, rigging, and sailing of a ship; each has his system; and the same vessel, laden by the judgement and orders of one captain, shall sail better or worse than when by the orders of another. Besides, it scarce ever happens that a ship is form'd, fitted for the sea, and sail'd by the same person. One man builds the hull, another rigs her, a third lades and sails her. No one of these has the advantage of knowing all the ideas and experience of the others, and, therefore, cannot draw just conclusions from a combination of the whole.

Even in the simple operation of sailing when at sea, I have often observ'd different judgements in the officers who commanded the successive watches, the wind being the same. One would have the sails trimm'd sharper or flatter than another, so that they seem'd to have no certain rule to govern by. Yet I think a set of experiments might be instituted, first, to determine the most proper form of the hull for swift sailing; next, the best dimensions and properest place for the masts; then the form and quantity of sails, and their position, as the wind may be; and, lastly, the disposition of the lading. This is an age of experiments, and I think a set accurately made and combin'd would be of great use. I am persuaded, therefore, that ere long some ingenious philosopher will undertake it, to whom I wish success.

We were several times chas'd in our passage, but outsail'd everything, and in thirty days had soundings. We had a good observation, and the captain judg'd himself so near our port, Falmouth, that, if we made a good run in the night, we might be off the mouth of that harbour in the morning, and by running in the night might escape the notice of the enemy's privateers, who often crus'd near the entrance of the channel. Accordingly, all the sail was set that we could possibly make, and the wind being very fresh and fair, we went right before it, and made great way. The captain, after his observation, shap'd his course, as he thought, so as to pass wide of the Scilly Isles; but it seems there is sometimes a strong indraught setting up St George's Channel, which deceives seamen and caused the loss of Sir Cloudesley Shovel's squadron. This indraught was probably the cause of what happened to us.

We had a watchman plac'd in the bow, to whom they often called, 'Look well out before there,' and he as often answered, 'Ay, ay'; but perhaps had his eyes shut, and was half asleep at the time, they sometimes answering, as is said, mechanically; for he did not see a light just before us, which had been hid by the studding-sails from the man at the helm, and from the rest of the watch, but by an accidental yaw of the ship was discover'd, and occasion'd a great alarm, we being very near it, the light appearing to me as big as a cartwheel. It was midnight, and our captain fast asleep; but Captain Kennedy, jumping-upon deck, and seeing the danger, ordered the ship to wear round, all sails standing; an operation dangerous to the masts, but it carried us clear, and we escaped shipwreck, for we were running right upon the rocks on which the lighthouse was erected. This deliverance impressed me strongly with the utility of lighthouses, and made me resolve to encourage the building more of them in America, if I should live to return there.

In the morning it was found by the soundings, etc., that we were near our port, but a thick fog hid the land from our sight. About nine o'clock the fog began to rise, and seem'd to be lifted up from the water like the curtain at a playhouse, discovering underneath, the town of Falmouth, the vessels in its harbour, and the fields that surrounded it. This was a most pleasing spectacle to those who had been so long without any other prospects than the uniform view of a vacant ocean, and it gave us the more pleasure as we were now free from the anxieties which the state of war occasion'd.

I set out immediately, with my son, for London, and we only stopped a little by the way to view Stonehenge on Salisbury Plain, and Lord Pembroke's house and gardens, with his very curious antiquities at Wilton. We arrived in London the 27th of July, 1757.

As soon as I was settled in a lodging Mr Charles had provided for me, I went to visit Dr Fothergill, to whom I was strongly recommended, and whose counsel respecting my proceedings I was advis'd to obtain. He was against an immediate complaint to government, and thought the proprietaries should first be personally appli'd to, who might possibly be induc'd by the interposition and persuasion of some private friends, to accommodate matters amicably. I then waited on my old friend and correspondent, Mr Peter Collinson, who told me that John Hanbury, the great Virginia merchant, had requested to be informed when I should arrive, that he might carry me to Lord Granville's, who was then President of the Council and wished to see me as soon as possible. I agreed to go with him the next morning. Accordingly Mr Hanbury called for me and took me in his carriage to that nobleman's, who receiv'd me with great civility; and after some questions respecting the present state of affairs in America and discourse thereupon, he said to me: 'You Americans have wrong ideas of the nature of your constitution; you contend that the king's instructions to his governors are not laws, and think yourselves at liberty to regard or disregard them at your own discretion. But those instructions are not like the pocket instructions given to a minister going abroad, for regulating his conduct in some trifling point of ceremony. They are first drawn up by judges learned in the laws; they are then considered, debated, and perhaps amended in Council, after which they are signed by the king. They are then, so far as they relate to you, the *law of the land*, for the king is the LEGISLATOR OF THE COLONIES.' I told his lordship this was new doctrine to me. I had always understood from our charters that our laws were to be made by our Assemblies, to be presented indeed to the king for his royal assent, but that being once given the king could not repeal or alter them. And as the Assemblies could not make permanent laws without his assent, so neither could he make a law for them without theirs. He assur'd me I was totally mistaken. I did not think so, however, and his lordship's conversation having a little alarm'd me as to what might be the sentiments of the court concerning us, I wrote it down as soon as I return'd to my lodgings. I recollected that about 20 years before, a clause in a bill brought into Parliament by the ministry had propos'd to make the king's instructions laws in the colonies, but the clause was thrown out by the Commons, for which we adored them as our friends and friends of liberty, till by their conduct towards us in 1765 it seem'd that they had refus'd that point of sovereignty to the king only that they might reserve it for themselves.

After some days, Dr Fothergill having spoken to the proprietaries, they agreed to a meeting with me at Mr T. Penn's house in Spring Garden. The conversation at first consisted of mutual declarations of disposition to reasonable accommodations, but I suppose each party had its own ideas of what should be meant by *reasonable*. We then went into consideration of our several points of complaint, which I enumerated. The proprietaries justify'd their conduct as well as they could, and I the Assembly's. We now appeared very wide, and so far from each other in our opinions as to discourage all hope of agreement. However, it was concluded that I should give them the heads of our complaints in writing, and they promis'd then to consider them. I did so soon after, but they put the paper into the hands of their solicitor, Ferdinand John Paris, who managed for them all their law business in their great suit with the neighbouring proprietary of Maryland, Lord Baltimore, which had subsisted 70 years, and wrote for them all their papers and messages in their dispute with the Assembly. He was a proud, angry man, and as I had occasionally in the answers of the Assembly treated his papers with some severity, they being really weak in point of argument and haughty in expression, he had conceived a mortal enmity to me, which discovering itself whenever we met, I declin'd the proprietary's proposal that he and I should discuss the heads of complaint between our two selves, and refus'd treating with anyone but them. They then by his advice put the paper into the hands of the Attorney and Solicitor-General for their opinion and counsel upon it, where it lay unanswered a year wanting eight days, during which time I made frequent demands of an answer from the proprietaries, but without obtaining any other than that they had not yet received the opinion of the Attorney and Solicitor-General. What it was when they did receive it I never learnt, for they did not communicate it to me, but sent a long message to the Assembly drawn and signed by Paris, reciting my paper, complaining of its want of formality, as a rudeness on my part, and giving a flimsy justification of their conduct, adding that they should be willing to accommodate matters if the Assembly would send out *some person of candour* to treat with them for that purpose, intimating thereby that I was not such.

The want of formality or rudeness was, probably, my not having address'd the paper to them with their assum'd titles of True and Absolute Proprietaries of the Province of Pennsylvania, which I omitted as not thinking it necessary in a paper, the intention of which was only to reduce to a certainty by writing, what in conversation I had delivered *viva voce*.

But during this delay, the Assembly having prevailed with Gov'r Denny to pass an act taxing the proprietary estate in common with the estates of the people, which was the grand point in dispute, they omitted answering the message.

When this act however came over, the proprietaries, counselled by Paris, determined to oppose its receiving the royal assent. Accordingly they petition'd the king in Council, and a hearing was appointed in which two lawyers were employ'd by them against the act, and two by me in support of it. They alledg'd that the act was intended to load the proprietary estate in order to spare those of the people, and that if it were suffer'd to continue in force, and the proprietaries who were in odium with the people, left to their mercy in proportioning the taxes, they would inevitably be ruined. We reply'd that the act had no such intention, and would have no such effect. That the assessors were honest and discrete men under an oath to assess fairly and equitably, and that any advantage each of them might expect in lessening his own tax by augmenting that of the proprietaries was too trifling to induce them to perjure themselves. This is the purport of what I remember as urged by both sides, except that we insisted strongly on the mischievous consequences that must attend a repeal, for that the money, £100,000, being printed and given to the king's use, expended in his service, and now spread among the people, the repeal would strike it dead in their hands to the ruin of many, and the total discouragement of future grants, and the selfishness of the proprietors in soliciting such a general catastrophe, merely from a groundless fear of their estate being taxed too highly, was insisted on in the strongest terms. On this, Lord Mansfield, one of the counsel rose, and beckoning me took me into the clerk's chamber, while the lawyers were pleading, and asked me if I was really of opinion that no injury would be done the proprietary estate in the execution of the act. I said certainly. 'Then,' says he, 'you can have little objection to enter into an engagement to assure that point.' I answer'd, 'None at all.' He then call'd in Paris, and after some discourse, his lordship's proposition was accepted on both sides; a paper to the purpose was drawn up by the Clerk of the Council, which I sign'd with Mr Charles, who was also an Agent of the Province for their ordinary affairs, when Lord Mansfield returned to the Council Chamber, where finally the law was allowed to pass. Some changes were however recommended and we also engaged they should be made by a subsequent law, but the Assembly did not think them necessary; for one year's tax having been levied by the act before the order of Council arrived, they appointed a committee to examine the proceedings of the assessors, and on this committee they put several particular friends of the proprietaries. After a full enquiry, they unanimously sign'd a report that they found the tax had been assess'd with perfect equity.

The Assembly looked into my entering into the first part of the engagement, as an essential service to the Province, since it secured the credit of the paper money then spread over all the country. They gave me their thanks in form when I return'd. But the proprietaries were enraged at Governor Denny for having pass'd the act, and turn'd him out with threats of suing him for breach of instructions which he had given bond to observe. He, however, having done it at the instance of the General, and for His Majesty's service, and having some powerful interest at court, despis'd the threats and they were never put in execution . . .

Unfinished

The Dogood Papers

The New-England Courant *No. 35*
From Monday March 26th to Monday April 2nd 1722

To the Author of the New-England Courant

SIR – It may not be improper in the first Place to inform your Readers, that I intend once a Fortnight to present them, by the Help of this Paper, with a short Epistle, which I presume will add somewhat to their Entertainment.

And since it is observed, that the Generality of People, nowadays, are unwilling either to commend or dispraise what they read, until they are in some measure informed who or what the Author of it is, whether he be *poor* or *rich, old* or *young, a Scholar* or *a Leather Apron Man*, etc., and give their Opinion of the Performance, according to the Knowledge which they have of the Author's Circumstances, it may not be amiss to begin with a short Account of my past Life and present Condition, that the Reader may not be at a Loss to judge whether or no my Lucubrations are worth his reading.

At the time of my Birth, my Parents were on Ship-board in their Way from *London* to *N. England*. My Entrance into this troublesome World was attended with the Death of my Father, a Misfortune, which tho' I was not then capable of knowing, I shall never be able to forget; for as he, poor Man, stood upon the Deck rejoicing at my Birth, a merciless Wave entered the Ship, and in one Moment carry'd him beyond Reprieve. Thus was the *first* day which I saw, the *last* that was seen by my Father; and thus was my disconsolate Mother at once made both a *Parent* and a *Widow*.

When we arrived at *Boston* (which was not long after) I was put to Nurse in a Country Place, at a small Distance from the Town, where I went to School, and pass'd my Infancy and Childhood in Vanity and Idleness, until I was bound out Apprentice, that I might no longer be a Charge to my Indigent Mother, who was put to hard Shifts for a Living.

My Master was a Country Minister, a pious good-natur'd young Man, & a Batchelor: He labour'd with all his Might to instil virtuous and godly Principles into my tender Soul, well knowing that it was the most suitable Time to make deep and lasting Impressions on the Mind, while it was yet untainted with Vice, free and unbias'd. He endeavour'd that I might be instructed in all that Knowledge and Learning which is necessary for our Sex, and deny'd me no Accomplishment that could possibly be attained in a Country Place, such as all Sorts of Needle-Work, Writing, Arithmetic, etc. and observing that I took a more than ordinary Delight in reading ingenious Books, he gave me the free Use of his Library, which tho' it was but small, yet it was well chose, to inform the Understanding rightly and enable the Mind to frame great and noble Ideas.

Before I had liv'd quite two Years with this Reverend Gentleman, my indulgent Mother departed this Life, leaving me as it were by my self, having no Relation on Earth within my Knowledge.

I will not abuse your patience with a tedious Recital of all the frivolous Accidents of my Life, that happened from this Time until I arrived to Years of Discretion, only inform you that I liv'd a cheerful Country Life, spending my leisure Time either in some innocent Diversion with the neighbouring Females, or in some shady Retirement, with the best of Company, *Books*. Thus I past away the Time with a Mixture of Profit and Pleasure, having no Affliction but what was imaginary, and created in my own Fancy; as nothing is more common with us Women, than to be grieving for nothing, when we have nothing else to grieve for.

As I would not engross too much of your Paper at once, I will defer the Remainder of my Story until my next Letter; in the meantime desiring your Readers to exercise their Patience, and bear with my Humours now and then, because I shall trouble them but seldom. I am not insensible of the Impossibility of pleasing all, but I would not willingly displease any; and for those who will take Offence where none is intended, they are beneath the Notice of

Your Humble Servant,

SILINC DOGOOD

☞ *As the Favour of Mrs Dogood's Correspondence is acknowledged by the Publisher of this Paper, lest any of her Letters should miscarry, he desires they may for the future be deliver'd at his Printing-House, or at the Blue Ball in Union Street, and no Questions shall be ask'd of the Bearer.*

The (pencilled above) 39 New-England Courant *No. 37*
From Monday April 9th to Monday April 16th 1722

To the Author of the New-England Courant *No. 2*

SIR – Histories of Lives are seldom entertaining, unless they contain something either admirable or exemplar: And since there is little or nothing of this Nature in my own Adventures, I will not tire your Readers with tedious Particulars of no Consequence, but will briefly, and in as few Words as possible relate, the most material Occurrences of my Life, and according to my Promise, confine all to this Letter.

MY Reverend Master who had hitherto remained a Batchelor (after much Meditation on the Eighteenth verse of the second Chapter of *Genesis*), took up a Resolution to marry; and having made several unsuccessful fruitless Attempts on the more topping Sort of our Sex, and being tir'd with making troublesome Journeys and Visits to no Purpose, he began unexpectedly to cast a loving Eye upon Me, whom he had brought up cleverly to his Hand.

THERE is certainly scarce any Part of a Man's Life in which he appears more silly and ridiculous, than when he makes his first Onset in Courtship. The awkward Manner in which my Master first discover'd his Intentions, made me, in spite of my Reverence to his Person, burst out into an unmannerly Laughter: However, having ask'd his Pardon, and with much ado compos'd my Countenance, I promis'd him I would take his Proposal into serious Consideration, and speedily give him an Answer.

As he had been a great Benefactor (and in a Manner a Father to me) I could not well deny his Request, when I once perceived he was in earnest. Whether it was Love, or Gratitude, or Pride, or all Three that made me consent, I know not; but it is certain, he found it no hard Matter, by the Help of his Rhetoric to conquer my Heart, and persuade me to marry him.

THIS unexpected Match was very astonishing to all the Country round about and served to furnish them with Discourse for a long Time after; some approving it, others disliking it, as they were led by their various Fancies and Inclinations.

WE lived happily together in the Height of conjugal Love and mutual Endearments, for near Seven Years in which Time we added Two likely Girls and a Boy to the Family of the *Dogoods:* But alas! When my Sun was in its meridian Altitude, inexorable unrelenting Death, as if he had envy'd my Happiness and Tranquillity, and resolv'd to make me entirely miserable by the Loss of so good an Husband, hastened his Flight to the Heavenly World, by a sudden unexpected Departure from this.

I HAVE now remained in a State of Widowhood for several Years, but it is a State I never much admir'd, and I am apt to fancy that I could be easily persuaded to marry again, provided I was sure of a good-humour'd, sober, agreeable Companion: But one, even with these few good Qualities, being hard to find, I have lately relinquished all Thoughts of that Nature.

AT present I pass away my leisure Hours in Conversation, either with my honest Neighbour *Rusticus* and his Family, or with the ingenious Minister of our Town, who now lodges at my House, and by whose Assistance I intend now and then to beautify my Writings with a Sentence or two in the learned Languages, which will not only be fashionable, and pleasing to those who do not understand it, but will likewise be very ornamental.

I SHALL conclude this with my own Character, which (one would think) I should be best able to give. *Know then*, That I am an Enemy to Vice, and a Friend to Virtue. I am one of an extensive Charity, and a great Forgiver of *private* Injuries: A hearty Lover of the Clergy and all good Men, and a mortal Enemy to arbitrary Government & unlimited Power. I am naturally very jealous for the Rights and Liberties of my Country: & the least appearance of an Encroachment on those invaluable Privileges, is apt to make my Blood boil exceedingly. I have likewise a natural Inclination to observe and reprove the Faults of others, at which I have an excellent Faculty. I speak this by Way of Warning to all such whose offences shall come under my Cognisance, for I never intend to wrap my Talent in a Napkin. To be brief; I am courteous and affable, good-humour'd (unless I am first provok'd), and handsome, and sometimes witty, but always,

SIR, Your Friend, and Humble Servant,

SILENCE DOGOOD

No 39
From Monday April 23rd to Monday April 30th 1722

To the Author of the New-England Courant No. 3

SIR – It is undoubtedly the Duty of all Persons to serve the Country they live in, according to their Abilities; yet I sincerely acknowledge, that I have hitherto been very deficient in this Particular, whether it was for want of Will or Opportunity, I will not at present stand to determine: Let it suffice, that I now take up a Resolution, to do for the future all that *lies in my Way* for the Service of my Countrymen.

I HAVE from my Youth been indefatigably studious to gain and treasure up in my Mind all useful and desirable Knowledge, especially such as tends to improve the Mind, and enlarge the Understanding: And as I have found it very beneficial to me, I am not without Hopes, that communicating my small Stock in this Manner, by Piecemeal to the Public, may be at least in some Measure useful.

I AM very sensible that it is impossible for me, or indeed any *one* Writer to please *all* Readers at once. Various Persons have different Sentiments; and that which is pleasant and delightful to one, gives another a Disgust. He that would (in this Way of Writing) please all, is under a Necessity to make his Themes almost as numerous as his Letters. He must one while be merry and diverting, then more solid and serious; one while sharp and satirical, then (to mollify that) be sober and religious; at *one* Time let the Subject be Politics, then let the next Theme be Love: Thus will everyone, one Time or other find something agreeable to his own Fancy, and in his Turn be delighted.

According to this Method I intend to proceed, bestowing now and then a few gentle Reproofs on those who deserve them, not forgetting at the same time to applaud those whose Actions merit Commendation. And here I must not forget to invite the ingenious Part of your Readers, particularly those of my own Sex to enter into a Correspondence with me, assuring them, that their Condescension in this Particular shall be received as a Favour, and accordingly acknowledged.

I THINK I have now finish'd the Foundation, and I intend in my next to begin to raise the Building. Having nothing more to write at present, I must make the usual excuse in such Cases, of *being in haste*, assuring you that I speak from my Heart when I call my self, The most humble and obedient of all the Servants your Merits have acquir'd,

SILENCE DOGOOD

Those who incline to favour Mrs Dogood with their Correspondence, are desir'd to send their Letters (directed to her) to the Publishers of this Paper.

The New-England Courant *No. 41*
From Monday May 7th to Monday May 14th 1722

An fum etiam nunc vel Græcè logui vel Latinè docendus?

CICERO

To the Author of the New-England Courant *No. IV*

SIR – DISCOURSING the other Day at Dinner with my Reverend Boarder, formerly mention'd (whom for Distinction sake we will call by the name of *Clericus*), concerning the Education of Children, I ask'd his Advice about my young Son *William*, whether or no I had best bestow upon him Academical Learning, or (as our Phrase is) *bring him up at our College:* He persuaded me to do it by all Means, using many weighty Arguments with me, and answering all the Objections that I could form against it; telling me withal, that he did not doubt but that the Lad would take his Learning very well, and not idle away his Time as too many there nowadays do. These words of *Clericus* gave me a Curiosity to inquire a little more strictly into the present Circumstances of that famous Seminary of Learning; but the Information which he gave me, was neither pleasant, nor such as I expected.

As soon as Dinner was over, I took a solitary Walk into my Orchard, still ruminating on *Clericus's* discourse with much consideration, until I came to my usual Place of Retirement under the *Great Apple Tree;* where having seated myself, and carelessly laid my Head on a verdant Bank, I fell by Degrees into a soft and undisturbed Slumber. My waking Thoughts remained with me in my Sleep, and before I awak'd again, I dreamt the following DREAM.

I FANCY'D I was travelling over pleasant and delightful Fields and Meadows, and thro' many small Country Towns and Villages; and as I pass'd along, all Places resounded with the Fame of the Temple of LEARNING: Every Peasant, who had wherewithal, was preparing to send one of his Children at least to this famous Place; and in this Case most of them consulted their own Purses instead of their Children's Capacities: So that I observed, a great many, yea, the most part of those who were travelling thither, were little better than Dunces and Blockheads. Alas! Alas!

At length I entered upon a spacious Plain, in the Midst of which was erected a large and stately Edifice: It was to this that a great Company of Youths from all Parts of the Country were going; so stepping in among the Crowd, I passed on with them, and presently arrived at the Gate.

THE Passage was Kept by two sturdy Porters named *Riches* and *Poverty*, and the latter obstinately refused to give Entrance to any who had not first gain'd the Favour of the former; so that I observed, many who came even to the very Gate, were obliged to travel back again as ignorant as they came, for want of this necessary Qualification. However, as a Spectator I gain'd Admittance, and with the rest entered directly into the Temple.

IN the Middle of the great Hall stood a stately and magnificent Throne, which was ascended to by two high and difficult Steps. On the Top of it sat LEARNING in awful State; she was apparelled wholly in Black, and surrounded almost on every Side with innumerable Volumes in all Languages. She seem'd very busily employ'd in writing something on half a Sheet of Paper, and upon Enquiry, I understood she was preparing a Paper, call'd *The New-England Courant*. On her Right Hand sat *English*, with a pleasant smiling Countenance, and handsomely attir'd; and on her left were seated several *Antique Figures* with their Faces veil'd. I was considerably puzzl'd to guess who they were, until one informed me (who stood beside me) that those Figures on her Left Hand, were *Latin, Greek, Hebrew*, etc. and that they were very much reserv'd, and seldom or never unveil'd their Faces here, and then to few or none, tho' most of those who have in this Place acquir'd so much Learning as to distinguish them from *English*, pretended to an intimate Acquaintance with them. I then enquir'd of him, what could be the Reason why they continued veil'd, in this Place especially: He pointed to the Foot of the Throne, where I saw *Idleness*, attended with *Ignorance*, and these (he informed me) were they, who first veil'd them, and still kept them so.

NOW I observed, that the whole Tribe who entered into the Temple with me, began to climb the Throne; but the Work proving troublesome and difficult to most of them, they withdrew their Hands from the Plough, and contented themselves to sit at the Foot, with Madam *Idleness* and her Maid *Ignorance*, until those who were assisted by Diligence and a docible Temper, had well nigh got up the first Step: But the Time drawing nigh in which they could no way avoid ascending, they were fain to crave the Assistance of those who had got up before them, and who, for the Reward perhaps of a *Pint of Milk*, or a *Piece of Plumb Cake*, lent the Lubbers a helping Hand, and sat them in the Eye of the World, upon a Level with themselves.

THE other Step being in the same Manner ascended, and the usual Ceremonies at an End, every Beetle-Skull seem'd well satisfy'd with his own Portion of Learning, tho' perhaps he was *e'en just* as ignorant as ever. And now the Time of their Departure being come, they march'd out of Doors to make Room for another Company, who waited for Entrance: And I, having seen all that was to be seen, quitted the Hall likewise, and went to make my Observations on those who were just gone out before me.

Some I perceiv'd took to Merchandising, others to Travelling, some to one Thing, some to another, and some to Nothing; and many of them from henceforth, for want of Patrimony, liv'd as poor as church Mice, being unable to dig, and asham'd to beg, and to live by their Wits it was impossible. But the most Part of the Crowd went along a large beaten Path, which led to a Temple at the further End of the Plain, call'd *The Temple of Theology*. The Business of those who were employ'd in this Temple being laborious and painful, I wonder'd exceedingly to see so many go towards it; but while I was pondering this Matter in my Mind, I spy'd *Pecunia* behind a Curtain, beckoning to them with her Hand, which Sight immediately satisfy'd me for whose Sake it was, that a great Part of them (I will not say all) travel'd that Road. In this Temple I saw nothing worth mentioning, except the ambitious and fraudulent Contrivances of *Plagius*, who (notwithstanding he had been severely reprehended for such Practices before) was diligently transcribing some eloquent Paragraphs out of *Tillotson's* Works, etc. to embellish his own.

Now I bethought my self in my Sleep, that it was Time to be at Home, and as I fancy'd I was travelling back thither, I reflected in my Mind on the extreme Folly of those Parents, who, blind to their Childrens Dullness, and insensible of the Solidity of their Skulls, because they think their Purses can afford it, will needs send them to the Temple of Learning, where, for want of a suitable Genius, they learn little more than how to carry themselves handsomely, and enter a Room genteelly (which might as well be acquir'd at a Dancing-School), and from whence they return, after Abundance of Trouble and Charge, as great Blockheads as ever, only more proud and self-conceited.

While I was in the midst of these unpleasant Reflections, *Clericus* (who with a Book in his Hand was walking under the Trees) accidentally awak'd me; to him I related my Dream with all its Particulars, and he, without much Study, presently interpreted it, assuring me, *That it was a lively representation of* HARVARD COLLEGE, *Etcetera*.

I remain, Sir,

Your Humble Servant,

SILENCE DOGOOD

The New-England Courant *No. 43*
From Monday May 21st to Monday May 28th 1722

Mulier muliere magis congruet – TERENCE

To the Author of the New-England Courant *No. V*

SIR – I SHALL here present your Readers with a Letter from one, who informs me that I have begun at the wrong End of my Business, and that I ought to begin at Home, and censure the Vices and Follies of my own Sex, before I venture to meddle with your's: Nevertheless, I am resolved to dedicate this Speculation to the Fair Tribe, and endeavour to show, that Mr *Ephraim* charges Women with being particularly guilty of Pride, Idleness, etc. wrongfully, inasmuch as the Men have not only as great a Share in those Vices as the Women, but are likewise in a great Measure the Cause of that which the Women are guilty of. I think it will be best to produce my Antagonist, before I encounter him.

To Mrs Dogood

MADAM – My Design in troubling you with this Letter is, to desire you would begin with your own Sex first: Let the first Volley of your Resentments be directed against *Female* Vice; let Female Idleness, Ignorance and Folly (which are Vices more peculiar to your Sex than to our's), be the Subject of your Satires, but more especially Female Pride, which I think is intolerable. Here is a large Field that wants Cultivation, and which I believe you are able (if willing) to improve with Advantage; and when you have once reformed the Women, you will find it a much easier Task to reform the Men, because Women are the prime Causes of a great many Male Enormities. This is all at present from

Your Friendly Wellwisher,

EPHRAIM CENSORIOUS

AFTER Thanks to my Correspondent for his Kindness in cutting out Work for me, I must assure him, that I find it a very difficult Matter to reprove Women separate from the Men; for what Vice is there in which the Men have not as great a Share as the Women? and in some have they not a far greater, as in Drunkenness, Swearing, etc.? And if they have, then it follows, that when a Vice is to be reproved, Men, who are most culpable, deserve the most Reprehension, and certainly therefore, ought to have it. But we will wave this point at present, and proceed to a particular Consideration of what my Correspondent calls *Female Vice*.

AS for Idleness, if I should *Query*, Where are the greatest Number of its Votaries to be found, with us or the Men? it might I believe be easily and truly answer'd, *With the latter*.

Preface to Poor Richard, 1733 (PHS)

Courteous Reader – I might in this place attempt to gain thy Favour, by declaring that I write Almanacs with no other View than that of the public Good; but in this I should not be sincere; and Men are nowadays too wise to be deceiv'd by Pretences how specious soever. The plain Truth of the Matter is, I am excessive poor, and my Wife, good Woman, is, I tell her, excessive proud; she cannot bear, she says, to sit spinning in her Shift of Tow, while I do nothing but gaze at the Stars; and has threatened more than once to burn all my Books and Rattling-Traps (as she calls my Instruments) if I do not make some profitable Use of them for the Good of my Family. The Printer has offer'd me some considerable share of the Profits, and I have thus begun to comply with my Dame's Desire.

Indeed this Motive would have had Force enough to have made me publish an Almanac many Years since, had it not been overpowered by my Regard for my good Friend and Fellow Student Mr *Titan Leeds*,*

* Titan Leeds replied in his 'American Almanac' for 1734 –
Kind Reader, Perhaps it may be expected that I should say something concerning an Almanac printed for the Year 1733, Said to be writ by Poor Richard or Richard Saunders, who for want of other matter was pleased to tell his Readers, that he had calculated my Nativity, and from thence predicts my Death to be the 17th of October, 1733. At 22 min. past 3 a-Clock in the Afternoon, and that these Provinces may not expect to see any more of his *(Titan Leeds)* Performances, and this precise Predicter who predicts to a Minute, proposes to succeed me in Writing of Almanacs; but notwithstanding his false Prediction, I have by the Mercy of God lived to write a Diary for the Year 1734, and to publish the Folly and Ignorance of this presumptuous Author. Nay, he adds another gross Falsehood in his said Almanac, viz. *That by my own Calculation, I shall survive until the 26th of the said Month* (October), which is as untrue as the former, for I do not pretend to that Knowledge, altho' he has usurped the Knowledge of the Almighty herein, and manifested himself a Fool and a Liar. And by the Mercy of God I have lived to survive this conceited Scribbler's Day and Minute whereon he has predicted my Death, and as I have supplied my Country with Almanacs for three seven Years by past, to general Satisfaction, so perhaps I may live to write when his Performances are Dead. *Thus much from your annual Friend, Titan Leeds.* October 18, 1733, 3 ho. 33 min. p.m.

whose Interest I was extremely unwilling to hurt: But this Obstacle (I am far from speaking it with Pleasure) is soon to be removed, since inexorable Death, who was never known to respect Merit, has already prepared the mortal Dart, the fatal Sister has already extended her destroying Shears, and that ingenious Man must soon be taken from us. He dies, by my Calculation made at his Request, on Oct. 17th 1733. 3 h. 29 m. p.m. at the very instant of the ☌ of ☉ and ☿ : By his own Calculation he will survive till the 26th of the same Month. This small Difference between us we have disputed whenever we have met these 9 Years past; but at length he is inclinable to agree with my Judgement: Which of us is most exact, a little Time will now determine. As therefore these Provinces may not longer expect to see any of his Performances after this Year, I think my self free to take up the Task, and request a share of the public Encouragement; which I am the more apt to hope for on this Account, that the Buyer of my Almanac may consider himself, not only as purchasing an useful Utensil, but as performing an Act of Charity, to his poor *Friend and Servant*

R. SAUNDERS

Poor Richard's Almanac, 1749

How to Get Riches

The Art of getting Riches consists very much in Thrift. All Men are not equally qualified for getting Money, but it is in the Power of everyone alike to practice this Virtue.

He that would be beforehand in the World, must be beforehand with his Business: It is not only ill Management, but discovers a slothful Disposition, to do that in the Afternoon, which should have been done in the morning.

Useful Attainments in your Minority will procure Riches in Maturity, of which Writing and Accounts are not the meanest.

Learning, whether Speculative or Practical, is, in Popular or Mixed Governments, the Natural Source of Wealth and Honour.

PRECEPT I
In Things of moment, on thy self depend,
Nor trust too far thy Servant or thy Friend:
With private views, thy Friend may promise fair,
And Servants very seldom prove sincere.

PRECEPT II
What can be done, with Care perform to Day,
Dangers unthought-of will attend Delay;
Your distant Prospects all precarious are,
And Fortune is as fickle as she's fair.

PRECEPT III
Nor trivial Loss, nor trivial Gain despise;
Molehills, if often heap'd, to Mountains rise:
Weigh every small Expense, and nothing waste,
Farthings long sav'd, amount to Pounds at last.

From Poor Richard's Almanac, 1756

The Wit of Conversation consists more in finding it in others, than showing a great deal yourself. He who goes out of your Company pleased with his own Facetiousness and Ingenuity, will the sooner come into it again. Most men had rather *please* than *admire* you, and seek less to be *instructed* and *diverted*, than *approved* and *applauded*, and it is certainly the most delicate Sort of Pleasure, to *please another*.

But that sort of *Wit*, which employs itself insolently in Criticising and Censuring, the Words and Sentiments of others in Conversation, is absolute *Folly*; for it answers none of the Ends of Conversation. He who uses it neither *improves* others, is *improved* himself, or pleases anyone.

As I spent some Weeks last Winter, in visiting my old Acquaintance in the *Jerseys*, great Complaints I heard for Want of money, and that leave to make more Paper Bills could not be obtained. *Friends and Countrymen*, my Advice on this Head shall cost you nothing, and if you will not be angry with me for giving it, I promise you not to be offended if you do not take it.

You spend yearly at least *two hundred thousand pounds*, it is said, in European, East-Indian and West-Indian commodities. Supposing one half of this expense to be in *things absolutely necessary*, the other half may be called *superfluities*, or, at best, conveniences, which, however, you might live without for one little year, and not suffer exceedingly. Now to save this half, observe these few directions;

1. When you incline to have new clothes, look first well over the old ones, and see if you cannot shift with them another year, either by scouring, mending, or even patching if necessary. Remember, a patch on your coat, and money in your pocket, is better and more creditable, than a writ on your back, and no money to take it off.

2. When you incline to buy China ware, Chintzes, India silks, or any other of their flimsy, slight manufactures, I would not be so hard with you, as to insist on your absolutely *resolving against it*; all I advise is, to

put it off (as you do your repentance) *till another year*, and this, in some respects, may prevent an occasion for repentance.

3. If you are now a drinker of punch, wine or tea, twice a day, for the ensuing year drink them but once a day. If you now drink them but once a day, do it but every other day. If you now do it but once a week, reduce the practice to once a fortnight. And, if you do not exceed in quantity as you lessen the times, half your expense in these articles will be saved.

4. When you incline to drink rum, fill the glass *half* with water.

Thus at the year's end, there will be a *hundred thousand pounds* more money in your country.

If paper money in ever so great a quantity could be made, no man could get any of it without giving something for it. But all he saves in this way, will be *his own for nothing*, and his country actually so much richer. Then the merchant's old and doubtful debts may be honestly paid off, and trading become surer thereafter, if not so extensive.

From Poor Richard's Almanac, 1757

How to make a STRIKING SUNDIAL, by which not only a Man's own Family, but all his Neighbours for ten Miles round, may know what a Clock it is, when the Sun shines, without seeing the Dial.

Choose an open Place in your Yard or Garden, on which the Sun may shine all Day without any Impediment from Trees or Buildings. On the Ground mark out your Hour Lines, as for a horizontal Dial, according to Art, taking Room enough for the Guns. On the Line for One o'Clock, place one Gun; on the Two o'Clock Line two Guns, and so of the rest. The Guns must all be charged with Powder, but Ball is unnecessary. Your Gnomon or Style must have twelve burning Glasses annex'd to it, and be so placed that the Sun shining through the Glasses, one after the other, shall cause the Focus or burning Spot to fall on the Hour Line of One, for Example, at One a Clock, and there kindle a Train of Gunpowder that shall fire one Gun. At Two a Clock, a Focus shall fall on the Hour Line of Two, and kindle another Train that shall discharge two Guns successively: and so of the rest.

Note, There must be 78 Guns in all. Thirty-two Pounders will be best for this Use; but 18 Pounders may do, and will cost less, as well as use less Powder, for nine Pounds of Powder will do for one Charge of each eighteen Pounder, whereas the Thirty-two Pounders would require for each Gun 16 Pounds.

Note also, That the chief Expense will be the Powder, for the Cannon once bought, will, with Care, last 100 Years.

Note moreover, that there will be a great Saving of Powder in Cloudy Days.

Kind Reader, Methinks I hear thee say, That is indeed a good Thing to know how the Time passes, but this Kind of Dial, notwithstanding the mentioned Savings, would be very Expensive; and the Cost greater than the Advantage, Thou art wise, my Friend, to be so considerate beforehand; some Fools would not have found out so much, till they had made the Dial and try'd it . . . Let all such learn that many a private and many a public Project, are like this Striking Dial, great Cost for little Profit.

Rules of Law Fit to be Observed in Purchasing
From an old Book

FIRST, see the Land which thou intend'st to buy
Within the Sellers title clear doth lie.
And that no Woman to it doth lay claim
By Dowry, Jointure, or some other Name.
That it may cumber. Know if bound or free
The Tenure stand, and that from each Feoffee
It be released: That the Seller be so old
That he may lawful sell, thou lawful hold.
Have special Care that it not mortgag'd lie,
Nor be entailed on Posterity.
Then if it stand in Statute bound or no:
Be well advised what Quit Rent out must go;
What Custom, Service hath been done of old,
By those who formerly the same did hold,
And if a wedded Woman put to Sale,
Deal not with her, unless she bring her Male.
For she doth under Covert-Baron go,
Altho' sometimes some also traffic so.
Have special Care to make thy Charter run
To thee, thine Heirs, Executors, Assigns,
For that beyond thy Life securely binds.
These Things forknown and done, you may prevent
Those Things rash Buyers many times repent.
And yet, when as you have done all you can
If you'd be sure, deal with an honest Man.

Very good Rules, these, and sweetly sung. If they are learnt by heart, and repeated often to keep them in Memory, they may happen to save the Purchaser more Pence than the Price of my Almanac. In Imitation of this old Writer, I have thoughts of turning Coke's Institutes, and all our Province Laws into Metre, hoping thereby to engage some of our young Lawyers and old Justices to read a little.

It is generally agreed to be Folly, to hazard the loss of a Friend, rather than to lose a Jest. But few consider how easily a Friend may be thus lost. Depending on the known Regard their Friends have for them, Jesters take more Freedom with Friends than they would dare to do with others, little thinking how much deeper we are wounded by an Affront from one we love. But the strictest Intimacy can never warrant

Freedoms of this Sort; and it is indeed preposterous to think they should; unless we can suppose Injuries are less Evils when they are done to us by Friends, than when they come from other Hands.

SOME ancient Philosophers have said, that Happiness depends more on the inward Disposition of Mind than on outward Circumstances; and that he who cannot be happy on any State, can be so in no State. To be happy, they tell us we must be content. Right. But they do not teach us how we may become content. Poor Richard shall give you a short good Rule for that. To be content look backward on those who possess less than yourself, not forward on those who possess more. If this does not make you content, you don't deserve to be happy.

> CONTENTMENT! Parent of Delight,
> So much a stranger to our Sight.
> Say, Goddess, in what happy Place
> Mortals behold thy blooming Face;
> Thy gracious Auspices impart,
> And for thy Temple choose my Heart.
> They whom thou deignest to inspire,
> Thy Science learn, to bound Desire;
> By happy Alchemy of Mind
> They turn to Pleasure all they find.
> Unmov'd when the rude Tempest blows,
> Without an Opiate they repose;
> And, cover'd by your Shield, defy
> The whizzing Shafts that round them fly;
> Nor, meddling with the Gods Affairs,
> Concern themselves with distant Cares;
> But place their Bliss in mental Rest,
> And feast upon the Good possest.

The Way to Wealth

Preface to Poor Richard Improved: 1758

COURTEOUS READER – I have heard that nothing gives an Author so great Pleasure, as to find his Works respectfully quoted by other learned Authors. This Pleasure I have seldom enjoyed; for tho' I have been, if I may say it without Vanity, an eminent Author of Almanacs annually now a full Quarter of a Century, my Brother Authors in the same Way, for what Reason I know not, have ever been very sparing in their Applauses, and no other Author has taken the least Notice of me, so that did not my Writings produce me some solid Pudding, the great Deficiency of Praise would have quite discouraged me.

I concluded at length, that the People were the best Judges of my Merit; for they buy my Works; and besides, in my Rambles, where I am not personally known, I have frequently heard one or other of my Adages repeated, with, as Poor Richard says, at the End on 't; this gave me some Satisfaction, as it showed not only that my Instructions were regarded, but discovered likewise some Respect for my Authority; and I own, that to encourage the Practice of remembering and repeating those wise Sentences, I have sometimes quoted myself with great Gravity.

Judge, then how much I must have been gratified by an Incident I am going to relate to you. I stopped my Horse lately where a great Number of People were collected at a Vendue of Merchant Goods. The Hour of Sale not being come, they were conversing on the Badness of the Times and one of the Company call'd to a plain clean old Man, with white Locks, 'Pray, Father Abraham, what think you of the Times? Won't these heavy Taxes quite ruin the Country? How shall we be ever able to pay them? What would you advise us to?' Father Abraham stood up, and reply'd, 'If you'd have my Advice, I'll give it you in short, for A Word to the Wise is enough, and many Words won't fill a Bushel, as Poor Richard says.' They join'd in desiring him to speak his Mind, and gathering round him, he proceeded as follows;

'Friends,' says he, 'and Neighbours, the Taxes are indeed very heavy, and if those laid on by the Government were the only Ones we had to pay, we might more easily discharge them; but we have many others, and much more grievous to some of us. We are taxed twice as much by our Idleness, three times as much by our Pride, and four times as much by our Folly; and from these Taxes the Commissioners cannot ease or deliver us by allowing an Abatement. However let us hearken to good Advice, and something may be done for us; God helps them that help themselves, as Poor Richard says, in his Almanac of 1733.

It would be thought a hard Government that should tax its People one-tenth Part of their Time, to be employed in its Service. But Idleness taxes many of us much more, if we reckon all that is spent in absolute Sloth, or doing of nothing, with that which is spent in idle Employments or Amusements, that amount to nothing. Sloth, by bringing on Diseases, absolutely shortens life. Sloth, like Rust, consumes faster than Labour wears; while the used Key is always bright, as Poor Richard says. But dost thou love Life, then do not squander Time, for that's the stuff Life is made of, as Poor Richard says. How much more than is necessary do we spend in sleep, forgetting that The sleeping Fox catches no Poultry, and that There will be sleeping enough in the Grave, as Poor Richard says.

If Time be of all Things the most precious, wasting Time must be, as Poor Richard says, the greatest Prodigality; since, as he elsewhere tells us, Lost Time is never found again; and what we call Time enough, always proves little enough: Let us then up and be doing, and doing to the Purpose; so by Diligence shall we do more with less Perplexity. Sloth makes all Things difficult, but Industry all easy, as Poor Richard says; and He that riseth late must trot all Day, and shall scarce overtake his Business at Night; while Laziness travels so slowly, that Poverty soon overtakes him, as we read in Poor Richard, who adds, Drive thy Business, let not that drive thee; and Early to Bed, and early to rise, makes a Man healthy, wealthy, and wise.

So what signifies wishing and hoping for better Times. We may make these Times better, if we bestir ourselves. Industry need not wish, as Poor Richard says, and he that lives upon Hope will die fasting. There are no Gains without Pains; then Help Hands, for I have no Lands, or if I have, they are smartly taxed. And, as Poor Richard likewise observes, He that hath a Trade hath an Estate; and he that hath a Calling, hath an Office of Profit and Honour; but then the

Trade must be worked at, and the Calling well followed, or neither the Estate nor the Office will enable us to pay our Taxes. If we are industrious, we shall never starve; for, as Poor Richard says, At the working Man's House Hunger looks in, but dares not enter. Nor will the Bailiff or the Constable enter, for Industry pays Debts, while Despair increaseth them, says Poor Richard. What though you have found no Treasure, nor has any rich Relation left you a Legacy, Diligence is the Mother of Good-luck as Poor Richard says and God gives all Things to Industry. Then plough deep, while Sluggards sleep, and you shall have Corn to sell and to keep, says Poor Dick. Work while it is called Today, for you know not how much you may be hindered Tomorrow, which makes Poor Richard say, One today is worth two Tomorrows, and farther, Have you somewhat to do Tomorrow, do it Today. If you were a Servant, would you not be ashamed that a good Master should catch you idle? Are you then your own Master, be ashamed to catch yourself idle, as Poor Dick says. When there is so much to be done for yourself, your Family, your Country, and your gracious King, be up by Peep of Day; Let not the Sun look down and say, Inglorious here he lies. Handle your Tools without Mittens; remember that The Cat in Gloves catches no Mice, as Poor Richard says. 'Tis true there is much to be done, and perhaps you are weak-handed, but stick to it steadily; and you will see great Effects, for Constant Dropping wears away Stones, and by Diligence and Patience the Mouse ate in two the Cable; and Little Strokes fell great Oaks, as Poor Richard says in his Almanac, the Year I cannot just now remember.

Methinks I hear some of you say, Must a Man afford himself no Leisure? I will tell thee, my friend, what Poor Richard says, Employ thy Time well, if thou meanest to gain Leisure; and, since thou art not sure of a Minute, throw not away an hour. Leisure, is Time for doing something useful; this Leisure the diligent Man will obtain, but the lazy Man never; so that, as Poor Richard says, A life of Leisure and a Life of Laziness are two Things. Do you imagine that Sloth will afford you more Comfort than Labour? No, for as Poor Richard says, Trouble springs from Idleness, and grievous Toil from needless Ease. Many without Labour, would live by their Wits only, but they break for want of Stock. Whereas Industry gives Comfort, and Plenty, and Respect: Fly Pleasures, and they'll follow you. The diligent Spinner has a large Shift; and now I have a Sheep and a Cow, every Body bids me good Morrow; all which is well said by Poor Richard.

But with our Industry, we must likewise be steady, settled, and careful, and oversee our own Affairs with our own Eyes, and not trust too much to others; for, as Poor Richard says

> I never saw an oft-removed Tree,
> Nor yet an oft-removed Family,
> That throve so well as those that settled be.

And again, Three Removes is as bad as a Fire; and again, Keep thy Shop, and thy Shop will keep thee; and again, If you would have your business done, go; if not, send. And again,

> He that by the Plough would thrive
> Himself must either hold or drive.

And again, The Eye of a Master will do more Work than both his Hands; and again, Want of Care does us more Damage than Want of Knowledge; and again, Not to oversee Workmen, is to leave them your Purse open. Trusting too much to others' Care is the Ruin of many; for, as the Almanac says, In the Affairs of this World, Men are saved, not by Faith, but by the Want of it; but a Man's own Care is profitable; for, saith Poor Dick, Learning is to the Studious, and Riches to the Careful, as well as Power to the Bold, and Heaven to the Virtuous, And farther, If you would have a faithful Servant, and one that you like, serve yourself. And again, he adviseth to Circumspection and Care, even in the smallest Matters, because sometimes A little Neglect may breed great Mischief; adding, for want of a Nail the Shoe was lost; for want of a Shoe the Horse was lost; and for want of a Horse the Rider was lost, being overtaken and slain by the Enemy; all for want of Care about a Horse-shoe Nail.

So much for Industry, my Friends, and Attention to one's own Business; but to these we must add Frugality, if we would make our Industry more certainly successful. A Man may, if he knows not how to save as he gets, keep his Nose all his life to the Grindstone, and die not worth a Groat at last. A fat Kitchen makes a lean Will, as Poor Richard says; and

> Many Estates are spent in the Getting,
> Since Women for Tea forsook Spinning and Knitting,
> And Men for Punch forsook Hewing and Splitting.

If you would be wealthy, says he, in another Almanac, think of Saving as well as of Getting: The Indies have not made Spain rich, because her Outgoes are greater than her Incomes.

Away then with your expensive Follies, and you will not then have so much Cause to complain of hard Times, heavy Taxes, and chargeable Families; for, as Poor Dick says,

> Women and Wine, Game and Deceit,
> Make the Wealth small and the Wants great.

And farther, What maintains one Vice, would bring up two Children. You may think perhaps, that a little Tea, or a little Punch now and then, Diet a little more costly, Clothes a little finer, and a little Entertainment now and then, can be no great Matter; but remember what Poor Richard says, Many a Little makes a Mickle; and farther, Beware of little expenses; A small Leak will sink a great Ship; and again, Who Dainties love, shall Beggars prove; and moreover, Fools make Feasts, and wise Men eat them.

Here you are all got together at this Vendue of Fineries and Knicknacks. You call them Goods; but if you do not take Care, they will prove Evils to some of you. You expect they will be sold cheap, and perhaps they may for less than they cost; but if you have no Occasion for them, they must be dear to you. Remember what Poor Richard says; Buy what thou hast no Need of, and ere long thou shalt sell thy Necessaries. And again, At a great Pennyworth pause a while: He means, that perhaps the Cheapness is apparent only, and not Real; or the bargain, by straightening thee in thy Business, may do thee more Harm than Good. For in another Place he says, Many have been ruined by buying good Pennyworths. Again, Poor Richard says, 'tis foolish to lay out Money in a Purchase of Repentance; and yet this Folly is practised every Day at Vendues, for want of minding the Almanac. Wise Men, as Poor Dick says, learn by others Harms, Fools scarcely by their own; but *felix quem faciunt aliena pericula cautum*. Many a one, for the Sake of Finery on the Back, have gone with a hungry Belly, and half-starved their Families. Silks and Satins, Scarlet and Velvets, as Poor Richard says, put out the Kitchen Fire.

These are not the Necessaries of Life; they can scarcely be called the Conveniences; and yet only because they look pretty, how many went to have them! The artificial Wants of Mankind thus become more numerous than the Natural; and, as Poor Dick says, for one poor Person, there are an hundred indigent. By these, and other Extravagancies, the Genteel are reduced to poverty, and forced to borrow of those whom they formerly despised, but who through Industry and Frugality have maintained their Standing; in which Case it appears plainly, that A Ploughman on his Legs is higher than a Gentleman on his Knees, as Poor Richard says. Perhaps they have had a small Estate left them, which they knew not the Getting of; they think, 'tis Day, and will never be Night; that a little to be spent out of so much, is not worth minding; A Child and a Fool, as Poor Richard says, imagine Twenty shillings and Twenty Years can never be spent but, always taking out of the Meal-tub, and never putting in, soon comes to the Bottom; as Poor Dick says, When the Well's dry, they know the Worth of Water. But this they might have known before, if they had taken his Advice; If you would know the Value of Money, go and try to borrow some; for, he that goes a borrowing goes a sorrowing; and indeed so does he that lends to such People, when he goes to get it in again. Poor Dick farther advises, and says,

> Fond Pride of Dress is sure a very Curse;
> E'er Fancy you consult, consult your Purse.

And again, Pride is as loud a Beggar as Want, and a great deal more saucy. When you have bought one fine Thing, you must buy ten more, that your Appearance may be all of a Piece; but Poor Dick says, 'Tis easier to suppress the first Desire, than to satisfy all that follow it. And 'tis as truly Folly for the Poor to ape the Rich, as for the Frog to swell, in order to equal the ox.

> Great Estates may venture more,
> But little Boats should keep near Shore.

'Tis, however, a Folly soon punished; for Pride that dines on Vanity, sups on Contempt, as Poor Richard says. And in another Place, Pride breakfasted with Plenty, dined with Poverty, and supped with Infamy. And after all, of what Use is this Pride of Appearance, for which so much is risked so much is suffered? It cannot promote Health, or ease Pain; it makes no Increase of Merit in the Person, it creates Envy, it hastens Misfortune.

> What is a Butterfly? At best
> He's but a Caterpillar dressed
> The gaudy Fop's his Picture just,

as Poor Richard says.

But what Madness must it be to run in Debt for these Superfluities! We are offered, by the Terms of this Vendue, Six Months' Credit; and that perhaps has induced some of us to attend it, because we cannot spare the ready Money, and hope now to be fine without it. But, ah, think what you do when you run in Debt; you give to another Power over your Liberty. If you cannot pay at the Time, you will be ashamed to see your Creditor; you will be in Fear when you speak to him; you will make poor pitiful sneaking Excuses, and by Degrees come to lose your Veracity, and sink into base downright lying; for, as Poor Richard says, The second Vice is Lying, the first is running in Debt. And again, to the same Purpose, Lying rides upon Debt's Back. Whereas a free-born Englishman ought not to be ashamed or afraid to see or speak to any Man living. But Poverty often deprives a Man of all Spirit and Virtue: 'Tis hard for an empty Bag to stand upright, as Poor Richard truly says.

What would you think of that Prince, or that Government, who should issue an Edict forbidding you to dress like a Gentleman or a Gentlewoman, on Pain of Imprisonment or Servitude? Would you not say, that you were free, have a Right to dress as you please, and that such an Edict would be a Breach of your Privileges, and such a Government tyrannical? And yet you are about to put yourself under that Tyranny, when you run in Debt for such Dress! Your Creditor has Authority, at his Pleasure to deprive you of your Liberty, by confining you in Gaol for Life, or to sell you for a Servant, if you should not be able to pay him! When you have got your Bargain, you may, perhaps, think little of Payment; but Creditors, Poor Richard tells us, have better Memories than Debtors; and in another Place says, Creditors are a superstitious Sect, great Observers of set Days and Times. The Day comes round before you are aware, and the Demand is made before you are prepared to satisfy it, Or if you bear your Debt in Mind, the Term which at first seemed so long, will, as it lessens, appear extremely short. Time will seem to have added Wings to his Heels as well as Shoulders. Those have a short Lent, saith Poor Richard, who owe Money to be paid at Easter. Then since, as he says, The Borrower is a Slave to the Lender, and the Debtor to the Creditor, disdain the Chain, preserve your Freedom; and maintain your Independency: Be industrious and free; be frugal and free. At present, perhaps, you may think yourself in thriving Circumstances, and that you can bear a little Extravagance without Injury; but,

> For Age and Want, save while you may;
> No Morning Sun lasts a whole Day,

as Poor Richard says. Gain may be temporary and uncertain, but ever while you live, Expense is constant and certain; and 'tis easier to build two Chimneys, than to keep one in Fuel, as Poor Richard says. So, Rather go to Bed supperless than rise in Debt.

> Get what you can, and what you get hold;
> 'Tis the Stone that will turn all your lead into Gold,

as Poor Richard says. And when you have got the Philosopher's Stone, sure you will no longer complain of bad Times, or the Difficulty of paying Taxes.

This Doctrine, my Friends, is Reason and Wisdom; but after all, do not depend too much upon your own Industry, and Frugality, and Prudence, though excellent Things, for they may all be blasted without the Blessing of Heaven; and therefore, ask that Blessing humbly, and be not uncharitable to those that at present seem to want it, but comfort and help them. Remember, Job suffered, and was afterwards prosperous.

And now to conclude, Experience keeps a dear School, but Fools will learn in no other, and scarce in that; for it is true, we may give Advice, but we cannot give Conduct, as Poor Richard says: However, remember this, They that won't be counselled, can't be helped, as Poor Richard says: and farther, That, if you will not hear Reason, she'll surely rap your knuckles.'

Thus the old Gentleman ended his Harangue. The People heard it, and approved the Doctrine, and immediately practised the contrary, just as if it had been a common Sermon; for the Vendue opened, and they began to buy extravagantly, notwithstanding, his Cautions and their own Fear of Taxes. I found the good Man had thoroughly studied my Almanacs, and digested all I had dropped on these Topics during the Course of Five and twenty Years. The frequent Mention he made of me must have tired anyone else, but my Vanity was wonderfully delighted with it, though I was conscious that not a tenth Part of the Wisdom was my own, which he ascribed to me, but rather the Gleanings I had made of the Sense of all Ages and Nations. However, I resolved to be the better for the Echo of it; and though I had at first determined to buy Stuff for a new Coat, I went away resolved to wear my old One a little longer. Reader, if thou wilt do the same, thy Profit will be as great as mine. I am, as ever, thine to serve thee,

RICHARD SAUNDERS
July 7th, 1757

On the Price of Corn, and Management of the Poor

To the Public

I am one of that class of people, that feeds you all, and at present is abused by you all; in short I am a *farmer*.

By your newspapers we are told, that God had sent a very short harvest to some other countries of Europe. I thought this might be in favour of Old England; and that now we should get a good price for our grain, which would bring millions among us, and make us flow in money; that to be sure is scarce enough.

But the wisdom of government forbade the exportation.

'Well,' says I, 'then we must be content with the market price at home.'

'No'; say my lords the mob, 'you sha'nt have that. Bring your corn to market if you dare; we'll sell it for you for less money, or take it for nothing.'

Being thus attacked by both ends *of the constitution*, the head and tail *of government*, what am I to do?

Must I keep my corn in the barn, to feed and increase the breed of rats? Be it so; they cannot be less thankful than those I have been used to feed.

Are we farmers the only people to be grudged the profits of our honest labour? And why? One of the late scribblers against us gives a bill of fare of the provisions at my daughter's wedding, and proclaims to all the world, that we had the insolence to eat beef and pudding! Has he not read the precept in the good Book, *Thou shalt not muzzle the mouth of the ox that treadeth out the corn*; or does he think us less worthy of good living than our oxen?

'O, but the manufacturers! the manufacturers! they are to be favoured, and they must have bread at a cheap rate!'

Hark ye, Mr Oaf; the farmers live splendidly, you say. And pray, would you have them hoard the money they get? Their fine clothes and furniture, do they make them themselves, or for one another, and so keep the money among them? Or do they employ these your darling manufacturers, and so scatter it again all over the nation?

The wool would produce me a better price, if it were suffered to go to foreign markets; but that, Messieurs the Public, your laws will not permit. It must be kept all at home, that our *dear* manufacturers may have it the cheaper. And then, having yourselves thus lessened our encouragement for raising sheep, you curse us for the scarcity of mutton!

I have heard my grandfather say, that the farmers submitted to the prohibition on the exportation of wool, being made to expect and believe, that, when the manufacturer bought his wool cheaper, they should also have their cloth cheaper. But the deuce a bit. It has been growing dearer and dearer from that day to this. How so? Why, truly, the cloth is exported; and that keeps up the price.

Now, if it be a good principle, that the exportation of a commodity is to be restrained, that so our people at home may have it the cheaper, stick to that principle, and go thorough-stitch with it. Prohibit the exportation of your cloth, your leather, and shoes, your iron ware, and your manufactures of all sorts, to make them all cheaper at home. And cheap enough they will be, I will warrant you; till people leave off making them.

Some folks seem to think they ought never to be easy till England becomes another Lubberland, where it is fancied that streets are paved with penny-rolls, the houses tiled with pancakes, and chickens, ready roasted, cry, 'Come eat me.'

I say, when you are sure you have got a good principle, stick to it, and carry it through. I hear it is said, that though it was *necessary and right* for the ministry to advise a prohibition of the exportation of corn, yet it was *contrary to law;* and also, that though it was *contrary to law* for the mob to obstruct wagons, yet it was *necessary and right.* Just the same thing to a tittle. Now they tell me, an act of indemnity ought to pass in favour of the ministry, to secure them from the consequences of having acted illegally. If so, pass another in favour of the mob. Others say, some of mob ought to be hanged, by way of example. If so – but I say no more than I have said before, *when you are sure that you have a good principle, go through with it.*

You say, poor labourers cannot afford to buy bread at a high price, unless they had higher wages. Possibly. But how shall we farmers be able to afford our labourers higher wages, if you will not allow us to get, when we might have it, a higher price for our corn?

By all that I can learn, we should at least have had a guinea a quarter more, if the exportation had been allowed. And this money England would have got from foreigners.

But, it seems, we farmers must take so much less, that the poor may have it so much cheaper.

This operates, then, as a tax for the maintenance of the poor. A very good thing you will say. But I ask, Why, a partial tax? why laid on us farmers only? If it be a good thing, pray, Messieurs the Public, take your share of it, by indemnifying us a little out of your public treasury. In doing a good thing, there is both honour and pleasure; you are welcome to your share of both.

For my own part, I am not so well satisfied of the goodness of this thing. I am for doing good to the poor, but I differ in opinion about the means. I think the best way of doing good to the poor, is, not making them easy *in* poverty, but leading or driving them *out* of it. In my youth, I travelled much, and I observed in different countries, that the more public provisions were made for the poor, the less they provided for themselves, and of course became poorer. And, on the contrary, the less was done for them, the more they did for themselves, and became richer. There is no country in the world where so many provisions are established for them; so many hospitals to receive them when they are sick or lame, founded and maintained by voluntary charities; so many almshouses for the aged of both sexes, together with a solemn general law made by the rich to subject their estates to a heavy tax for the support of the poor. Under all these obligations, are our poor modest, humble, and thankful? And do they use their best endeavours to maintain themselves, and lighten our shoulders of this burthen? On the contrary, I affirm, that there is no country in the world in which the poor are more idle, dissolute, drunken, and insolent. The day you passed that act, you took away from before their eyes the greatest of all inducements to industry, frugality, and sobriety, by giving them a dependence on somewhat else than a careful accumulation during youth and health, for support in age or sickness.

In short, you offered a premium for the encouragement of idleness, and you should not now wonder, that it has had its effect in the increase of poverty. Repeal that law, and you will soon see a change in their manners. *Saint Monday* and *Saint Tuesday* will soon cease to be holidays. Six *days shalt thou labour*, though one of the old commandments long treated as out of date, will again be looked upon as a respectable precept; industry will increase, and with it plenty among the lower people; their circumstances will mend, and more will be done for their happiness by inuring them to provide for themselves, than could be done by dividing all your estates among them.

Excuse me, Messieurs the Public, if, upon this *interesting* subject, I put you to the trouble of reading a little of *my* nonsense. I am sure I have lately read a great deal of *yours*, and therefore from you (at least from those of you who are writers) I deserve a little indulgence.

I am yours, etc.,

ARATOR

Advice to a Young Tradesman [1748]

To My Friend, A. B. – As you have desired it of me, I write the following hints, which have been of service to me, and may, if observed, be so to you.

Remember, that *time* is money. He that can earn ten shillings a day by his labour, and goes abroad, or sits idle, one half of that day, though he spends but sixpence during his diversion or idleness, ought not to reckon *that* the only expense; he has really spent, or rather thrown away, five shillings besides.

Remember, that *credit* is money. If a man lets his money lie in my hands after it is due, he gives me the interest, or so much as I can make of it during that time. This amounts to a considerable sum where a man has good and large credit, and makes good use of it.

Remember, that money is of the prolific, generating nature. Money can beget money, and its offspring can beget more, and so on. Five shillings turned is six, turned again it is seven and three-pence, and so on till it becomes an hundred pounds. The more there is of it, the more it produces every turning, so that the profits rise quicker and quicker. He that kills a breeding sow, destroys all her offspring to the thousandth generation. He that murders a crown, destroys all that it might have produced, even scores of pounds.

Remember, that six pounds a year is but a groat a day. For this little sum (which may be daily wasted either in time or expense unperceived) a man of credit may, on his own security, have the constant possession and use of an hundred pounds. So much in stock, briskly turned by an industrious man, produces great advantage.

Remember this saying, *The good paymaster is lord of another man's purse*. He that is known to pay punctually and exactly to the time he promises, may at any time, and on any occasion, raise all the money his friends can spare. This is sometimes of great use. After industry and frugality, nothing contributes more to the raising of a young man in the world than punctuality and justice in all his dealings; therefore never keep borrowed money an hour beyond the time you promised, lest a disappointment shut up your friend's purse for ever.

The most trifling actions that affect a man's credit are to be regarded. The sound of your hammer at five in the morning, or nine at night, heard by a creditor, makes him easy six months longer; but, if he sees you at a billiard-table, or hears your voice at a tavern, when you should be at work, he sends for his money the next day; demands it, before he can receive it, in a lump.

It shows, besides, that you are mindful of what you owe; it makes you appear a careful as well as an honest man, and that still increases your credit.

Beware of thinking all your own that you possess, and of living accordingly. It is a mistake that many people who have credit fall into. To prevent this, keep an exact account for some time, both of your expenses and your income. If you take the pains at first to mention particulars, it will have this good effect: you will discover how wonderfully small, trifling expenses mount up to large sums, and will discern what might have been, and may for the future be saved, without occasioning any great inconvenience.

In short, the way to wealth, if you desire it, is as plain as the way to market. It depends chiefly on two words, *industry* and *frugality*; that is, waste neither *time* nor *money*, but make the best use of both. Without industry and frugality nothing will do, and with them everything. He that gets all he can honestly, and saves all he gets (necessary expenses excepted), will certainly become *rich*, if that Being who governs the world, to whom all should look for a blessing on their honest endeavours, doth not, in his wise providence, otherwise determine.

AN OLD TRADESMAN

*Journal of a Voyage from London to Philadelphia (LC)**

Journal of Occurrences in my Voyage to Philadelphia on board the Berkshire, *Henry Clark, Master, from London*

Friday, July 22nd, 1726 – Yesterday in the afternoon we left London, and came to an anchor off Gravesend about eleven at night. I lay ashore all night, and this morning took a walk up to the Windmill Hill, from whence I had an agreeable prospect of the country for above twenty miles round, and two or three reaches of the river, with ships and boats sailing both up and down, and Tilbury Fort on the other side, which commands the river and passage to London. This Gravesend is a *cursed biting* place; the chief dependence of the people being the advantage they make of imposing upon strangers. If you buy anything of them, and give half what they ask, you pay twice as much as the thing is worth. Thank God, we shall leave it tomorrow.

Saturday, July 23rd – This day we weighed anchor and fell down with the tide, there being little or no wind. In the afternoon we had a fresh gale, that brought us down to Margate, where we shall lie at anchor this night. Most of the passengers are very sick. Saw several porpoisies, etc.

Sunday, July 24th – This morning we weighed anchor, and coming to the Downs, we set our pilot ashore at Deal, and passed through. And now, whilst I write this, sitting upon the quarterdeck, I have methinks one of the pleasantest scenes in the world before me. 'Tis a fine, clear day, and we are going away before the wind with an easy, pleasant gale. We have near fifteen sail of ships in sight, and I may say in company. On the left hand appears the coast of France at a distance, and on the right is the town and castle of Dover, with the green hills and chalky cliffs of England, to which we must now bid farewell. Albion, farewell!

---

* From a transcript in the Library of Congress.

Monday, July 25th – All the morning calm. After noon sprung up a gale at East; blew very hard all night. Saw the isle of Wight at a distance.

Tuesday, July 26th – Contrary winds all day, blowing pretty hard. Saw the Isle of Wight again in the evening.

Wednesday, July 27th – This morning, the wind blowing very hard at West, we stood in for the land, in order to make some harbour. About noon we took on board a pilot out of a fishing shallop, who brought the ship into Spithead off Portsmouth. The captain, Mr Denham, and myself went on shore, and, during the little time we stayed, I made some observations on the place.

Portsmouth has a fine harbour. The entrance is so narrow that you may throw a stone from Fort to Fort; yet it is near ten fathom deep, and bold close to; but within there is room enough for five hundred, or, for aught I know, a thousand sail of ships. The town is strongly fortified, being encompassed with a high wall and a deep and broad ditch, and two gates, that are entered over drawbridges; besides several forts, batteries of large cannon, and other outworks, the names of which I know not, nor had I time to take so strict a view as to be able to describe them. In war time, the town has a garrison of 10,000 men; but at present 'tis only manned by about 100 Invalids. Notwithstanding the English have so many fleets of men-of-war at sea at this time, I counted in this harbour above thirty sail of 2nd, 3rd, and 4th Rates, that lay by unrigged, but easily fitted out upon occasion, all their masts and rigging lying marked and numbered in storehouses at hand. The King's yards and docks employ abundance of men, who, even in peace time, are constantly building and refitting men-of-war for the King's Service.

Gosport lies opposite to Portsmouth, and is near as big, if not bigger; but, except the fort at the mouth of the harbour, and a small outwork before the main street of the town, it is only defended by a mud wall, which surrounds it, and a trench or dry ditch of about ten feet depth and breadth. Portsmouth is a place of very little trade in peace time; it depending chiefly on fitting out men-of-war. Spithead is the place where the Fleet commonly anchor, and is a very good riding-place. The people of Portsmouth tell strange stories of the severity of one *Gibson*,* who was governor of this place in the Queen's time, to his soldiers, and show you a miserable dungeon by the town gate, which they call *Johnny Gibson's Hole*, where, for trifling misdemeanours, he

* Sir John Gibson (1637–1717) was lieutenant-governor of Portsmouth, 1689–1717. – Ed.

used to confine his soldiers till they were almost starved to death. It is a common maxim, that, without severe discipline, 'tis impossible to govern the licentious rabble of soldiery. I own, indeed, that if a commander finds he has not those qualities in him that will make him beloved by his people, he ought, by all means, to make use of such methods as will make them fear him, since one or the other (or both) is absolutely necessary; but Alexander and Cæsar, those renowned generals, received more faithful service, and performed greater actions, by means of the love their soldiers bore them, than they could possibly have done, if, instead of being beloved and respected, they had been hated and feared by those they commanded.

Thursday, July 28th – This morning we came on board, having lain on shore all night. We weighed anchor and with a moderate gale, stood in for Cowes, in the Isle of Wight, and came to an anchor before the town about eleven o'clock. Six of the passengers went on shore, and diverted themselves till about 12 at night; and then got a boat, and came on board again, expecting to sail early in the morning.

Friday, July 29th – But the wind continuing adverse still, we went ashore again this morning, and took a walk to Newport, which is about four miles distant from Cowes, and is the metropolis of the island. Thence we walked to Carisbrooke, about a mile further, out of curiosity to see that castle, which King Charles the First was confined in; and so returned to Cowes in the afternoon, and went on board in expectation of sailing.

Cowes is but a small town, and lies close to the seaside, pretty near opposite to Southampton on the main shore of England. It is divided into two parts by a small river that runs up within a quarter of a mile of Newport, and is distinguished by East and West Cowes. There is a fort built in an oval form, on which there are eight or ten guns mounted for the defence of the road. They have a post-office, a custom-house, and a chapel of ease. And a good harbour for ships to ride in in easterly and westerly winds.

All this afternoon I spent agreeably enough at the draft-board. It is a game I much delight in; but it requires a clear head, and undisturbed; and the persons playing, if they would play well, ought not much to regard the *consequence* of the game, for that diverts and withdraws the attention of the mind from the game itself, and makes the player liable to make many false open moves; and I will venture to lay it down for an infallible rule, that, if two persons *equal* in judgement play for a considerable sum, he that loves money most shall lose; his anxiety for the success of the game confounds him. Courage is almost as requisite for the good conduct of this game as in a real battle; for, if the player imagines himself opposed by one that is much his superior in skill, his mind is so intent on the defensive part, that an advantage passes unobserved.

Newport makes a pretty prospect enough from the hills that surround it; (for it lies down in a bottom). The houses are beautifully intermixed with trees, and a tall, old-fashioned steeple rises in the midst of the town, which is very ornamental to it. The name of the church I could not learn; but there is a very neat market-house, paved with square stone, and consisting of eleven arches. There are several pretty handsome streets, and many well-built houses and shops, well stored with goods. But I think Newport is chiefly remarkable for oysters, which they send to London and other places, where they are very much esteemed, being thought the best in England. The oyster-merchants fetch them, as I am informed, from other places, and lay them upon certain beds in the river (the water of which is it seems excellently adapted for that purpose) a-fattening; and when they have lain a suitable time they are taken up again, and made fit for sale.

When we came to Carisbrooke, which, as I said before, is a little village about a mile beyond Newport, we took a view of an ancient church that had formerly been a priory in Romish times, and is the first church, or the mother-church, of the island. It is an elegant building, after the old Gothic manner, with a very high tower, and looks very venerable in its ruins. There are several ancient monuments about it; but the stone of which they are composed is of such a soft, crumbling nature, that the inscriptions are none of them legible. Of the same stone are almost all the tombstones, etc., that I observed in the island.

From this church (having crossed over the brook that gives the name to the village, and got a little boy for a guide), we went up a very steep hill, through several narrow lanes and avenues, till we came to the castle gate. We entered over the ditch (which is now almost filled up, partly by the ruins of the mouldering walls that have tumbled into it, and partly by the washing down of the earth from the hill by the rains), upon a couple of brick arches, where I suppose formerly there was a drawbridge. An old woman who lives in the castle, seeing us strangers walk about, sent and offered to show us the rooms if we pleased, which we accepted. This castle, as she informed us, has for many years been the seat of the governors of the island; and the rooms and hall, which are very large and handsome, with high, arched roofs, have all along been kept handsomely furnished, every succeeding governor buying the furniture of his predecessor; but, Cadogan, the last governor, who succeeded General Webb,* refusing to purchase it, Webb stripped it clear of all, even the hangings, and left nothing but bare walls. The floors are several of them of plaster of Paris, the art of making which, the woman told us, was now lost.

The castle stands upon a very high and steep hill, and there are the remains of a deep ditch round it; the walls are thick, and seemingly well contrived; and certainly it has been a very strong hold in its time, at least before the invention of great guns. There are several breaches in the ruinous walls, which are never repaired (I suppose they are purposely neglected), and the ruins are almost everywhere overspread with ivy. It is divided into the lower and the upper castle, the lower enclosing the upper, which is of a round form, and stands upon a promontory, to which you must ascend by near an hundred stone steps; this upper castle was designed for a retreat in case the lower castle should be won, and is the least ruinous of any part except the stairs before mentioned, which are so broken and decayed, that I was almost afraid to come down again when I was up, they being but narrow, and no rails to hold by.

From the battlements of this upper castle (which they call the *Coop*), you have a fine prospect of the greatest part of the island, of the sea on one side, of Cowes road at a distance, and of Newport as it were just below you. There is a well in the middle of the Coop, which they called the bottomless well, because of its great depth; but it is now half filled up with stones and rubbish, and is covered with two or three loose planks; yet a stone, as we tried, is near a quarter of a minute in falling before you hear it strike. But the well that supplies the inhabitants at present with water is in the lower castle, and is thirty fathoms deep. They draw their water with a great wheel, and with a bucket that holds near a barrel. It makes a great sound if you speak in it, and echoed the flute which we played over it very sweetly. There are but seven pieces of ordnance mounted upon the walls, and those in no very good order; and the old man, who is the gunner and keeper of the castle, and who sells ale in a little house at the gate, has in his possession but six muskets (which hang up at his wall) and one of them wants a lock. He told us that the castle, which had now been built 1203 years, was first founded by one Whitgert, a Saxon, who conquered the island, and that it was called Whitgertsburg for many ages.

* General John Richmond Webbe was governor of the Isle of Wight 1710 to 1716. He was succeeded by William, first Earl Cadogan. – ED.

That particular piece of building, which King Charles lodged in during his confinement here, is suffered to go entirely to ruin, there being nothing standing but the walls. The island is about sixty miles in circumference, and produces plenty of corn and other provisions, and wool as fine as Cotswold; its militia having the credit of equalling the soldiery, and being the best disciplined in England. — was once, in King William's time, entrusted with the government of this island. At his death it appeared he was a great villain, and a great politician; there was no crime so damnable which he would stick at in the execution of his designs, and yet he had the art of covering all so thick, that with almost all men in general, while he lived, he passed for a saint. What surprised me was, that the silly old fellow, the keeper of the castle, who remembered him governor, should have so true a notion of his character as I perceived he had. In short, I believe it is impossible for a man, though he has all the cunning of a devil, to live and die a villain, and yet conceal it so well as to carry the name of an honest fellow to the grave with him, but someone, by some accident or other, shall discover him. Truth and sincerity have a certain distinguishing native lustre about them, which cannot be perfectly counterfeited; they are like fire and flame, that cannot be painted.

The whole castle was repaired and beautified by Queen Elizabeth, and strengthened by a breastwork all round without the walls, as appears by this inscription in one or two places upon it.

1598
E. R.
40

Saturday, July 30th – This morning about eight o'clock we weighed anchor, and turned to windward till we came to Yarmouth, another little town upon this island, and there cast anchor again, the wind blowing hard, and still westerly. Yarmouth is a smaller town than Cowes; yet, the buildings being better, it makes a handsomer prospect at a distance, and the streets are clean and neat. There is one monument in the church, which the inhabitants are very proud of, and which we went to see. It was erected to the memory of Sir Robert Holmes,* who had formerly been governor of the island. It is his statue in armour, somewhat bigger than the life, standing on his tomb, with a

* Sir Robert Holmes (1622–1692) was governor of the Isle of Wight from 1668 to his death.

truncheon in his hand, between two pillars of porphyry. Indeed, all the marble about it is very fine and good; and they say it was designed by the French King for his palace at Versailles, but was cast away upon this island, and by Sir Robert himself in his lifetime applied to this use, and that the whole monument was finished long before he died; (though not fixed up in that place) the inscription likewise (which is very much to his honour) being written by himself. One would think either that he had no defect at all, or had a very ill opinion of the world, seeing he was so careful to make sure of a monument to record his good actions and transmit them to posterity.

Having taken a view of the church, town, and fort, on which there are seven large guns mounted, three of us took a walk up further into the island; and, having gone about two miles, we headed a creek that runs up one end of the town, and then went to Freshwater Church, about a mile nearer the town, but on the other side of the creek. Having stayed here some time it grew dark, and my companions were desirous to be gone, lest those whom we had left drinking where we dined in the town should go on board and leave us. We were told, that it was our best way to go straight down to the mouth of the creek, and that there was a ferry boy that would carry us over to the town. But when we came to the house the lazy whelp was in bed, and refused to rise and put us over; upon which we went down to the waterside, with a design to take his boat, and go over by ourselves. We found it very difficult to get the boat, it being fastened to a stake, and the tide risen near fifty yards beyond it; I stripped all to my shirt to wade up to it; but missing the causeway, which was under water, I got up to my middle in mud. At last I came to the stake; but, to my great disappointment, found she was locked and chained. I endeavoured to draw the staple with one of the thole-pins, but in vain; I tried to pull up the stake, but to no purpose; so that, after an hour's fatigue and trouble in the wet and mud, I was forced to return without the boat.

We had no money in our pockets, and therefore began to conclude to pass the night in some haystack, though the wind blew very cold and very hard. In the midst of these troubles one of us recollected that he had a horse-shoe in his pocket, which he found in his walk, and asked me if I could not wrench the staple out with that. I took it, went, tried, and succeeded, and brought the boat ashore to them. Now we rejoiced and all got in, and, when I had dressed myself, we put off. But the worst of all our troubles was to come yet; for, it being high water and the tide over all the banks, though it was moonlight we could not discern the channel of the creek; but, rowing heedlessly straight forward, when we were got about half way over, we found ourselves aground on a mud bank; and, striving to row her off by putting our oars in the mud, we broke one and there stuck fast, not having four inches water. We were now in the utmost perplexity, not knowing what in the world to do; we could not tell whether the tide was rising or falling; but at length we plainly perceived it was ebb, and we could feel no deeper water within the reach of our oar.

It was hard to lie in an open boat all night exposed to the wind and weather; but it was worse to think how foolish we should look in the morning, when the owner of the boat should catch us in that condition, where we must be exposed to the view of all the town. After we had strove and struggled for half an hour and more, we gave all over, and sat down with our hands before us, despairing to get off; for, if the tide had left us, we had been never the nearer; we must have sat in the boat, as the mud was too deep for us to walk ashore through it, being up to our necks. At last we bethought ourselves of some means of escaping, and two of us stripped and got out, and thereby lightening the boat, we drew her up upon our knees near fifty yards into deeper water; and then with much ado, having but one oar, we got safe ashore under the fort; and, having dressed ourselves and tied the man's boat, we went with great joy to the Queen's Head, where we left our companions, whom we found waiting for us, though it was very late. Our boat being gone on board, we were obliged to lie ashore all night; and thus ended our walk.

Sunday, July 31st – This morning the wind being moderated, our pilot designed to weigh, and, taking advantage of the tide, get a little further to windward. Upon which the boat came ashore, to hasten us on board. We had no sooner returned and hoisted in our boat, but the wind began again to blow very hard at west, insomuch that, instead of going any further, we were obliged to weigh and run down again to Cowes for the sake of more secure riding, where we came to an anchor again in a very little time; and the pudding, which our mess made and put into the pot at Yarmouth, we dined upon at Cowes.

Monday, August 1st – This morning all the vessels in the harbour put out their colours in honour of the day, and it made a very pretty appearance. The wind continuing to blow hard westerly, our mess resolved to go on shore, though all our loose corks were gone already. We took with us some goods to dispose of, and walked to Newport to make our market, where we sold for three shillings in the pound less than the prime cost in London; and, having dined at Newport, we returned in the evening to Cowes, and concluded to lodge on shore.

Tuesday, August 2nd – This day we passed on shore, diverting ourselves as well as we could; and, the wind continuing still westerly, we stayed on shore this night also.

Wednesday, August 3rd – This morning we were hurried on board, having scarce time to dine, weighed anchor, and stood away for Yarmouth again, though the wind is still westerly; but, meeting with a hoy when we were near halfway there, that had some goods on board for us to take in, we tacked about for Cowes, and came to anchor there a third time, about four in the afternoon.

Thursday, August 4th – Stayed on board till about five in the afternoon, and then went on shore and stopped all night.

Friday, August 5th – Called up this morning and hurried aboard, the wind being Northwest. About noon we weighed and left Cowes a third time, and, sailing by Yarmouth, we came into the channel through the Needles; which passage is guarded by Hurst Castle, standing on a spit of Land which runs out from the main land of England within a mile of the Isle of Wight. Towards night the wind veered to the Westward, which put us under apprehensions of being forced into port again: but presently after it fell a flat calm, and then we had a small breeze that was fair for half an hour, when it was succeeded by a calm again.

Saturday, August 6th – This morning we had a fair breeze for some hours, and then a calm that lasted all day. In the afternoon I leaped overboard and swam round the ship to wash myself. Saw several porpoises this day. About eight o'clock we came to an anchor in forty fathom water against the tide of flood, somewhere below Portland, and weighed again about eleven, having a small breeze.

Sunday, August 7th – Gentle breezes all this day. Spoke with a ship, the Ruby, bound for London from Nevis, off the Start of Plymouth. This afternoon spoke with Captain Homans in a ship bound for Boston, who came out of the river when we did, and had been beating about in the channel all the time we lay at Cowes in *the Wight*.

Monday, August 8th – Fine weather, but no wind worth mentioning, all this day; in the afternoon saw the Lizard.

Tuesday, August 9th – Took our leave of the land this morning. Calms the fore part of the day. In the afternoon a small gale; fair. Saw a Grampus.

Wednesday, August 10th – Wind N. W. Course S. W. about four Knots.

By observation in latitude 48° 50'. Nothing remarkable happened.

Thursday, August 11th – Nothing remarkable. Fresh gale all day.

Friday, August 12th; Saturday, 13th; Sunday, 14th – Calms and fair breezes alternately.

Monday, 15th; Tuesday, 16th; Wednesday, 17th – No contrary winds, but calm and fair breezes alternately.

Thursday, August 18th – Four dolphins followed the ship for some hours; we struck at them with the fizgig, but took none.

Friday, August 19th – This day we have had a pleasant breeze at East. In the morning we spied a sail upon our larboard bow, about two leagues' distance. About noon she put out English colours, and we answered with our ensign, and in the afternoon we spoke with her. She was a ship, of New York, Walter Kippen, master, bound from Rochelle, in France, to Boston, with salt. Our captain and Mr — went on board, and stayed till evening, it being fine weather. Yesterday, complaints being made that Mr G—n, one of the passengers, had, with a fraudulent design, marked the cards, a court of justice was called immediately, and he was brought to his trial in form. A Dutchman, who could speak no English, deposed by his interpreter that, when our mess was on shore at Cowes, the prisoner at the bar marked all the Court cards on the back with a pen.

I have sometimes observed, that we are apt to fancy the person that cannot speak intelligibly to us, proportionably stupid in understanding, and, when we speak two or three words of English to a foreigner, it is louder than ordinary, as if we thought him deaf, and that he had lost the use of his ears as well as his tongue. Something like this I imagine might be the case of Mr G—n; he fancied the Dutchman could not see what he was about, because he could not understand English, and therefore boldly did it before his face.

The evidence was plain and positive; the prisoner could not deny the fact, but replied in his defence, that the cards he marked were not those we commonly played with, but an imperfect pack, which he afterwards gave to the cabin-boy. The attorney-general observed to the court, that it was not likely he should take the pains to mark the cards without some ill design, or some further intention than just to give them to the boy when he had done, who understood nothing at all of cards. But another evidence being called deposed that he saw the prisoner in the main-top one day, when he thought himself unobserved, marking a pack of cards on the backs, some with the print of a dirty thumb, others with the top of his finger, etc. Now, there being but two packs on board, and the prisoner having just confessed the marking of one, the Court perceived the case was plain. In fine the jury brought him in guilty, and he was condemned to be carried up to the round-top, and made fast there, in view of all the ship's company, during the space of three hours, that being the place where the act was committed, and to pay a fine of two bottles of brandy. But the prisoner resisting authority and refusing to submit to punishment, one of the sailors stepped up aloft and let down a rope to us, which we, with much struggling, made fast about his middle, and hoisted him up into the air, sprawling, by main force. We let him hang, cursing and swearing, for near a quarter of an hour; but at length, he crying out Murder! and looking black in the face, the rope being overtaut about his middle, we thought proper to let him down again; and our mess have excommunicated him till he pays his fine, refusing either to play, eat, drink, or converse with him.

Saturday, August 20th – We shortened sail all last night and all this day, to keep company with the other ship. About noon Captain Kippen and one of his passengers came on board and dined with us; they stayed till evening. When they were gone, we made sail and left them.

Sunday, August 21st – This morning we lost sight of the Yorker, having a brisk gale of wind at East. Towards night a poor little bird came on board us, being almost tired to death, and suffered itself to be taken by the hand. We reckon ourselves near two hundred leagues from land, so that no doubt a little rest was very acceptable to the unfortunate wanderer, who 'tis like, was blown off the coast in thick weather, and could not find its way back again. We receive it hospitably, and tender it victuals and drink; but he refuses both, and I suppose will not live long. There was one came on board some days ago, in the same circumstances with this, which I think the cat destroyed.

Monday, August 22nd – This morning I saw several flying-fish, but they were small. A favourable wind all day.

Tuesday, August 23rd; Wednesday, 24th – Fair winds, nothing remarkable.

Thursday, August 25th – Our excommunicated shipmate thinking proper to comply with the sentence the court passed upon him, and expressing himself willing to pay the fine, we have this morning received him into unity again. Man is a sociable being, and it is, for aught I know, one of the worst of punishments to be excluded from

Society. I have read abundance of fine things on the subject of solitude, and I know 'tis a common boast in the mouths of those that affect to be thought wise, *that they are never less alone than when alone*. I acknowledge solitude an agreeable refreshment to a busy mind; but were these thinking people obliged to be always alone, I am apt to think they would quickly find their very being insupportable to them. I have heard of a gentleman, who underwent seven years' close confinement, in the Bastille, at Paris. He was a man of sense, he was a thinking man, but being deprived of all conversation, to what purpose should he think; for he was denied even the instruments of expressing his thoughts in writing. There is no burden so grievous to man as time that he knows not how to dispose of. He was forced at last to have recourse to this invention; he daily scattered pieces of paper about the floor of his little room, and then employed himself in picking them up again and sticking them in rows and figures on the arm of his elbow-chair; and he used to tell his friends, after his release, that he verily believed, if he had not taken this method he should have lost his senses. One of the philosophers, I think it was Plato, used to say, that he had rather be the veriest stupid block in nature, than the possessor of all knowledge without some intelligent being to communicate it to.

What I have said may in a measure account for some particulars in my present way of living here on board. Our company is in general very unsuitably mixed, to keep up the pleasure and spirit of conversation: and, if there are one or two pair of us that can sometimes entertain one another for half an hour agreeably, yet perhaps we are seldom in the humour for it together. I rise in the morning and read for an hour or two, perhaps, and then reading grows tiresome. Want of exercise occasions want of appetite, so that eating and drinking afford but little pleasure. I tire myself with playing at Draughts, then I go to cards; nay, there is no play so trifling or childish, but we fly to it for entertainment. A contrary wind, I know not how, puts us all out of good humour; we grow sullen, silent, and reserved, and fret at each other upon every little occasion. 'Tis a common opinion among the ladies, that if a man is ill-natured he infallibly discovers it when he is in liquor. But I who have known many instances to the contrary, will teach them a more effectual method to discover the natural temper and disposition of their humble servants. Let the ladies make one long sea-voyage with them, and, if they have the least spark of ill-nature in them, and conceal it to the end of the voyage, I will forfeit all my pretensions to their favour. The wind continues fair.

Friday, August 26th – The wind and weather fair till night came on; and then the wind came about, and we had hard squalls, with rain and lightning, till morning.

Saturday, August 27th – Cleared up this morning, and the wind settled westerly. Two dolphins followed us this afternoon; we hooked one, and struck the other with the fizgig; but they both escaped us, and we saw them no more.

Sunday, August 28th – The wind still continues westerly, and blows hard. We are under a reefed mainsail and foresail.

Monday, August 29th – Wind still hard west. Two dolphins followed us this day; but we struck at them, but they both escaped.

Tuesday, August 30th – Contrary wind still. This evening, the moon being near full, as she rose after eight o'clock, there appeared a rainbow in a western cloud, to windward of us. The first time I ever saw a rainbow in the night, caused by the moon.

Wednesday, August 31st – Wind still west; nothing remarkable.

Thursday, Sept. 1st – Bad weather, and contrary winds.

Friday, Sept. 2nd – This morning the wind changed; a little fair. We caught a couple of dolphins, and fried them for dinner. They eat indifferent well. These fish make a glorious appearance in the water; their bodies are of a bright green, mixed with a silver colour, and their tails of a shining golden yellow; but all this vanishes presently after they are taken out of their element, and they change all over to a light gray. I observed that cutting off pieces of a just-caught, living dolphin for baits, those pieces did not lose their lustre and fine colours when the dolphin died, but retained them perfectly. Everyone takes notice of that vulgar error of the painters, who always represent this fish monstrously crooked and deformed, when it is, in reality, as beautiful and well-shaped a fish as any that swims. I cannot think what could be the original of this chimera of theirs (since there is not a creature in nature that in the least resembles their dolphin) unless it proceeded at first from a false imitation of a fish in the posture of leaping, which they have since improved into a crooked monster, with a head and eyes like a bull, a hog's snout, and a tail like a blown tulip. But the sailors give me another reason though a whimsical one, viz. that as this most beautiful fish is only to be caught at sea, and that very far to the Southward, they say the painters wilfully deform it in their representations, lest pregnant women should long for what it is impossible to procure for them.

Saturday, September 3rd; Sunday, 4th; Monday, 5th – Wind still westerly; nothing remarkable.

Tuesday, September 6th – This afternoon the wind still continuing in the same quarter, increased till it blew a storm, and raised the sea to a greater height than I had ever seen it before.

Wednesday, September 7th – The wind is somewhat abated, but the sea is very high still. A dolphin kept us company all this afternoon; we struck at him several times, but could not take him.

Thursday, September 8th – This day nothing remarkable has happened, but I am so indolent that – Contrary wind.

Friday, September 9th – This afternoon we took four large dolphins, three with a hook and line, and the fourth we struck with a fizgig. The bait was a candle with two feathers stuck in it, one on each side, in imitation of a flying-fish, which are the common prey of the dolphins. They appeared extremely eager and hungry, and snapped up the hook as soon as ever it touched the water. When we came to open them, we found in the belly of one a small dolphin, half-digested. Certainly they were half-famished, or are naturally very savage, to devour those of their own species.

Saturday, September 10th – This day we dined upon the dolphins we caught yesterday, three of them sufficing the whole ship, being twenty-one persons.

Sunday, September 11th – We have had a hard gale of wind all this day, accompanied with showers of rain. 'Tis uncomfortable being upon deck; and, though we have been all together all day below, yet the long continuance of these contrary winds has made us so dull, that scarce three words have passed between us.

Monday, September 12th; Tuesday, 13th – Nothing remarkable; wind contrary.

Wednesday, September 14th – This afternoon, about two o'clock, it being fair weather and almost calm, as we sat playing drafts upon deck, we were surprised with a sudden and unusual darkness of the sun, which, as we could perceive, was only covered with a small, thin cloud; when that was passed by, we discovered that that glorious luminary laboured under a very great eclipse. At least ten parts out of twelve of him were hid from our eyes, and we were apprehensive he would have been totally darkened.

Thursday, September 15th – For a week past, we have fed ourselves with the hopes, that the change of the moon (which was yesterday) would bring us a fair wind; but, to our great mortification and disappointment, the wind seems now settled in the westward, and shows as little signs of an alteration as it did a fortnight ago.

Friday, September 16th – Calm all this day. This morning we saw a *Tropic bird*, which flew round our vessel several times. It is a white fowl, with short wings; but one feather appears in his tail, and does not fly very fast. We reckon ourselves about half our voyage; latitude 38 and odd minutes. These birds are said never to be seen further north than the latitude of 40.

Saturday, September 17th – All the forenoon the calm continued; the rest of the day some light breezes easterly; and we are in great hopes the wind will settle in that quarter.

Sunday, September 18th – We have had the finest weather imaginable all this day, accompanied with what is still more agreeable, a fair wind. Everyone puts on a clean shirt and a cheerful countenance, and we begin to be very good company. Heaven grant that this favourable gale may continue! for we have had so much of turning to windward, that the word *helm-a-lee* is become almost as disagreeable to our ears as the sentence of a judge to a convicted malefactor.

Monday, September 19th – The weather looks a little uncertain, and we begin to fear the loss of our fair wind. We see Tropic birds every day, sometimes five or six together; they are about as big as pigeons.

Tuesday, September 20th – The wind is now westerly again, to our great mortification; and we are come to a allowance of bread, two biscuits and a half a day.

Wednesday, September 21st – This morning our steward was brought to the gears and whipped, for making an extravagant use of flour in the puddings, and for several other misdemeanours. It has been perfectly calm all this day, and very hot. I was determined to wash myself in the sea today, and should have done so, had not the appearance of a Shark, that mortal enemy to swimmers, deterred me; he seemed to be about five foot long, moves round the ship at some distance, in a slow, majestic manner, attended by near a dozen of those they call Pilot-fish, of different sizes; the largest of them is not so big as a small mackerel, and the smallest not bigger than my little finger. Two of these diminutive Pilots keep just before his nose, and he seems to govern himself in his motions by their direction; while the rest surround him on every side indifferently. A shark is never seen without a retinue of these, who are his purveyors, discovering and distinguishing his prey for him; while he in turn gratefully protects them from the ravenous, hungry dolphin. They are commonly counted a very greedy fish; yet this refuses to meddle with the bait thrown out for him. 'Tis likely he has already made a full meal.

Thursday, September 22nd – A fresh gale at West all this day. The shark has left us.

Friday, September 23rd – This morning we spied a sail to windward of us about two leagues. We showed our jack upon the ensign-staff, and shortened sail for them till about noon, when she came up with us. She was a snow, from Dublin, bound for New York, having upwards of fifty servants on board of both sexes; they all appeared upon deck, and seemed very much pleased at the sight of us. There is really something strangely cheering to the spirits in the meeting of a ship at sea, containing a society of creatures of the same species and in the same circumstances with ourselves, after we had been long separated and excommunicated as it were from the rest of mankind. My heart fluttered in my breast with joy, when I saw so many human countenances, and I could scarce refrain from that kind of laughter, which proceeds from some degree of inward pleasure. When we have been for a considerable time tossing on the vast waters, far from the sight of any land or ships, or any mortal creature but ourselves (except a few fish and sea-birds), the whole world, for aught we know, may be under a second deluge, and we, like Noah and his company in the ark, the only surviving remnant of the human race.

The two Captains have mutually promised to keep each other company; but this I look upon to be only matter of course, for if ships are unequal in their sailing, they seldom stay for one another, especially strangers. This afternoon, the wind, that had been so long contrary to us, came about to the eastward (and looks as if it would hold), to our no small satisfaction. I find our messmates in a better humour, and more pleased with their present condition, than they have been since they came out; which I take to proceed from the contemplation of the miserable circumstances of the passengers on board our neighbour, and making the comparison. We reckon ourselves in a kind of paradise, when we consider how they live, confined and stifled up with such a lousy, stinking rabble, in this hot sultry latitude.

Saturday, September 24th – Last night we had a very high wind, and very thick weather; in which we lost our consort. This morning early we spied a sail ahead of us, which we took to be her; but presently after we spied another, and then we plainly perceived, that neither of them could be the snow; for one of them stemmed with us, and the other bore down directly upon us, having the weather-gauge of us. As the latter drew near, we were a little surprised, not knowing what to make of her; for by the course she steered, she did not seem designed for any port, but looked as if she intended to clap us aboard immediately. I could perceive concern in every face on board; but she presently eased us of our apprehensions by bearing away astern of us. When we hoisted our jack, she answered with French colours, and presently took them down again; and we soon lost sight of her. The other ran by us in less than half an hour, and answered our jack with an English ensign; she stood to the Eastward, but the wind was too high to speak with either of them. About nine o'clock we spied our consort, who had got a great way ahead of us. She, it seems, had made sail during the night, while we lay by, with our mainyard down, during the hard gale. She very civilly shortened sail for us, and this afternoon we came up with her; and now we are running along very amicably together, side by side, having a most glorious fair wind.

> On either side the parted billows flow
> While the black ocean foams and roars below.

Sunday, September 25th – Last night we shot ahead of our consort pretty far. About midnight, having lost sight of each other, we shortened sail for them: but this morning they were got as far ahead of us as we could see, having run by us in the dark unperceived. We made sail and came up with them about noon; and if we chance to be ahead of them again in the night, we are to show them a light, that we may not lose company by any such accident for the future. The wind still continues fair, and we have made a greater run these last four-and-twenty hours than we have done since we came out. All our discourse, now, is of Philadelphia, and we begin to fancy ourselves ashore already. Yet a small change of weather, attended by a westerly wind, is sufficient to blast all our blooming hopes, and quite spoil our present good humour.

Monday, September 26th – The wind continued fair all night. In the twelve o'clock watch our consort, who was about a league ahead of us, showed us a light, and we answered with another. About six o'clock this morning we had a sudden hurry of wind at all points of the compass, accompanied with the most violent shower of rain I ever saw, insomuch that the sea looked like a *cream dish*. It surprised us with all our sails up, and was so various, uncertain, and contrary, that the mizzen topsail was full, while the head sails were all aback; and before the men could run from one end of the ship to the other, 'twas about again. But this did not last long ere the wind settled to the NorthEast again, to our great satisfaction. Our consort fell astern of us in the storm, but made sail and came up with us again after it was over. We hailed one another on the morrow, congratulating upon the continuance of the fair wind, and both ran on very lovingly together.

Tuesday, September 27th – The fair wind continues still. I have laid a bowl of punch, that we are in Philadelphia next Saturday se'nnight; for we reckon ourselves not above 150 leagues from land. The snow keeps us company still.

Wednesday, September 28th – We had very variable winds and weather last night, accompanied with abundance of rain; and now the wind is come about westerly again, but we must bear it with patience. This afternoon we took up several branches of gulf-weed (with which the sea is spread all over, from the Western Isles to the coast of America); but one of these branches had something peculiar in it. In common with the rest, it had a leaf about three quarters of an inch long, indented like a saw, and a small yellow berry, filled with nothing but wind; besides which it bore a fruit of the animal kind, very surprising to see. It was a small shell-fish like a heart, the stalk by which it proceeded from the branch being partly of a grisly kind. Upon this one branch of the weed, there were near forty of these vegetable animals; the smallest of them, near the end, contained a substance somewhat like an oyster, but the larger were visibly animated, opening their shells every moment, and thrusting out a set of unformed claws, not unlike those of a crab; but the inner part was still a kind of soft jelly. Observing the weed more narrowly, I spied a very small crab crawling among it, about as big as the head of a tenpenny nail, and of a yellowish colour, like the weed itself. This gave me some reason to think, that he was a native of the branch; that he had not long since been in the same condition with the rest of those little embryos that appeared in the shells, this being the method of their generation; and that, consequently, all the rest of this odd kind of fruit might be crabs in due time. To strengthen my conjecture, I have resolved to keep the weed in salt water, renewing it every day till we come on shore, by this experiment to see whether any more crabs will be produced or not in this manner.

I remember that the last calm we had, we took notice of a large crab upon the surface of the sea, swimming from one branch of weed to another, which he seemed to prey upon; and I likewise recollect that at Boston, in New England, I have often seen small crabs with a shell like a snail shell upon their backs, crawling about in the salt water; and likewise at Portsmouth in England. It is like Nature has provided them hard shell to secure them till their own proper shell has acquired a sufficient hardness, which once perfected, they quit their old habitation and venture abroad safe in their own strength. The various changes that silkworms, butterflies, and several other insects go through, make such alterations and metamorphoses not improbable. This day the captain of the snow with one of his passengers came on board us; but the wind beginning to blow, they did not stay dinner, but returned to their own vessel.

Thursday, September 29th – Upon shifting the water in which I had put the weed yesterday, I found another crab, much smaller than the former, who seemed to have newly left his habitation. But the weed begins to wither, and the rest of the embryos are dead. This newcomer fully convinces me, that at least this sort of crabs are generated in this manner. The snow's captain dined on board us this day. Little or no wind.

Friday, September 30th – I sat up last night to observe an eclipse of the moon, which the calendar, calculated for London, informed us would happen at five o'clock in the morning, Sept. 30. It began with us about eleven last night, and continued till near two this morning, darkening her body about six digits, or one half; the middle of it being about half an hour after twelve, by which we may discover that we are in a meridian of about four hours and half from London, or 67½ degrees of Longitude, and consequently have not much above one hundred leagues to run. This is the second eclipse we have had within these fifteen days. We lost our consort in the night, but saw him again this morning nearly two leagues to the windward. This afternoon we spoke with him again. We have had abundance of dolphins about us these three or four days; but we have not taken any more than one, they being shy of the bait. I took in some more gulf-weed today with the boat-hook, with shells upon it like that before mentioned, and three living perfect crabs, each less than the nail of my little finger. One of them had something particularly observable, to wit, a thin piece of the white shell which I before noticed as their covering while they remained in the condition of embryos, sticking close to his natural shell upon his back. This sufficiently confirms me in my opinion of the manner of their generation. I have put this remarkable crab with a piece of the gulf-weed, shells, etc., into a glass phial filled with salt water (for want of spirits of wine) in hopes to preserve the curiosity till I come on shore. The wind is SouthWest.

Saturday, October 1st – Last night our consort, who goes incomparably better upon a wind than our vessel, got so far to windward and ahead of us, that this morning we could see nothing of him, and it is like shall see him no more. These SouthWests are hot, damp winds, and bring abundance of rain and dirty weather with them.

Sunday, October 2nd – Last night we prepared our line with a design to sound this morning at four o'clock; but the wind coming about again to the northwest, we let it alone. I cannot help fancying the water is changed a little, as is usual when a ship comes within soundings, but 'tis probable I am mistaken; for there is but one besides myself of my opinion, and we are very apt to believe what we wish to be true.

Monday, October 3rd – The water is now very visibly changed to the eyes of all except the Captain and Mate, and they will by no means allow it; I suppose because they did not see it first. Abundance of dolphins are about us, but they are very shy, and keep at a distance. Wind NorthWest.

Tuesday, October 4th – Last night we struck a dolphin, and this morning we found a flying-fish dead under the windlass. He is about the bigness of a small mackerel, a sharp head, a small mouth, and a tail forked somewhat like a dolphin, but the lowest branch much larger and longer than the other, and tinged with yellow. His back and sides of a darkish blue, his belly white, and his skin very thick. His wings are of a finny substance, about a span long, reaching, when close to his body from an inch below his gills to an inch above his tail. When they fly it is straight forward (for they cannot readily turn), a yard or two above the water; and perhaps fifty yards in the furthest before they dip into the water again, for they cannot support themselves in the air any longer than while their wings continue wet. These flying-fish are the common prey of the dolphin, who is their mortal enemy. When he pursues them, they rise and fly; and he keeps close under them till they drop, and then snaps them up immediately. They generally fly in flocks, four or five, or perhaps a dozen together and a dolphin is seldom caught without one or more in his belly. We put this flying-fish upon the hook, in hopes of catching one, but in a few minutes they got it off without hooking themselves; and they will not meddle with any other bait.

Tuesday Night – Since eleven o'clock we have struck three fine dolphins, which are a great refreshment to us. This afternoon we have seen abundance of grampuses, which are seldom far from land; but towards evening we had a more evident token, to wit, a little tired bird, something like a lark, came on board us, who certainly is an American, and 'tis likely was ashore this day. It is now calm. We hope for a fair wind next.

Wednesday, October 5th – This morning we saw a heron, who had lodged aboard last night. 'Tis a long-legged, long-necked bird, having, as they say, but one gut. They live upon fish, and will swallow a living eel thrice, sometimes, before it will remain in their body. The wind is west again. The ship's crew was brought to a short allowance of water.

Thursday, October 6th – This morning abundance of grass, rock-weed, etc., passed by us; evident tokens that land is not far off. We hooked a dolphin this morning, that made us a good breakfast. A sail passed by us about twelve o'clock, and nobody saw her till she was too far astern to be spoken with. 'Tis very near calm; we saw another sail ahead this afternoon; but, night coming on, we could not speak with her, though we very much desired it; she stood to the northward, and it is possible might have informed us how far we are from land. Our artists on board are much at a loss. We hoisted our jack to her, but she took no notice of it.

Friday, October 7th – Last night, about nine o'clock, sprung up a fine gale at NorthEast, which run us in our course at the rate of seven miles an hour all night. We were in hopes of seeing land this morning, but cannot. The water, which we thought was changed, is now as blue as the sky; so that, unless at that time we were running over some unknown shoal, our eyes strangely deceived us. All the reckonings have been out these several days; though the captain says 'tis his opinion we are yet a hundred leagues from land; for my part I know not what to think of it; we have run all this day at a great rate, and now night is come on we have no soundings. Sure the American continent is not all sunk under water since we left it.

Saturday, October 8th – The fair wind continues still; we ran all night in our course, sounding every four hours, but can find no ground yet, nor is the water changed by all this day's run. This afternoon we saw an *Irish Lord,* and a bird which flying looked like a yellow duck. These, they say, are not seen far from the coast. Other signs of lands have we none. Abundance of large porpoises ran by us this afternoon, and we were followed by a shoal of small ones, leaping out of the water as they approached. Towards evening we spied a sail ahead, and spoke with her just before dark. She was bound from New York for Jamaica, and left Sandy Hook yesterday about noon, from which they reckon themselves forty-five leagues distant. By this we compute that we are not above thirty leagues from our Capes, and hope to see land tomorrow.

Sunday, October 9th – We have had the wind fair all the morning; at twelve o'clock we sounded, perceiving the water visibly changed, and struck ground at twenty-five fathoms, to our universal joy. After dinner one of our mess went up aloft to look out, and presently pronounced the long wished-for sound, LAND! LAND! In less than an hour we could decry it from the deck, appearing like tufts of trees. I could not discern it so soon as the rest; my eyes were dimmed with the suffusion of two small drops of joy. By three o'clock we were run in within two leagues of the land, and spied a small sail standing along shore. We would gladly have spoken with her, for our captain was unacquainted with the Coast, and knew not what land it was that we saw. We made all the sail we could to speak with her. We made a signal of distress; but all would not do, the ill-natured dog would not come near us. Then we stood off again till morning, not caring to venture too near.

Monday, October 10th – This morning we stood in again for land; and we that had been here before all agreed that it was Cape Henlopen; about noon we were come very near, and to our great joy saw the pilot-boat come off to us, which was exceeding welcome. He brought on board about a peck of apples with him; they seemed the most delicious I ever tasted in my life; the salt provisions we had been used to gave them a relish. We had extraordinary fair wind all the afternoon, and ran above a hundred miles up the Delaware before ten at night. The country appears very pleasant to the eye, being covered with woods, except here and there a house and plantation. We cast anchor when the tide turned, about two miles below Newcastle, and there lay till the morning tide.

Tuesday, October 11th – This morning we weighed anchor with a gentle breeze, and passed by Newcastle, whence they hailed us and bade us welcome. It is extreme fine weather. The sun enlivens our stiff limbs with his glorious rays of warmth and brightness. The sky looks gay, with here and there a silver cloud. The fresh breezes from the woods refresh us; the immediate prospect of liberty, after so long and irksome confinement, ravishes us. In short, all things conspire to make this the most joyful day I ever knew. As we passed by Chester, some of the company went on shore, impatient once more to tread on *terra firma*, and designing for Philadelphia by land. Four of us remained on board, not caring for the fatigue of travel when we knew the voyage had much weakened us. About eight at night, the wind failing us, we cast anchor at Redbank, six miles from Philadelphia, and thought we must be obliged to lie on board that night; but, some young Philadelphians happening to be out upon their pleasure in a boat, they came on board, and offered to take us up with them; we accepted of their kind proposal, and about ten o'clock landed at Philadelphia, heartily congratulating each upon our having happily completed so tedious and dangerous a voyage. Thank God!

Notes to the Autobiography

page 7, Twyford   Near Winchester – the country home of one of Franklin's intimate friends, Dr Jonathan Shipley, Bishop at St Asaph's in Wales. At Twyford, Franklin wrote the first section of the Autobiography, covering the years 1706–31.

page 7, Dear Son   William Franklin, who became tory Governor of New Jersey (1762).

page 8, Franklin   In medieval times the term Franklin designated a freeman, owner of land.

page 9, January 6th   Benjamin Franklin was born on Sunday, January 6th, 1706, Old Style, or January 17th, New Style. The Julian calendar, established in the régime of Julius Caesar, was superseded in 1582 by the Gregorian calendar, promulgated by Pope Gregory XIII. Unlike the other Western European countries, England refused to adopt the Pope's reform, and in the eighteenth century an error of eleven days existed. It was not until 1752 that Parliament caused the change to be made.

page 10, Conventicle   During the first five years (1660–65) of Charles II's reign, laws were passed to crush the power of the Dissenters and to strengthen the position of the Church of England. Penalties were imposed against those holding conventicles, nonconformist gatherings for religious worship.

page 10, Boston   Franklin was born in Milk Street, near the Old South Church.

page 10, Cotton Mather   His *Magnalia Christi Americana* (London, 1702) is one of the most important books for the colonial period. He was sometime minister at Boston's North Church a voluminous writer and active politician as well as a conservative theologian.

page 11, Because to be a Libeller   These verses are from Peter Folger's *A Looking-Glass for the Times, or the Former Spirit of New England Revived in this Generation* (1676).

page 11, Sherburne   Now called Nantucket.

page 11, Character   Refers to shorthand characters.

page 11, Grammar school Latin was the chief course of study in the Boston grammar school. In his *Proposals Relating to the Education of Youth in Pennsylvania* (1749), Franklin attacked the over-emphasis on Latin and Greek in the schools

page 11, Arithmetic This confessed failure in arithmetic is surprising, inasmuch as, later in life, Franklin worked out ingenious, mathematical squares and circles.

page 13, Marble The original having broken into pieces, public-spirited Bostonians erected, in 1827, a granite obelisk over the grave, with Franklin's original inscription on a bronze tablet.

page 14, Mather's Bonifacius. An Essay upon the Good that is to be Devised and Designed by those who desire to answer the Great End of Life, and to do good while they live (Boston, 1710).

page 15, Poetry Franklin here records his 'fancy to poetry' at the age of twelve. Further attempts at versifying were made later in *Poor Richard's Almanac*.

page 15, Grub Street A London street inhabited by impecunious and mediocre writers.

page 15, Argument Throughout his public life Franklin avoided public discussions on controversial subjects. His early aversion to argument probably accounts for his extraordinary capacity for making friends.

page 16, Spectator Notable for contributions from the pens of Addison and Steele, this daily was published in London, 1711–12. The preface of A. Millar's London edition of the Autobiography (1799) observes: 'Dr Franklin tells us, in his life, that he was an assiduous imitator of Addison, and from some of these papers it will be admitted that he was not an unhappy one. The public will be amused with following a great philosopher in his relaxations, and observing in what respects philosophy tends to elucidate and improve the most common subjects.' That he was greatly influenced by Addison, Bunyan, and Defoe is evident throughout his writings.

page 17, Vegetable Diet The idea was suggested by Thomas Tryon's *The Way to Health, long Life and Happiness or a Discourse of Temperance* (1691), published originally as *Health's Grand Preservative; or, The Woman's Best Doctor* (1682).

page 19, Immodest Words This quotation is not from Pope. The couplet is adapted from the Earl of Roscommon's *Essay on Translated Verse*, reputed to have contained the first definite statement of the principles of poetic diction. Lord Roscommon (1630–85), English poet, was a nephew of Thomas Wentworth Earl of Strafford.

page 19, New England Courant First issued August 21, 1721, it was the fourth newspaper in America. The first number of the *Boston News-Letter* appeared on April 24th, 1704, being the first newspaper in America. The *Boston Gazette* made its bow on December 21, 1719, and the *American Weekly Mercury* (Philadelphia) a day later. James Franklin's *New England Courant* was, indeed, the first to offer original contributions by the colonists themselves, and was not merely a rehash of the London papers.

page 22, William Bradford His printery was first established in Philadelphia in 1665, the first outside of New England. In 1693 Bradford removed to New York where Franklin met him.

page 22, Aquila Rose A Philadelphia poet and man of affairs.

page 22, Kill Kill van Kull, the inlet between Staten Island and the New Jersey shore.

page 23, Cotton Charles Cotton's *Scarronides, or Virgil Travestie* (1664–70), a burlesque of the *Æneid*.

page 25, Meeting-house Prominent Quakers worshipped in this Meeting-House of the Society of Friends, at the southwest corner of Second and High (Market) Streets, until 1810.

page 25, Market Market sheds were erected in the centre of High Street (now Market Street), near the Delaware wharves, in early Philadelphia. As the city spread westward the markets were extended until they finally reached Thirteenth Street. In 1859 they were removed to make way for trolley cars.

page 25, Crooked Billet This inn was located at the wharves above Chestnut Street.

page 26, Keimer Samuel Keimer is said to have been one of the Camisards or Protestants of the Cevennes, persecuted by Louis XIV. They indulged in miraculous prophecies and trances.

page 28, Both Governments Pennsylvania and Delaware.

page 29, Piece of Eight Spanish dollar containing eight reals, each worth 12½ cents.

page 31, Burnet William Burnet was appointed Governor of New York and New Jersey, April 19th, 1720.

page 34, Miss Read Deborah Read. She was married to Franklin, September 1st, 1730; died December 19th, 1774. She does not appear to have been an inspiring companion for her versatile husband.

page 34, James Ralph He went to England with Franklin and became a freelance writer and political propagandist. He wrote a *History of England during the Reigns of King William, Queen Anne and King George 1* (1744–6).

page 38, Little Britain A London street.

page 38, Pistole   Spanish coin, worth about four dollars.

page 38, Wilkes   Robert Wilkes was a well-known London comedian and actor. He made his first appearance in 1691, as Othello, and played important roles in a long series of plays at the famous Drury Lane and Haymarket Theatres between 1699 and his death in 1732. At times he was also one of the managers of these theatres.

page 38, Paternoster Row   A street near St Paul's Cathedral, London still a book-publishers' section.

page 39, Wollaston   William Wollaston's *The Religion of Nature Delineated* (1722). This dissertation was an attempt to prove the identity of religion and morality.

page 39, Dr Mandeville   Bernard Mandeville, a Dutchman living in England a large part of his life, expressed his cynical views regarding society in *The Fable of the Bees, or Private Vices Public Benefits* (1705).

page 39, Dr Pemberton   Henry Pemberton was a physician and author, associated for a time with Sir Isaac Newton. He wrote *A View of Sir I. Newton's Philosophy* (1728).

page 39, Sir Hans Sloane   He was not only an esteemed physician but also a distinguished collector whose library and curios were assembled after his death and opened to public view, forming the nucleus of the British Museum (1759).

page 40, Young's Satires   Edward Young's *Love of Fame, the Universal Passion*, Satire IV. Young was an English poet. The title mentioned is one of a series of seven satires on *The Universal Passion*, published between 1725 and 1728.

page 41, Chapel   A printing-house was called a chapel by the workers. The *bien venu* was an initiation fee of so many gallons of beer demanded of the newcomer.

page 43, College   The College at Chelsea, founded by James I in 1609 was used in Franklin's time as a home for needy military officers.

page 43, Don Saltero   Once a servant to Sir Hans Sloane. Naturally, therefore, James Salter (Don Saltero) learned to prize curious objects. His house in Cheyne Walk, Chelsea, served as a combination barber-shop, museum, and coffee-shop.

page 43, Blackfriars   The swim here recorded covered a distance of about three miles. Franklin was an exceptionally strong swimmer, and he thoroughly enjoyed the water. He discussed the art and technique of swimming in letters to Oliver Neave (date unknown) and to Barbeu Dubourg (1773), both of which are printed in Nathan G. Goodman's *The Ingenious Dr Franklin*, pp. 41–9.

page 45, Journal   This journal of the voyage from London to

Philadelphia is included in this volume. Franklin's *plan* for the regulation of his conduct in life has never been found.

page 50, Dryden A misquotation from *Œdipus*, Act III, Scene I. The correct wording is:

> Whatever is, is in its causes just
>
> Since all things are by Fate. But purblind man . . .

page 52, Junto This organisation was at once a literary, scientific and social club for the intelligent citizen, regardless of wealth or social position. The membership was limited to twelve. Books were discussed, public policies examined, business problems analysed, and scientific theories presented and explained. Members of the Junto were to seek the truth and work for the common good. The question and answer method was used in the meetings where such subjects were discussed as: 'How may the phenomena of vapours be explained?', 'What is the reason that the tides rise higher in the Bay of Fundy than the Bay of Delaware?'; 'Why does the flame of candle tend upwards in a spire?'; 'Which is the best form of government and what was that form which first prevailed among mankind?'; 'Is it consistent with the principles of liberty in a free government to punish a man as a libeller who speaks the truth?'

page 54, Paper Keimer's weekly newspaper was called *The Universal Instructor in all Arts and Sciences and Pennsylvania Gazette*. Franklin became owner of the paper on October 2nd, 1729, and changed the title to *The Pennsylvania Gazette*, a semi-weekly chock-full of Franklin's wit and wisdom.

page 54, Governor Burnet The governor's instructions called for a salary of a thousand pounds, but the legislature insisted on fixing the amount of the salary.

page 56, About the Year 1729 July 14th, 1730.

page 60, Library This first subscription library in America has continued to the present day. It is located at Juniper and Locust Streets, Philadelphia, with an important offspring, the Ridgway Branch, at Broad and Christian Streets. It is still a private library, for the use of shareholders only, although the reading rooms are open to the public. Many of the Library's first one hundred titles, ordered from England in 1731 by Franklin, are preserved in the Ridgway Branch, which boasts valuable manuscript collections and copious files of early American newspapers.

page 74, O Vitae O philosophy, guide of life. O seeker of virtues and ejector of vices. One day really lived in keeping with thy instructions is to be preferred to an eternity of sin.

page 75, Scheme of Order Throughout his entire life Franklin had great difficulty in filing his papers and records systematically. The meticulous John Adams, when he arrived in Paris on a diplomatic mission during the War for Independence, was disturbed at Franklin's lack of method in filing official papers.

page 78, Humility Until the end of his life Franklin maintained a liberal viewpoint in his relations with others. Never assuming a superior air, he avoided controversies and disputes. His attitude is well expressed at the close of a letter on electrical experiments, addressed to John Lining, March 18th, 1755: 'Those who affect to be thought to know everything, and so undertake to explain everything, often remain long ignorant of many things that others could and would instruct them in, if they appeared less conceited.'

page 81, Richard Saunders An English almanac publisher of the period.

page 81, Poor Richard's Almanac This Almanac was published by Franklin from 1733 to 1758 inclusive, and contained, in addition to Franklin's own essays and humorous sketches, weather predictions; time of tides; dates of fairs, courts, household recipes; planetary motions; and holidays; important historical dates and facts; description of the highways and roads; medical advice; and proverbs. Franklin used the Almanac as a medium for preaching and for advancing his own ideas, especially on industry, frugality and virtue. The most notable essay is the *Way to Wealth*, being the preface to the Almanac for 1758 (and not the 'harangue of a wise old man of 1757'), being a collection of the best words of wisdom from Poor Richard during a quarter of a century. An almanac of some sort was considered indispensable in the homes of the colonists. The circulation of *Poor Richard's Almanac* reached 10,000 copies annually.

page 82, Socratic Dialogue The dialogue and the discourse appeared on June 23rd and July 7th, 1730; and not 'about the beginning of 1735' as Franklin recorded.

page 83, Pamphlets See Paul Leicester Ford's *A List of Books Written by, or Relating to Benjamin Franklin* (1889), page 15.

page 84, Chess Franklin was intensely interested in chess. In April, 1757, he wrote to his wife from New York for 'two or three little pieces on the game of chess among my books on the shelves'. In 1779 he wrote a short essay on the moral rules of chess. In this paper he warns the player to 'snatch not eagerly at every advantage offered by his [the adversary's] unskilfulness or inattention; but point out to him kindly, that by such a move he places or leaves a piece in danger and unsupported and that by another he will put his king in a perilous situation, etc. by this general civility . . . you may, indeed, happen to lose the game to your opponent; but you will win what is better, his esteem, his respect, and his affection, together with the silent approbation and good-will of impartial spectators.' Today Franklin's Library Company of Philadelphia (Ridgway Branch) owns one of the world's largest collections of books on chess.

page 87, Colonel Spotswood   Alexander Spotswood was governor of Virginia when the first regular post line was established in 1717. In 1730 he was elevated to the position of Postmaster-general of America at a salary of three hundred pounds a year, plus ten per cent of the net profit. Franklin, after serving as Philadelphia's Postmaster, became comptroller, supervising several offices, and then (1753) joint Postmaster-General.

page 88, Union Fire Company   Organised December 7th, 1736. Franklin was also interested in fireproof construction – see especially his letter to Samuel Rhoads, June 26th, 1770, and February 10th, 1771: A. H. Smyth: *Life and Writings of Benjamin Franklin*, V, p. 265 and p. 305.

page 88, Reverend Mr Whitefield   George Whitefield, one of the most popular preachers ever known in England, worked with John and Charles Wesley in the cradle years of Methodism. Sent as a missionary to Georgia in 1738, Whitefield preached throughout the colonies. He reached Philadelphia in November, 1739, and began preaching in Christ Church, Second Street above Market. This edifice being too small, a building was erected by public subscription on Fourth Street near Arch and later became the home of the Academy and College of Philadelphia, the parent of the University of Pennsylvania.

page 90, Mr Benezet   Anthony Benezet, American philanthropist, was an early advocate of the abolition of slave trade and the education of the negro. He came to America from France and settled in Philadelphia, 1731. In 1767 he published: *A Caution to Great Britain and Her Colonies, in a Short Representation of the Calamitous State of the Enslaved Negroes of the British Dominion*.

page 90, Germantown   About eight miles northwest of central Philadelphia, and reached by Germantown Road, now a busy thoroughfare.

page 91, Front Street   The first street east of Second Street and the first west of the Delaware River. From Franklin's account one conjectures that Whitefield could be heard at a distance of almost one hundred and fifty yards.

page 93, Philosophical Society   The idea of such an organisation was discussed in the Junto, but the first public suggestion seems to have been made in Franklin's paper: 'A Proposal For Promoting Useful

Knowledge Among the British Plantations in America' (May 14th, 1743). He proposed calling the body *The American Philosophical Society* and advocated that such subjects be discussed as botany, medicine, mineralogy, mathematics, chemistry, physics, topography, agriculture, art, 'and all philosophical experiments that let light into the nature of things, tend to increase the power of man over matter, and multiply the conveniences or pleasures of life.' Six of the first nine members of the new organisation were members of the Junto. Franklin, himself, was President of the Society from 1764 until his death. The American Philosophical Society, the oldest scientific body in this country, dates its organisation back to 1727 when the Junto was founded; the 200th anniversary was celebrated in 1927. The Society owns more than 13,000 Franklin letters and papers, about eighty per-cent of the Franklin papers extant. Its library, consisting of 90,000 volumes, is extremely valuable. There are four hundred American members and sixty foreign. For many years the Society was quartered in an old building adjoining Independence Hall in Philadelphia; in 1932 it was decided to erect a monumental home at Sixteenth Street and the Parkway.

page 94, Clinton   George Clinton was colonial governor, 1741–53.

page 96, James Logan   He came to Philadelphia in 1699 and acted as business secretary to the Penn family. His country home, 'Stenton', is in excellent state of preservation and is open to the public (Seventeenth and Courtland Streets, Philadelphia).

page 97, Dunkers   A sect of German-American Baptists who came to America in 1719. No church organisation was perfected until 1723. The Church of the Brethren at 6613 Germantown Avenue, Germantown, Philadelphia, is the Mother church of this sect. The front section of the present building was erected in 1770.

page 98, Iron-Furnace   Warwick Furnace, Chester County, Pennsylvania.

page 98, Fireplaces   For many years Franklin was interested in stoves. His lengthy letter to Jan Ingenhousz (August 28th, 1785) is especially entertaining and instructive. It deals with *The Causes and Cure of Smoky Chimneys* – see Smyth: *Life and Writings of Benjamin Franklin*, IX, pp. 413–43.

page 99, Proposals   *Proposals Relating to the Education of Youth in Pennsylvania* (1749) was written and distributed by Franklin with the hope that 'some public spirited Gentlemen' would finance an Academy for the youth of the Province. Franklin advocated that less emphasis be placed on Latin and Greek and more on one's native tongue, practical training in agriculture, and courses in the history of commerce. English and history were to be the major subjects, the first to insure clarity and correctness in speech and writing, the second to provide a background and approach to geography and other subjects. A facsimile reprint of the original 'Proposals' was issued by The University of Pennsylvania Press in 1931.

page 100, University of Philadelphia The University of Pennsylvania traces its origin to the Charity School (1740) and to its successor, the Academy organised by Franklin (1749) and first opened in January, 1751. It became the College of Philadelphia (1775); and in 1779 was designated a University, and in 1791 the institution assumed the name of the University of Pennsylvania.

page 101, Magic Squares A square containing numbers arranged in such a manner that the sum of each row equals the sum of any other row. Two of Franklin's squares are reproduced in Nathan G. Goodman's *The Ingenious Dr Franklin*, pp. 106–9.

page 102, Hospital The Pennsylvania Hospital, founded in 1751, was the first in the Province. The first patient was admitted for treatment on February 10th, 1752. This hospital was the first in the country to care adequately for insane patients. It is located at Eighth and Spruce Streets, Philadelphia, and maintains five hundred forty beds; its department of Mental and Nervous Diseases maintains two hundred forty beds, and its Institute of Mental Hygiene, one hundred twenty.

page 104, Revd Gilbert Tennent The Second Presbyterian Church, now located at Twenty-first and Walnut Streets, was organised by Gilbert Tennent in 1743.

page 105, Lamps Copies of Franklin's lamps light the pavement in front of Independence Hall today.

page 106, Dr Fothergill Dr John Fothergill was a distinguished English physician and botanist. One of the first descriptions of diphtheria to appear in English is to be found in his pamphlet: *Account of the Sore Throat attended with Ulcers* (1748).

page 106, Craven Street Franklin boarded in the home of a widow, Mrs Margaret Stevenson, at 7 Craven Street, just off the Strand.

page 109, College of Cambridge Harvard College.

page 110, My Plan Franklin's *Papers Relating to a Plan of Union of the Colonies* (1754) are printed in Smyth: *Life and Writings of Benjamin Franklin*, III, pp. 197–226.

page 112, War The French and Indian War (Seven Years' War) (1756–63).

page 118, George Croghan A celebrated Indian trader in Pennsylvania.

In 1767 he sent Franklin a box of elephants' tusks and teeth. On August 5th, 1767, Franklin wrote Croghan: 'I return you many thanks for the box of elephants' tusks and grinders. They are extremely curious on many accounts; no living elephants having been seen in any part of America by any of the Europeans settled there, or remembered in any tradition of the Indians. It is also puzzling to conceive what should have brought so many of them to die on the same spot; and that no such remains should be found in any other part of the continent, except in that very distant country, Peru . . . It is remarkable, that elephants now inhabit naturally only hot countries where there is no winter, and yet these remains are found in a winter country; and it is no uncommon thing to find elephants' tusks in Siberia, in great quantities, when their rivers overflow, and wash away the earth, though Siberia is still more a wintry country than that on the Ohio; which looks as if the earth had anciently been in another position, and the climates differently placed from what they are at present . . .'

page 119, French Friends This march of the French troops was in connection with the siege of Yorktown which fell on October 19th, 1781.

page 120, David Hume Scotch historian and philosopher.

page 122, Dialogue Franklin's dialogue, and the militia act appeared in the *Gentleman's Magazine*, February and March, 1756.

page 125, Bethlehem About fifty-five miles north of Philadelphia.

page 128, Mr P. Collinson Peter Collinson was an English naturalist and antiquarian who first published Franklin's papers on electricity London, 1751, as *Experiments and Observations on Electricity, made at Philadelphia in America, by Benjamin Franklin*. New and enlarged editions were issued from time to time. The 1769 edition was translated into French (1773) by Barbeu Dubourg as *Œuvres de M. Franklin*. In a letter to Collinson, July 29, 1750, Franklin first suggested a method of testing the theory that lightning and electricity are identical – See Smyth's *Life and Writings of Benjamin Franklin*, II, pp. 426–545.

page 128, Glass Tube Franklin's original primitive electrical machines can be seen in the Library Company of Philadelphia, and in the Benjamin Franklin Memorial and the Franklin Institute.

page 129, Cave Edward Cave founded the *Gentleman's Magazine*, one of the earliest and most valuable literary journals of the eighteenth century.

page 130, Kite In a letter to Peter Collinson, October 19th, 1752, Franklin details the method of constructing a kite with which to draw electricity from the clouds. See *The Ingenious Dr Franklin*, pp. 115–16.

page 132, Proprietary The sons of William Penn, Thomas and Richard, who nominated the Governor of the Province of Pennsylvania.

page 132, Agent Franklin's first foreign mission, in 1757, was successful. He brought about the assessment of the surveyed lands of the Proprietaries (the Penns).

page 137, Ship-building Franklin's knowledge of ship-building and maritime matters in general was extensive. He located the Gulf Stream and charted it; he experimented on the relationship between the depth of water and the speed of boats, he observed the behaviour of oil on water; he wrote on tides and suggested water-tight compartments in ship-building. See especially his letter to David Le Roy, written at sea in August 1785: Smyth: *Life and Writings of Benjamin Franklin*, IX, pp. 372–413.

page 139, My Son William Franklin.

page 139, 1757 Here terminates the Autobiography as first published by William Temple Franklin, in 1818, and subsequent editors. The paragraphs that follow, written in the last year of Franklin's life, were first published in English by John Bigelow in 1868.

Wordsworth American Library

IRVING BACHELLER
Eben Holden

AMBROSE BIERCE
Can Such Things Be?

KATE CHOPIN
The Awakening

JAMES FENIMORE COOPER
The Deerslayer

STEPHEN CRANE
The Red Badge of Courage
Maggie: A Girl of the Streets

RICHARD HENRY DANA JR
Two Years Before the Mast

FREDERICK DOUGLASS
*The Life and Times of
Frederick Douglass*

THEODORE DREISER
Sister Carrie

BENJAMIN FRANKLIN
*Autobiography of
Benjamin Franklin*

ZANE GREY
Riders of the Purple Sage

EDWARD E. HALE
The Man Without a Country

NATHANIEL HAWTHORNE
The House of the Seven Gables
The Scarlet Letter

HENRY JAMES
Washington Square
The Awkward Age

JACK LONDON
The Iron Heel
Call of the Wild/White Fang

HERMAN MELVILLE
Moby Dick

HARRIET BEECHER STOWE
Uncle Tom's Cabin

MARK TWAIN
*The Man That
Corrupted Hadleyburg*
*The Tragedy of Pudd'nhead
Wilson*

HENRY DAVID THOREAU
Walden

EDITH WHARTON
Ethan Frome
The House of Mirth

OWEN WISTER
The Virginian